Goal-focused Coaching

This book offers a comprehensive, practical guide to goal-focused coaching. Addressing a significant gap in the literature, Ives and Cox contextualise goal-focused coaching within the broader coaching framework and explain the efficacy of this approach across a number of contexts and applications.

The book draws on behavioural science, rather than humanistic psychology, to provide a well-researched, evidence-based guide that includes:

- A detailed examination of the theoretical underpinnings of this approach;
- A discussion of the skills, models and formats for goal-focused coaching;
- Cutting edge insights into barriers to coaching and managing the coaching relationship;
- Summaries, vignettes, references and diagrams to aid learning.

Goal-focused Coaching will be of interest to students taking classes in coaching, as well as professional executive coaches.

Yossi Ives is chairman of Tag International Development, UK. He is a life coach with a PhD in goal-focused coaching, and is the author of several books.

Elaine Cox is director of the Coaching and Mentoring programme at Oxford Brookes University, UK. She has published extensively, and is editor of the *International Journal of Evidence Based Coaching and Mentoring*.

Goal-focused Coaching

Theory and Practice

Yossi Ives and Elaine Cox

NEW YORK AND LONDON

First published 2012
by Routledge
605 Third Avenue, New York, NY 10017
4 Park Square, Milton Park, Abingdon, Oxon OX14 4RN

Routledge is an imprint of the Taylor & Francis Group, an informa business

Library of Congress Cataloging-in-Publication Data
Ives, Yossi.
   Goal-focused coaching : theory and practice / Yossi Ives and Elaine
Cox. — 1st ed.
   p. cm.
   Includes bibliographical references and index.
   1. Personal coaching. 2. Executive coaching. I. Cox, Elaine. II. Title.
   BF637.P36I845 2012
   658.3'124—dc23
   2012002849

Typeset in Garamond MT
by Swales & Willis Ltd, Exeter, Devon

ISBN 13: 978-0-415-80895-8 (hbk)

This book is dedicated

to a dear friend
Ricardo Leiman

In loving memory of
Frank (Anthony Francis) Stirling

and
Grant Ledgerwood
who would have enjoyed this book

Contents

List of Illustrations

Figures

Tables

Boxes

Foreword

Goals: The Core of the Coaching Enterprise

Without a doubt, goals are the core of the coaching enterprise. Clients come to coaching for many and varied reasons. They may want to make changes in their business, adjust to life or work transitions, improve their health, become more productive, more creative, more insightful, they may want to develop a greater understanding of themselves and the social systems in which they live and work, or improve their work or business performance. Whatever the reason, these all involve indentifying, defining and then pursuing goals. Indeed it can be said that human beings are goal-oriented organisms. Without goals we would not get out of bed in the morning, get dressed, deal with the day-to-day activities of life or get back in bed at the end of the day. Goals, as internalised representations of desired states and outcomes, in many ways represent the psychology of what it means to be human, and more specifically, what it means to be ourselves as individuals. Our goals define us personally and distinguish us from our fellows.

Given that goals are so central to the lived human experience, it is remarkable that so little of the coaching literature has addressed the use of goals in coaching. Where goals are discussed they tend to have been considered in a somewhat cursory or dismissive manner, often with a passing or superficial reference to SMART goals (Specific, Measurable, Attractive, Realistic and Time-framed – or similar terms). Strangely, some commentators have even stated that they don't use goals, or avoid their use in coaching.

Apart from the somewhat amusing observation that the aim of avoiding the use of goals in coaching is in itself a goal, this situation strongly suggests that goals are really not well understood in the coaching community.

This is a shame, not least because goal theory comprises a rich and complex body of knowledge which has the potential to help coaches make explicit connections to the broader evidence base, develop more sophisticated coaching techniques and skills, and further the professionalising of this exciting and vibrant industry.

It is this context that makes this book such a welcome addition to the coaching literature. In this book you will find an intelligent and well-informed exposition of a goal-focused approach to coaching that outlines a comprehensive theory of goal-focused coaching including methodologies, relationship management, action planning, motivation and commitment as well as core questioning and listening skills – and for the more pedantic academically-minded amongst us, it is fully referenced through-out!

The coaching industry has really come a long way in the past ten years. From little more than a perceived fad, we have seen the emergence of a vibrant industry focused on facilitating purposeful, positive change and staking a solid claim in terms of respectability in organisational contexts, and in areas such as health and well-being. As coaching methodologies continue to develop, we are in need of literature that explicitly links emergent coaching practices to the established behavioural sciences. In this way new and exciting coaching applications can remain grounded in research and coherent theory. This book does just that. There is knowledge here that will enrich the practice and understanding of coaching for both novices and experts.

This is an important book in coaching. Enjoy!

Anthony M. Grant, PhD
Coaching Psychology Unit
University of Sydney

Acknowledgements

A book is like a child. From the moment it is conceived, it is a commitment for life; it may have a beginning, but it never truly has an end. As with a child, parents try to shape its character, but it invariably assumes a life and character of its own. As it takes a village to raise a child, it takes more than the authors to turn a book into a successful reality. We each have people in our 'village' that we want to recognise:

Yossi

I express my thanks to my once academic supervisor and now cherished colleague Dr Elaine Cox, for her scholarship and humanity – both deep in equal measure.

I am also grateful to Peter Jackson and Dr Christian Ehrlich, for their feedback and advice, and to Oxford Brookes University where my research was conducted. It has been a source of inspiration and a rock of support.

My wife, Rivkie, and our children Chaya, Miriam, Meir, Ahuva, Dina, Dov and Rosie, have graciously made way for another member of our family – this book. The least I can do is acknowledge their patience, love and enthusiasm for everything I do. The support from my parents and parents-in-law is much appreciated, as is the doting interest from Grandma.

Similarly, the support received from my colleagues at Tag, Dr Amos Avgar, Matti Fruhman, Prof Bernard Jackson and Dr Michael ben Avie, is much appreciated.

I humbly offer thanks to the Almighty for the opportunity to study and learn, to share and to teach knowledge, to contribute in some small way to human progress and enlightenment.

Elaine

I wish to thank my colleague Peter Jackson for his insightful comments on draft chapters of this book and to acknowledge the contribution of Claire Patrick to the action research we undertook together in the retail support sector.

I especially want to thank my husband, Chris, for his tolerance, enduring support and love.

1 Introduction

Aims

- To explain Goal-focused Coaching (GFC);
- To outline the need for a theory of GFC;
- To provide a guide to reading the book and give an outline of the chapters that follow.

This book is aimed at filling a significant gap in the coaching literature. It combines a practical guide to the goal-focused approach to coaching with a theoretical underpinning in order to substantiate the approach and explain its efficacy across a number of contexts and applications.

Despite its importance in coaching practice, goal-focused coaching (hereafter referred to as GFC) is an area that has not so far attracted significant attention in the coaching literature. There have been occasional short chapters in books, most of which link GFC with brief coaching or solution-focused coaching, but do not explain the differences. In addition, there are a few notable academic writings (e.g. Cavanagh & Grant, 2010; Grant & O'Connor, 2010). However, notwithstanding the explosion of interest in and writing about coaching, the nature and application of GFC has been largely (and inexplicably) ignored. In fact, while most approaches to coaching involve the setting of goals (Garvey, Stokes & Megginson, 2009) GFC is currently very much a practice without a theory.

This book will therefore provide a much-needed comprehensive practical and theoretical guide to GFC. It will explain the unique dimensions of the approach while embracing the broader coaching processes and techniques. It also discusses a variety of applications of coaching that are made possible through a goal focus. The book contains more than 30 original diagrams and tables and numerous other user-friendly features, such as summaries, vignettes and useful references and tips. It is designed to meet the needs of busy practitioners, but at the same time to pay attention to scholarly accuracy and the importance of the theoretical foundations. The book capitalises on doctoral research and so has a wide-ranging theoretical orientation, which informs a new and systematic presentation of GFC.

A key aim of this book, as suggested, is to synthesise extant research into a theory of GFC. The book therefore draws on a range of theories, including goal theories, self-determination theories, motivation theories in education, self-regulated learning, social cognitive theory, self-regulation and volition theories, goal-focused coaching and solution-focused coaching.

To achieve this aim, it is first necessary to clarify the role and establish a definition of GFC. Following this, in the second section of this chapter, we justify the need for a theory of GFC, discussing the current eclectic and atheoretical nature of coaching in some detail and suggesting that coaches should make use of more thoroughgoing theoretical explorations in order to understand their work and provide a better service. In the third section, we outline our structure for the book.

Defining GFC

Based on a review of numerous coaching approaches (drawn primarily from coaching handbooks such as Drake, Brennan & Gørtz, 2008; Palmer & Whybrow, 2007; Passmore, 2005; Peltier, 2001; Stober & Grant, 2006) it emerges that coaching approaches can be divided into two main applications: coaching to modify people's actions (external) and coaching to change people's attitudes (internal).

This distinction is akin to Peltier's (2001) bifurcation of coaching into two main categories: executive coaching (internal, attitudinal) and a day-to-day management activity (external). It also shares some similarity with Summerfield's (2006) division between 'acquisitional' coaching (acquires a new ability) versus 'transformational' coaching (undergoes personal change). GFC, we identify as being essentially about raising performance and supporting effective action, rather than addressing feelings and generating deep reflection. We suggest that GFC primarily aims for a level of operational change, rather than psychological restructuring (Hall & Duval, 2004) and looks primarily to make small, incremental improvements (Jackson & McKergow, 2008). According to this conception, its foremost intention is to promote immediate enhancement of productivity, rather than personal transformation of the coachee.

The approach to coaching taken in this book is rooted in the cognitive perspective. As we explore at length in Chapter 3, GFC presents coaching as an effective tool for managing the relationship between attributions and expectancies and goal-related activity. People's actions are viewed as being more the result of cognition, attribution and expectancy than habit, drive and need. GFC foregrounds the role of conscious decisions and of goals in the process of human functioning (Bandura, 1986, 2001). Cognitive and environmental factors are viewed as more influential than stable personality dispositions. Thus, our conception of coaching marginalises trait, entity and personality type constructs in favour of directionality and level of aspiration (Pintrich & Schunk, 2003), including both internally-focused subconscious factors such as attributions and emotions as well as externally-focused, conscious factors such as goals. GFC also recognizes the centrality of self-efficacy beliefs, as they play a decisive role in influencing behaviour (Bandura, 1986) by impacting on choice, effort and determination (Bandura & Cervone, 1983; Schunk, 1991), and cognitive engagement (Schunk, 1984).

A key element of GFC is the role of goals as regulators of action. Goal theorists view life as a cyclical process of establishing and pursuing goals that energise and direct people's activities (Ford, 1992; Latham, 2007; Locke & Latham, 1990). Consciously setting a goal stimulates a rigorous set of activities that focus the mind towards reaching the goal. Therefore, the most successful way of improving goal performance is to address the individual's situated, immediate, conscious, personal goals (Locke & Latham, 2006).

GFC is thus viewed as a self-regulation tool. Self-regulation can be defined as the process whereby coachees activate and sustain the cognitions, behaviours and affects oriented towards attainment of their goals (Pintrich, 2000; Zimmerman, 1989). Self-regulation maintains concentration and directs effort by managing attentional and self-regulatory resources (Baumeister & Vohs, 2007; Mischel & Ayduk, 2007). Within this theoretical framework, interventions that seek to boost self-regulation are perceived as highly effective in bringing about positive outcomes by raising performance levels and by influencing future self-efficacy judgements.

However, the features of the goal, the directional variables, are the key factors for successful self-regulation (Rawsthorne & Elliot, 1999), and for maximising goal setting effectiveness. Goal setting is about discrepancy management, crafting the careful balance that is required to achieve optimum goal-oriented motivation. We shall explain further in Chapter 8 that disaggregating the goal is the key objective of goal implementation (Carver & Scheier, 1998).

Monitoring progress is also a key part of self-regulation and is at the heart of coaching since, as Carver & Scheier (1998 p. 34) claim, "increases in *self-focus* can promote increases in *task-focus*," facilitating appropriate adjustments to the goal (Carver, 2007). Feedback is viewed as crucial in both self-regulation and motivation theory (Carver & Scheier, 1998; Pintrich & Schunk, 1996) and is highlighted in coaching texts (Parsloe & Wray, 2000; Whitmore, 2003). However, in GFC, feedback is recursive and is primarily used to inform future decisions and motivate future actions: it is intended to assess past performance and compare to goals set, rather than facilitate long-term learning and development (Ives, 2008).

In this book we will argue that GFC should be classified as a distinct variety of coaching, encompassing the various forms of coaching that are goal- or solution-focused, including:

(1) Brief coaching (Berg & Szabo, 2005), which argues that short and focused interventions can be effective in generating lasting change;
(2) Solution-focused coaching (Grant, 2003; Jackson & McKergow, 2008) which discourages problem analysis and promotes identifying and building on what works;
(3) Goal-oriented models (Alexander & Renshaw, 2005; Grant, 2006; Greene & Grant, 2006) that view goal setting and action planning as central to the coaching process.

A fundamental feature of GFC is its relative disinterest in directly addressing underlying motives or resolving conflicting issues (Jackson & McKergow, 2008;

Whitmore, 2003). Goal-oriented approaches adopt a practical stance towards their coachee's problems and avoid delving into the underlying aspects of the coachee's life, in contrast to many other approaches to coaching that seek to address deeper dimensions of personality (Peterson, D. B., 2006; Snyder, 1995). Grant (2006 p. 156) argues that coaching supports "solution construction in preference to problem analysis," and Jackson and McKergow (2008 p. 25) insist that "understanding why things are how they are does little to help you decide what to do." Proponents of goal-oriented coaching thus view coaching as a method of helping coachees to reframe their challenges as practical problems, and to help them discover the required internal and external resources. Goal-oriented approaches generally focus on specific aims, seeking to integrate an ongoing self-regulatory process into daily modes of behaviour, rather than aiming for a clear life-changing breakthrough.

The Need for a Theory of GFC

As suggested above, from a reading of the many books and articles on coaching that have been published in recent years it could be concluded that coaching is the victim of an identity crisis, and that "creating a unique identity of coaching is still an unresolved problem" (Bachkirova, Cox & Clutterbuck, 2010 p. 3). Coaching is often given contradictory interpretations and incompatible connotations. We therefore believe it is vital for the various forms of coaching to be clarified and defined and this book contributes towards remedying the problem for GFC and related approaches.

Although there has been a growth in evidence-based coaching (Skiffington & Zeus, 2003; Stober & Grant, 2006), most of what has been written on coaching is decidedly non-scientific. Rigorous studies looking at the effects of coaching are sparse, as are studies about the most effective coaching methods. While there have been repeated calls for research to be undertaken (Jackson, 2008; O'Broin & Palmer, 2006), the coaching field remains mostly uncharted territory (Garvey et al., 2009). Additionally, little of the 'evidence' that is used to inform coaching practice is built on empirical research into coaching; rather it relies on a range of theories from other helping fields, such as adult learning (Cox, 2006), humanist psychotherapy (Stober, 2006), personal development (Berger, 2006), and positive psychology (Kauffman, 2006). In fact, as Garvey et al. (2009 p. 25) argue coaching is in the 'swampy lowlands', lacking a firm research base. What little research there is they lament for being "fragmented, partisan and impressionistic" (p. 40). They further note that "there are almost more surveys of the field bemoaning its quality than there are quality studies doing something to improve the situation" (p. 45).

Moreover, there appears to be a lack of clear evidence for the transfer of ideas and techniques from these disciplines to the field of coaching: Drake (2008 p. 20) argues that "coaching would gain more credibility if coaches would make more explicit and transparent the connections between their theoretical base, practice methods and client results," and while coaches insist that their work is distinct from therapeutic approaches, many continue to cite evidence from psychotherapy without empirical evidence of its relevance to the coaching discipline (Bachkirova, 2007). Linley (2006

p. 4) for example, suggests that there is potential for benefiting from the 'common factors' between the therapy and coaching and advocates adopting lessons from the therapy literature, if nothing else "as a basis from which to construct critical coaching research questions." However, the areas of commonality are a matter of considerable debate and we agree with Stober, Wildflower and Drake (2006 p. 3) who acknowledge that "evidence based coaches would do well to first evaluate the evidence's applicability" to coaching before extrapolating from other disciplines.

The assumption is that best practice and scientific data derived from other fields, after appropriate adjustment, is relevant to coaching. While this is possibly a plausible argument, it is largely unsubstantiated (Palmer & Whybrow, 2007) in that the research just does not exist. The problem of extrapolation is considerably worse for GFC approaches. Here, we would argue that the comparison to personal development and therapeutic interventions, for instance, is less justified, rendering research and evidence on the effectiveness of GFC particularly crucial and our task in this book vital.

Besides a weak *evidence* base, then, coaching lacks *theoretical* underpinning (Jackson, 2008). However, there is little consensus about which core theoretical principles underlie coaching (Gray, 2006): for the most part principles have been rooted in an assortment of psychological disciplines, such as gestalt (Allan & Whybrow, 2007), cognitive behavioural therapy (CBT) and rational emotive behaviour therapy (REBT) (Auerbach, 2006; Ducharme, 2004; Neenan, 2006; Palmer & Szymanska, 2007; Peltier, 2001; Sherrin & Caiger, 2004), psychoanalysis (Allcorn, 2006; Lee, 2010), behavioural psychology (Alexander, 2006; Peterson, D. B., 2006; Skiffington & Zeus, 2003;), appreciative inquiry (Gordon, 2008), solution-focused therapy (de Shazer, 1988), and person-centred psychotherapy (de Haan, 2008; Joseph, 2010; Pemberton, 2006; Stober, 2006).

Thus, most of the theoretical foundations attributed to coaching are drawn from a variety of disciplines (Williams, P., 2008), and are transplanted into coaching, rather than being empirically tested in the field or developed organically from practice. Books that explore the roots of coaching sometimes read as a catalogue of ideas drawn from across the full range of mainly psychology literature, displaying little in terms of theoretical integration. In fact, it would seem that authors often embrace conflicting paradigms without acknowledging that this is happening, as identified by Cox (2005), Bachkirova, et al. (2010) and Ives (2008). Furthermore, those works that explore the theoretical foundations of coaching often celebrate eclecticism, a tendency which has been justifiably criticised for lacking coherence (Jackson, 2008).

Jackson (2008) advocates challenging the overly eclectic, theory-free approach to coaching, and cautions that not recognising inherent theory risks leaving coaching without any serious foundations. Similarly, Barner and Higgins (2007 p. 149) argue that problems occur when coaches fail to clarify their predominant theoretical orientation: "When we lack a clear understanding of the theory base that shapes our practice, we are less likely to adapt our practice to those shortcomings and constraints that accompany the particular model that we employ." In our view, an empirical, evidence-based approach is essential since it extends knowledge beyond the idiosyncratic eclecticism of the individual coach and feeds into a more complete, theoretical commons that can become a resource for the profession.

Coaching is versatile and can be applied to a diverse range of circumstances, needs and types of people and so it is only natural that it will encompass a wide range of approaches to meet those needs, address those circumstances and suit those people. Furthermore, specific models or approaches will be relevant at different times or situations. Thus, coaching theory rightly needs to acknowledge the diversity of legitimate approaches that the coaching discipline encompasses. However, in practice such coaching theory has been left largely undeveloped. What each coaching approach needs is its own theory: an organised logical basis for its proposed course of action.

Nothing as Practical as a Good Theory

To allay the concerns that many practitioners have regarding theory, it needs to be noted that theory need not be abstract, and it need not be removed from real-life knowledge. Schön (1991) distinguished between 'technical rationality,' which is taught didactically and 'theories in use,' which are accumulated through experience. He argued that the latter are superior. Coaching theory, too, can be generated by subjecting the experiences of coaches to careful analysis and thoughtful consideration. Coaching practice needs increasing levels of critical inquiry to challenge assumptions, research effectiveness and ensure the healthy development of the discipline.

Theory is not about establishing strict cause and effect, which is not desirable and arguably is not even possible, as no two human situations are ever identical. However, revealing social mechanisms, patterns and systems, much like meteorologists or economists do, can help to guide the person towards more intelligent decision-making. What jurisprudence is for law, coaching theory is for coaching practice. Much as engineers are taught the physics behind design, so too coaches should be master designers of coaching interventions. To do this, however, they need to be deeply familiar with the thinking behind their work. For example, not all goals are equally effective (Deci & Ryan, 2002; Locke & Latham, 1990) and a coach who understands the thinking behind goal construction can better facilitate effective goal setting. A more theoretical exposition of GFC would do a great service to coaching by adding coherence to the overall landscape, enabling coaching researchers and practitioners to assess more effectively what is appropriate and what is inappropriate for coaching.

Eclecticism

As described above, recent coaching work has drawn from an eclectic range of theoretical bases. Adult learning theories have been identified as a key foundation (Bachkirova et al., 2010; Cox, 2006; Gray, 2006). Similarly, adult development (Berger, 2006; Hudson, 1999), leadership development (Brennan, 2008) and personal construct psychology (Duignan, 2007) have been incorporated into coaching models. Several philosophical approaches have also been highlighted as offering a backdrop to coaching, such as linguistics (Flaherty, 2005), existentialism (Peltier, 2001; Spinelli & Horner, 2007; Spinelli, 2010) and spiritualism (Whitmore & Einzig, 2006). Feldman and Lankau (2005 p. 845) comment that coaching is so diverse that it is difficult to "put constructs around the construct itself." This makes it even more essential to have a theory of goal-focused coaching to mitigate this confusion.

However, undermining the development of theory in coaching has been the widespread support for and practice of eclecticism in the coaching literature (Snyder, 1995) defined by Hackman and Wageman (2005 p. 270) as "activities that derive from no particular theoretical perspective but have considerable face validity nonetheless." According to P. Williams (2008 p. 6), "coaching is a multidisciplinary, multi-theory synthesis," incorporating a range of theories of behaviour change and is a "synthesis of tools from other fields" (p. 21). Skiffington and Zeus (2003 p. xii) say that behavioural coaching, "a fusion of many disciplines, can also be seen as a montage, or synthesis of different forms into a new shape." What is less clear is the theoretical validity and coherence of this 'new shape.' Ironically, they argue that coaching "demands a conceptual framework that will provide a common language and a basis for research and create a blueprint for coaching practice and education" (p. 29)[1]. Flaherty (2005 p. 11) invokes pragmatism as the philosophical underpinning of coaching, arguing that in coaching "practical outcomes replace theoretical constructs." Parsloe and Wray (2000) likewise argue that coaching focuses on practice rather than theory, on praxis not psychology. Some coaches even promote their coaching model as *creative* for "combining contradictory models" (Grimley, 2007 p. 198).

Further exacerbating theoretical confusion, some coaching models combine strands from various psychological approaches that regard each other as incompatible and incommensurable, and those advocating these models do little to resolve these theoretical and practical contradictions. For example, Palmer and Szymanska (2007 p. 89) describe their cognitive–behavioural approach as "problem-oriented, goal- and solution-focused," seemingly overlooking that solution-focused is the opposite of problem-oriented. Similarly, coaching models that are claimed to be forward-focused allow room to address past experiences and to analyse the *causes* of the mistakes (e.g. Jackson & McKergow, 2008; O'Connell and Palmer, 2007; Palmer and Szymanska, 2007).

Indeed, Grant (2007 p. 24) acknowledges that "eclectic pragmatic utilitarianism, the 'use whatever works, and if it works, do more of it' philosophy, heavily influenced the early development of the contemporary commercial coaching industry." He adds that the diversity fostered by eclecticism has often tended towards an uncritical anti-intellectualism that closes down scientific and objective investigation. By contrast, Grant lauds the scientist–practitioner model in psychology for its openness to scientific debate and rigorous evaluation. The popularisers of coaching in the UK came from a sports background (e.g. Downey, 2003; Gallwey, 2002; Whitmore, 2003) and failed, for the most part, to make those principles explicit. Rogers (2008 p. 18) similarly states that "coaching, by and large, is a more pragmatic trade drawing on borrowed theory," and that "currently, practice leads theory." However, Jackson (2008) justly challenges coaching's 'can-do' culture of pragmatism and its talk of coaching as a practical discipline, which disguises the theoretical issues that underpin the development of coaching. Jackson (2008 p. 77) also points out that in the eyes of many coaches "there is a conflation of theory with speculation, and academia with the *un*real."

We also agree with de Haan (2008) that for coaching to be effective, it needs to be rooted in a clear methodology. In our view, combining conflicting approaches leads to one cancelling out the other and may impair both approaches from functioning properly. As Kauffman and Bachkirova (2008 p. 107) acknowledge, "sometimes these [diverse coaching] perspectives supplement each other, and sometimes they contradict each other." De Haan (2008) further cautions against adopting a pluralistic attitude, claiming that it is not possible to combine approaches at will and that sticking to a particular approach is important: "An important common factor is therefore the adoption and application of a *preferred approach*, something that eclectic, pluralistic or nihilistic coaches wouldn't do" (p. 55). A key aim of this book, therefore, is to articulate clear boundaries of GFC and explore a wide range of coaching issues through the goal-focused lens. We examine, for example, the art of questioning, relationship management and the use of feedback, and other key features of coaching, from a goal-focused perspective, all the while identifying the similarities and distinctions with other coaching paradigms.

Atheoreticism

While some coaching writers argue that their approach is rooted in a firm body of theory, others, as we identify above, claim that their approach is not theory based (Jackson & McKergow, 2008; McKergow and Korman 2009; Parsloe & Wray, 2000; Whitmore, 2003). Moreover, some goal-focused approaches, in particular solution-focused coaching, also claim to be atheoretical. Advocates suggest a theory of no theory in which solutions and techniques are invented anew each time in place of a set methodology (Berg & Szabo, 2005; Greene & Grant, 2003; Jackson & McKergow, 2008; McKergow & Korman, 2009). However, we would argue that all coaching approaches are necessarily based on a range of assumptions that are theoretical in nature, even if their advocates have not sought to articulate them in an overtly theoretical manner. Furthermore, as Grant and O'Connor (2010) show, it is inevitable that the coach will have a working hypothesis that guides his work. In our analysis, if the theoretical position of approaches such as solution-focused coaching remains largely unspoken, their techniques cannot be effectively enhanced, or indeed challenged. Rogers (2008) suggests that an atheoretical stance may be both a strength and a weakness, but in our view, the risks of adopting an atheoretical stance are too great.

Similarly some 'integrated' approaches (Passmore, 2006; Skiffington & Zeus, 2003) lack a consistent theoretical framework. For example, Skiffington and Zeus (2003 p. xii) argue that their behavioural coaching aims to facilitate learning, engender self-knowledge, and foster self-regulation of thinking and feeling – elements not normally associated with behavioural psychology, as Passmore (2007) notes. However, Passmore (2007 p. 79) similarly combines diverse elements, such as behaviourism, humanist psychology and psychoanalysis. A legitimate integrated approach would properly synthesise the various elements into a cohesive and theoretically coherent system, in which each part genuinely fits it and makes sense in relation to each other. 'Integrated' should not mean merely a potpourri of assorted techniques and models drawn together according to the personal taste of the particular coach. Coaching is in need of an organic basis for its own practice, informed by other disciplines, but ultimately true to its own essence. We agree with Drake that coaching needs to be "a primary activity rather than a derivative one" (Drake, 2008 p. 20) as it aspires to professionalise (Grant & Cavanagh, 2004).

A key casualty of this atheoreticism has been the boundary of the coaching discipline, which at times is so porous as to provide little coherence. Some coaches broaden coaching to include such diverse functions that it becomes unclear what the essence of coaching is. For many coaches, coaching has ceased to be a defined approach and has transmogrified into a business service influenced by a coaching-type approach. Indeed some coaches acknowledge that there has been a blurring of distinction between coaching and related disciplines (e.g. Skiffington and Zeus, 2003 p. 15). If coaching is to become a recognized discipline, rather than a general orientation, it needs theoretical integrity. Furthermore, in order for coaches to design coaching interventions effectively, they need to be deeply familiar with the thinking behind coaching practice. Some approaches to coaching have strayed far from the original task of coaching and what distinguishes it from therapy, which is, we would argue, its focus on action. Of course, there are many ways of stimulating action, some less direct than others, but coaching is invariably about making a practical change in the coachees' lives.

Human beings are goal-focused (Locke & Latham, 1990), and effective goal-pursuit is crucial to success in human endeavour (Bandura, 2001). GFC is therefore a vital form of coaching, harnessing a key driver for personal and organisational success. Yet little research has been conducted into GFC models. Therefore, in this book we are concerned with developing the theoretical foundation of GFC, which will add the 'how' and 'why' to the 'what', 'where' and 'when'– so that it is possible to judge when and where this particular approach is suitable and to better tailor the approach to specific circumstances. A car mechanic, who has only been taught how to fix a car, but not how a car works, is hardly a mechanic and will have very restricted abilities. Thus, a key objective of this book is to recommend a theoretical framework for GFC, setting out the psychological mechanisms that are involved, the boundaries of the approach and its main professional objectives.

This book, then, addresses a huge gap in the theory and practice of coaching. It foregrounds GFC theory rather than focusing on therapeutic or personal development models. It follows Kanfer (1990) and locates the foundations of goal-focused approaches to coaching within self-regulation theories (Baumeister & Vohs, 2007; Carver & Scheier, 1998; Kanfer, Ackerman, Murtha, Dugdale & Nelson, 1994), social cognitive psychology (Bandura, 1996, 2001) and goal theories (Ford, 1992; Locke & Latham, 1990).

About this Book

This well-researched yet practical book is based on a doctoral study (Ives, 2010) that explored the application and impact of goal-focused coaching in an adult education context. The study adopted an iterative (cyclical) action research methodology, introducing and studying a coaching intervention designed to help students establish clearly defined learning objectives, plan the action steps they needed to take to achieve it and to commit and motivate themselves to achieve their goals.

It adopted a traditional Lewinian (Lewin, 1946) approach to action research, emphasising development of *theoretical* knowledge rather than emancipatory and collaborative elements typical of more recent styles of action research (e.g. McNiff & Whitehead, 2005). The action research followed those who emphasise theory building, transferability and validity (Coghlan & Brannick, 2001; Eden & Huxham, 1996).

Research conclusions were based on data collected from focus group sessions and semi-structured interviews with participants of the coaching, as well as observation notes. Data analysis was conducted using coding methods from grounded theory (Glaser & Strauss, 1967; Strauss & Corbin, 1990), which facilitate a gradual transition from facts to theory (Charmaz, 2008).

Thus this book is based on significant empirical work undertaken by the authors and should be of interest to a wide range of readers. The business community is naturally goal-oriented and the book will be particularly useful to them. However, it is highly relevant to other sectors such as healthcare and education, and to life coaching. The book can be read linearly in order to assimilate the progression of the theory. Alternatively, readers may prefer to begin with Chapters 8, 9 and 10 which focus directly on the GFC model that is developed and described throughout the book, returning to the theoretical and process discussions later.

The GFC model has three main dimensions: Goal Setting, Action Planning and Commitment, which are established aspects of much coaching theory and practice and are rooted in the goal setting and motivational literature. We call this the 3W model of coaching, which is fundamentally about three core activities: goal setting (what), action planning (how and when) and motivation (why). These core areas are discussed in detail in Chapters 8, 9 and 10. Figure 1.1 illustrates the model and provides a concept map of the GFC process which will be described in subsequent chapters.

This map is not intended to provide a rigid sequential process, but aims to highlight how GFC, despite being a complex approach, is fundamentally about these core activities. While the map focuses on goal setting, action planning and motivation as the core activities of GFC in keeping with the ideas set out in later chapters, it also includes a range of elements considered necessary for successful goal-related activity, such as:

- Addressing barriers to coaching
- Considering group goals
- Reviewing options

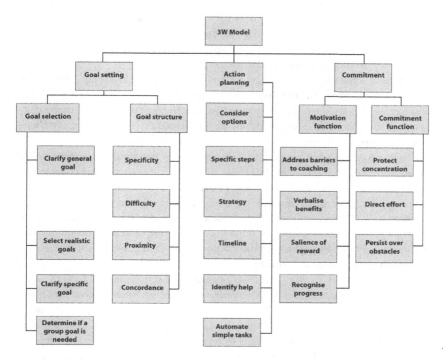

Figure 1.1 Goal-Focused Coaching: A Concept Map

- Seeking help
- Ensuring goal-related skills
- Monitoring progress.

Through the chapters that follow, we extend the exploration of GFC from the management of human relations, exploring a variety of aspects of the coaching relationship, to the core goal-related coaching activities, as summarised in Figure 1.1.

Chapter 2 – What is Goal-focused Coaching? – explains the goal-focused approach by contrasting it with other forms of coaching and identifying its unique characteristics, strengths and weakness in various contexts. It also discusses its relationship with the two other coaching 'paradigms': developmental and therapeutic. In particular, it proposes three axes around which revolve the key distinctions in approaches to coaching: (1) directive or non-directive, (2) personal-developmental or goal-focused and (3) therapeutic or performance-driven.

Chapter 3 – Goal-focused Coaching Theory – sets out the role of goals in coaching. It presents GFC as a self-regulation tool that operates in the intersection between antecedent influences, such as attributions and expectancies, and the goal choices that lead to actions. By facilitating more effective goals, GFC leads to raised performance, which in turn enhances self-efficacy.

Chapter 4 – Goal-focused Methodology – argues that the goal-focused coaching paradigm has two key features: it is forward-focused and it is driven by incremental change. It argues that goal-focused coaching is effective in leveraging small concrete actions to support positive change and thereby raise self-efficacy, an element critical to motivation and performance.

Chapter 5 – Relationship Management in Goal-focused Coaching – focuses on the importance of an effective coaching alliance. The chapter investigates the barriers to coaching and how they may be overcome. In particular it explores the challenges of the coachee's misconceptions about the coach's role, and the coachee's potential suspicion, resentment, dependence and indifference.

Chapter 6 – The Coaching Cycle – discusses how handling the beginning and ending of the coaching is crucial to the goal-focused approach. This chapter also covers handling breaks in the coaching and dealing with turbulence in the coaching context, both of which impinge on the goal-focus of the coaching process.

Chapter 7 – Team, Group and Peer Coaching with a Goal Focus – discusses the relative opportunities and risks of individual, peer, group and team coaching. This chapter suggests new insights into the strengths and weaknesses of these coaching formats in an organisational context.

Chapter 8 – Goal Setting – presents optimal goal setting as vital to GFC. This chapter examines key elements in effective goal setting, such as goal proximity, specificity and difficulty, and it suggests a two tier goal-setting process. The chapter also proposes a unique role for feedback in GFC, suggesting that the primary function of self-awareness and feedback is to feed into more effective goal-setting.

Chapter 9 – Action Planning – describes how breaking down the goal makes it seem more attainable and enables its smooth implementation. This chapter draws on new research into automaticity that suggests that developing task strategies allows the goal to be pursued below consciousness, which helps to conserve attentional and regulatory resources.

Chapter 10 – Commitment in Goal-focused Coaching – highlights how GFC aims to raise performance and motivation. This chapter explores a range of factors that influence commitment, such as intrinsic motivation, self-concordance, and participation in goal setting. The chapter will also draw on new research into raising commitment to the goal.

Chapter 11 – Questioning and Listening Skills – discusses how questions and listening, while always important in any coaching paradigm, have a subtly distinctive role in GFC. Questions primarily aim at raising awareness and gaining clarity, and listening is primarily about creating an empty space for the coachee's thoughts.

Chapter 12 – The Complete GFC Process – summarises key issues relating to GFC and presents a new 20-part map of the complete goal-focused process, with commentary and advice on each stage. The chapter also describes areas where GFC may be effective, providing real case studies and initial research results from a variety of contexts, including adult education, relationship work with singles and the training of prison officers.

2   What Is Goal-focused Coaching?

Aims

- To explain the goal-focused approach;
- To identify the unique characteristics of GFC and compare these with other approaches;
- To propose three broad coaching paradigms: therapeutic, developmental and goal-focused.

This chapter clarifies the role and extends the definition of Goal-Focused Coaching (GFC). As mentioned in Chapter 1, like other emerging disciplines, coaching struggles with problems of identity and definition, seemingly because of the explosion of coaching approaches available (Bachkirova et al., 2010; de Haan, 2008; Garvey et al., 2009). Coaching texts often present contradictory accounts about the nature and purpose of coaching, with commentators adding to the confusion by offering widely diverging definitions. For example, according to Stober (2006 p. 17) "coaching is above all about human growth and change," whereas D. B. Peterson (2006 p. 51) asserts that "the purpose of coaching is to change behaviour." Cavanagh (2006 p. 313) declares that "coaching is a journey in search of patterns," while in the view of Grant (2006 p. 156) "coaching is a goal-focused, solution-focused process."

Pemberton (2006) defines coaching by its emphasis on raising awareness, while other conceptions focus on enhancing the coachee's abilities (Costa & Garmston, 2002) and development (Carter, 2001) aimed at building competence (Moen & Skaalvik, 2009). By contrast, some coaches view coaching as primarily *performance*-related: "optimising people's potential and performance" (Whitmore, 2003 p. 97) or "to focus, motivate and support others in achieving their goal" (Parsloe & Wray, 2000 p. 183). According to these definitions, coaching is an intervention aimed at helping coachees to focus on and achieve their clearly defined goals. Many coaches combine several foci in their definition (Gray, 2006; Downey, 2003), suggesting that "coaching is about facilitating a client's performance, experience, learning and growth and about actualising goals" (Linder-Pelz & Hall, 2008 p. 43).

Thus, there is a need for greater clarity about the underpinnings of the coaching construct, especially in the context of an ever wider range of helping interventions

(D'Abate, Eddy & Tannenbaum, 2003; Parker, Hall & Kram, 2008). Additionally, as described in the previous chapter, coaching has relied on the theoretical influences of a range of mostly therapeutic or personal-development approaches, and while it has been immeasurably enriched by the injection of these ideas and techniques, these have often been accepted unquestioningly, leading to increased confusion about the precise nature of coaching and what it is designed to achieve.

This chapter aims to clarify the particular characteristics of GFC, which, we argue, is currently obscured amongst the burgeoning ideas and practices in the coaching orbit. GFC has its own unique philosophy, but is sometimes overshadowed by what appear to be more complete approaches to coaching. In this chapter we begin to delineate GFC as a distinct coaching paradigm.

The chapter is divided into four main sections. In the first section, in order to position goal-focused coaching, some popular, yet diverse types of coaching are identified. The diversity of approaches is then discussed, and the second section identifies some of the core criteria of coaching and also examines the disputed criteria. While the multifaceted nature of many coaching approaches precludes easy categorisation, our analysis of the rapidly expanding coaching literature (based on a textual analysis[1] of a considerable number of chapters drawn from coaching handbooks, such as Drake, 2008; Passmore, 2005; Peltier, 2001; Stober & Grant, 2006) suggests that there are three main axes around which revolve the key distinctions in approaches to coaching: directive or non-directive; personal-developmental or goal-focused and therapeutic or performance-driven. These three are discussed in some detail in section two. In the third section a comparative analysis is made, mapping eight coaching approaches against the three axes. In summary, we discuss the position of goal-focused coaching in relation to these other forms of coaching.

The Emergence of Diverse Approaches

Here eight different approaches to coaching are identified and the objectives of each given in order to begin to classify the qualities of each that are indispensable to the core meaning of coaching.[2]

Coaching from a humanist perspective – Based upon Rogerian person-centred principles (Rogers, 1959, 1980), coaching from this perspective views positive change and self-actualisation as a driving force in the human psyche (Stober, 2006). Coaching, from this point of view, capitalises on a person's inherent tendency to self-actualise and looks to stimulate a person's inherent growth potential. This approach draws from psychotherapy a strong emphasis on the practitioner–coachee relationship, suggesting that the relationship itself (its warmth and positive regard) is a main ingredient for growth. It also promotes a holistic approach, requiring the coach to address all aspects of the person.

Behaviour based approach – A behaviour based approach acknowledges the complexity of both human beings and their environment, but nevertheless focuses on facilitating practical change rather than psychological adjustments (Peterson, D. B., 2006). This approach is action focused insofar as it looks to the future and seeks to create change and imbed it in real-life contexts, but it still leans heavily towards personal development, emphasising the need for coachee learning. To a lesser degree, it adopts a therapeutic emphasis on the coaching relationship, as it primarily "strives to engender self-knowledge and self-regulation of thinking, feelings and actions" (Skiffington & Zeus, 2003 p. xii).

Adult development approach – The adult development approach has two strands. The first is rooted in lifecourse development theories and is well described by Palmer and Panchal (2011). This approach takes account of how motivation changes across the lifespan and suggests that coaches need to be aware of this and other lifecourse issues. The second adult development approach is based on constructive-developmental theories, which claim that as people develop they become more aware of and open to a mature understanding of authority and responsibility, and display greater tolerance to ambiguity. Coaching from this perspective is predicated upon the idea of stages of development and it suggests that coaching at each stage needs to focus on stage-of-development related issues (Bachkirova, 2011; Bachkirova & Cox, 2007; Berger, 2006).

Cognitive coaching – Auerbach (2006) claims that although coaching must address the multiple facets of the individual, it is primarily a cognitive method. A fundament of cognitive coaching is the view that feelings and emotions are the product of thoughts: they are a person's perceptions, interpretations, mental attitudes and beliefs. Cognitive therapy helps clients replace maladaptive and inaccurate cognitions (Burns, 1990). Auerbach argues that a primary function of the coach is to assist the coachee in challenging and overcoming their maladaptive and distorted perceptions.

Adult learning approach – This approach seeks to use coaching to stimulate deep learning. It draws from a range of adult-learning theories, such as andragogy (Knowles, 1975, 1984), reflective practice (Boud, Cohen and Walker, 1994) and experiential learning (Kolb, 1984), which collectively argue that adults learn by reflecting on experiences. Cox (2006) argues that, similarly, coaching can be seen as a learning approach designed to nurture goal-focused, self-directed learners who draw on their reservoir of previous experience with a view to solving real-life dilemmas. Gray (2006) and Askew and Carnell (2011) advocate a transformative learning coaching model that seeks to raise the coachee's critical reflection in order to question assumptions. They suggest that coaching has become a tool in the increasing shift towards informal, self-directed learning in organisations.

A positive psychology model – Kauffman (2006) argues that coaching should work to identify and build on the coachee's strengths and should seek to engender hope and happiness. Positive psychology seeks to encourage people to look to what is good and going well in their lives to reinforce a positive disposition. Positive emotions, it is argued, widens a person's focus of attention and broadens access to the person's intellectual and psychological resources, resulting in improved performance. While certain aspects of the positive coaching model can be used to achieve specific goals, it would seem that it is primarily designed to effect general enhancement and life balance.

Systemic approach – Coaching using a systemic framework is about helping the coachee to recognize hitherto unrecognized patterns of behaviour and forms of feedback, and in so doing to see their experiences in new ways (Peltier, 2001). It also encourages a holistic view, in which various other parts of the system may have relevance to the issue at hand. Humans are complex adaptive systems insofar as they consist of a combination of interacting factors that are affected by change and can respond to changed circumstances (see Carver & Scheier, 1998 chap. 14). A systemic coaching model seeks to foreground complexity, unpredictability and contextual factors, and highlights the importance of small changes; it encourages openness, growth and creativity. This approach views the balance between stability and instability as optimal for performance (Cavanagh, 2006).

Goal-focused approaches – The foregoing approaches may be contrasted with a goal-focused approach that sees the primary function of coaching as fostering the coachee's self-regulation. According to Grant (2006 p. 153), "coaching is essentially about helping individuals regulate and direct their interpersonal and intrapersonal resources to better attain their goals." The primary method is assisting the coachee to identify and form well-crafted goals and develop an effective action plan. The role of the coach here is to stimulate ideas and action and to ensure that the goals are consistent with the coachee's main life values and interests, rather than working on helping the coachee to adjust his/her values and beliefs. In this conception, coaching primarily aims to raise performance and support effective action, rather than to address feelings and thoughts, which it is assumed will be indirectly addressed through actual positive results (Grant, 2003). This approach encompasses brief coaching (Berg & Szabo, 2005) and solution-focused coaching which both aim to achieve results in a comparatively short space of time and normally focus on a relatively defined issue or goal.

The approaches described are distinct and each offers unique possibilities for coaching practice. As we shall argue, there are fundamental differences that emerge in relation to the definition and purpose of coaching. In Table 2.1 the objectives of each approach demonstrate subtle differences between approaches.

Table 2.1 Approaches to Coaching: Quotes selected from Stober & Grant (2006)

Type of coaching	Objective of coaching
Humanist	"Coaching is above all about human growth and change" (Stober, 2006 p. 17)
Behaviourist	"The purpose of coaching is to change behaviour" (Peterson, 2006 p.51)
Adult development	Coaching is about helping coachees develop and grow in maturity
Cognitive coaching	Coaching is foremost about developing adaptive thoughts
Adult learning	A learning approach that helps self-directed learners to reflect on and grow from their experiences
Positive psychology	"Shift attention away from what causes and drives pain to what energises and pulls people forward" (Kauffman, 2006 p. 220)
Systemic coaching	"Coaching is a journey in search of patterns" (Cavanagh, 2006 p. 313)
Goal-focused	"Coaching is a goal-oriented, solution-focused process" (Grant, 2006 p. 156)."

In the chronology of the emergence of the coaching discipline, coaching was originally directive, conceived as guidance, teaching or instruction. As coaching emerged as a distinct discipline, it began to be regarded as a form of facilitation or a people-management style, and as strictly non-directive. Increasingly, however, non-directive coaching, in its search for relevant theory, has adopted therapeutic elements, especially those drawn from Rogers (1980) and we need to consider whether aspects of these are incommensurable and incompatible, and whether there are basic features that form the core definition of coaching.

Core and Disputed Criteria of Coaching

As noted, some conceptions of coaching are strongly performance related. For example, according to Evered and Selman (1989), "to coach means to convey a valued colleague from where he or she is to where he or she wants to be," and Grant (2003 p. 254) defines life coaching as a "collaborative solution-focused, result-orientated and systematic process in which the coach facilitates the enhancement of life experience and goal attainment in the personal and/or professional life of normal, non-clinical clients." According to this perspective, coaching is an intervention aimed at raising coachee attainment by deploying open-ended questions that provoke thought, raise awareness, and inspire motivation and commitment.

However, other descriptions of coaching include a focus on developing the coachee's abilities. Costa and Garmston (2002 p. 21), for example, identify the aim of coaching as enhancing another's self-directedness: the other's ability to self-manage, monitor and modify. Coaches, they argue, "apply specific strategies to enhance another person's perceptions, decisions, and intellectual functions." Carter (2001 p. 15) refers to coaching as "work-related *development* for senior and professional managers" (emphasis added) and many definitions of coaching incorporate elements of both performance and development. According to Gray (2006 p. 476), "the coached client is someone who wants to reach a higher level of performance, personal satisfaction or learning," and Downey (2003 p. 15) suggests that it is "the art of facilitating the performance, learning and development of another." Linder-Pelz and Hall (2008 p. 43) state that "coaching is about facilitating a client's performance, experience, learning and growth and about actualising goals."

From an analysis of the literature, with very few exceptions, it may be said that the following features are common to the full range of coaching approaches:

- A systematic process designed to facilitate development (change), whether cognitive, emotional or behavioural;
- Intended for a non-clinical population;
- An individualised, tailor-made approach;
- Aims to encourage coachees to take charge of their life;
- Based on the twin growth areas of awareness and responsibility;
- Reliant on the skills of listening and questioning;
- Involves a collaborative and egalitarian relationship, rather than one based on authority;

- Creates a relationship within which coachees agree to be held accountable for their choices;
- Designed to access the inner resourcefulness of coachee and built on their wealth of knowledge, experience and intuition.

One final feature is core to the overwhelming majority of approaches:

- Focused on the achievement of a clear stated goal, rather than problem analysis.

However, while the foregoing list gives the impression of a broad base of agreement across the coaching literature, in fact there are issues of sharp divergence, relating to the nature of the coaching relationship, the function of coaching, and the scope of the coaching intervention. These issues are of paramount importance to some approaches and have the capacity to provoke intense disagreement and polarise opinion. For example:

- Do coaches need domain-specific expertise or knowledge?
- Do coaches only 'ask' or may they also 'tell'?
- Is coaching primarily designed to foster personal growth or to raise performance?
- How central is the coaching relationship to the coaching process?
- Is it essential for coaching to adopt an holistic view?
- Is coaching primarily designed to address feelings or actions?
- Should coaching aim to address the coachee's values?

To aid coherence, we suggest that there are three main clusters of issues around which to categorise coaching approaches:

(1) directive or non-directive;
(2) developmental or goal-focused; and
(3) therapeutic or performance-driven.

While these three areas are independent of each other, goal-focused approaches to coaching are non-directive, goal-focused and performance-driven. These clusters are now discussed in more detail.

Directive versus Non-directive

Grant and Stober (2006 p. 363) note that the issue of 'coach as advice giver' is 'controversial.' For example, D. B. Peterson and Hicks (1996 p. 14) advocate a more directive role when they suggest that "coaching is the process of equipping people with the tools, knowledge, and opportunities they need to develop themselves." Stober and Grant (2006 p. 2) cite Parsloe's early definition of coaching in which coaching is "directly concerned with the immediate improvement of performance and development of skills by a form of tutoring or instructing." Druckman and Bjork (1991 p. 61) portray coaching as guidance from an expert with a view to align the coachee's performance with that of the teacher, and in Hudson (1999 p. 6) a coach is described as a facilitator but also a guide.

These early and often partially directive conceptions generally gave way to a non-directive understanding of coaching. For example, Whitmore (2003) suggests that the hands-off approach should be applied whenever possible, and Parsloe and Wray (2000 p. 47) later argue that "the more rapidly a coach can move from a hands-on to hands-off style the faster improvement in performance will be achieved." This is because performance is enhanced when "control and respon-sibility is transferred from the coach to the learner." According to this view, the coach manages the process rather than the content of the coachee's development and the coach is advised to lead from behind (Jackson & McKergow, 2008), should be inclined to give as little advice as possible (de Haan, 2008) and should not seek to influence the coachee (Bresser & Wilson, 2006). Bresser and Wilson (2006) limit the control of the coach to the process of coaching (time-keeping, ensuring clear goals, holding the coachee accountable, keeping the coachee on track), rather than the content (area of focus, choosing goals and strategies, deciding on timeframe). Stober and Grant (2006 p. 363) conclude that a coach can deliver "excellent out-comes purely through facilitating a process that operationalises the principles of coaching, rather than through an instructor mode that emphasises the delivery of expert knowledge."

Stober (2006) also argues that she is drawing on the humanist therapeutic tra-dition when she suggests coaches need to facilitate another's growth rather than direct it. However, we would argue that the non-directive approach GFC is dis-tinct from its therapeutic counterpart in humanistic therapy. Humanistic thera-pies, that have (sometimes uncritically) influenced coaching approaches, are based on Rogers' (1980) conceptions of person-centred counselling and unconditional positive regard, but there are important differences between these approaches and the non-directive, client-centred approach adopted in coaching (see Cox, 2012c). We would argue that in coaching, particularly GFC, there is less emphasis on the moment-to-moment psychological state of the client (the truth of the client's 'state' being a positivist notion that is inherent in Rogers', and other therapists', work) and more on what is being constructed by the coach and client in relation to the production and maintenance of goals. GFC is constructivist and is driven by a belief that the client is constantly changing and updating, whereas the non-directive, person-centred approach of Rogers is a realist theory built on the idea that within the client there is a person, a self, to be understood and 'fixed.'

It could also be argued that, with the recent growth in therapeutic influences on coaching, a partial return towards guidance has been witnessed. Cavanagh (2006 p. 342), for example, insists that expert knowledge is critical to coaching, without which, he says, the coach is no more than a "well-meaning amateur." Furthermore, some coaches advocate sharing with the coachee the theoretical models being used (Chapman, Best & Van Casteren, 2003). Cavanagh (2006 p. 337) further argues that, 'overly client-centric approaches' which insist that the solution is within the coachee, are simplistic, arguing that "sometimes no matter how long we ask the solution does not emerge, because it is not 'in' the client, nor are the raw materials available for it to emerge via a process of questioning" (p. 337). Grant and Stober (2006 p. 363) on the other hand, do not see these approaches as so diverse. They maintain that the two approaches (emphasis on content vs. emphasis on process) are not 'categorically different' but lie on a continuum, and the coach should be guided by what is best for the coachee. They assert that a skilled coach would know when it is appropriate to act as authoritative expert and when to act as facilitator.

However, we would argue that guidance is broadly unsuited to coachee-centric approaches such as GFC. Such coaching approaches preference a totally non-directive stance, and they are generally targeted only at relatively defined issues and goals, where it is entirely reasonable to consider that the coachee could work out the solution.

A strict non-directive approach would insist that coaching is almost *entirely* about questioning and is not about directing. While goal-focused approaches recognize the occasional need for the coach to suggest a solution, we would argue that for most problems the solutions are relatively obvious but that the coachee needs to refocus from dwelling on the problem towards seeking a solution. In this respect, the role of the coach is to conduct the process not to direct the outcome, and in this view one of the most valuable skills of the coach is to know how not to interfere!

Directive versus Non-directive – How Coachee Centric?

- Is the coach essentially a facilitator or also a guide?
- Should the coach be advising or sticking to an 'ask-not-tell' approach?
- Does the coach need domain specific expertise or knowledge?
- Should coaches be encouraged to share their theoretical ideas?

Development-focused or Goal-focused

While there is a general consensus that coaching is forward-focused, coaching approaches diverge significantly in the extent to which they advocate delving into the subterranean aspects, the issues that lurk beneath the surface. Snyder (1995) highlights how some coaches adopt a pragmatic approach towards their coachee's problems, while others adopt an exploratory style that seeks to uncover the underlying issues. More explicitly, Reding and Collins (2008 p. 178) argue that "as the profession of coaching matures, coaches are being called on to go deeper with their coachees. Coachees [. . .] are looking for coaching relationships that facilitate deeper explorations." Similarly, from a cognitive–behavioural position, Neenan (2006) posits that simply following a goal-oriented action plan is usually insufficient as the coachee is often confronted with self-limiting beliefs and thoughts. Nevertheless, Neenan (2006 p. 94) argues that the practical side of coaching can be neglected by an unhealthy interest in the psychological aspects of the coaching: "some coaches, particularly from counselling backgrounds, are too eager to 'dig deep' into psychological issues or overly focus on them before there is evidence to warrant such an investigation."

Many coaches then are steeped in a therapeutic model and carry a deficit–conflict perspective (Kauffman & Scouler, 2004), which Kauffman (2006) argues leads them to look to identify pathology and problems. Based upon positive psychology, Kauffman (2006 p. 220) argues that coaches "shift attention away from what causes and drives pain to what energises and pulls people forward." Solution-focused approaches have been found wanting for being superficial (e.g. Ellis, 1997) and it has been argued that coaching needs to go 'deeper' to be successful (Kilberg, 2004). However, as Grant (2006 p. 80) argues, problems invariably surface on their own: "There is no need to go looking for 'deeper' underlying issues."

Writing from a behavioural perspective, D. B. Peterson (2006) argues that insight-oriented questions are not at the heart of coaching and Jackson and McKergow (2008) suggest that often the quickest and most effective way of solving the problem is not to try to solve it but to sidestep it. Grant (2006) similarly suggests that coaching supports "solution construction in preference to problem analysis," the latter being a more therapeutic mode (although Brockbank [2008 p. 138] suggests that combining behavioural and cognitive elements "can lead to coaching which is problem-solving and solution-focused"). Proponents of goal-focused or solution-focused coaching view coaching as a method of helping coachees to reframe their challenges as practical problems, and help them generate the required internal and external resources.

All approaches to coaching include consideration of context as part of the coaching format, and recognize that coaching needs to be adjusted in accordance with the specific environment. However, coaching approaches vary in the extent to which they prioritise a holistic approach. In particular, approaches to coaching based upon family therapy (Peltier, 2001) and systems thinking (Cavanagh, 2006) explore the wider context, the complex layers of subsystems (systems approach). In contrast, goal-focused approaches generally focus on specific aims. They seek to integrate an ongoing self-regulatory process into daily modes of behaviour, rather than aiming for a comprehensive breakthrough.

The conflicting tendencies described above also support varying time remits for the coaching process. Personal-development and in particular therapeutic approaches typically require an extended time period to effect change. Hudson (1999 p. 19) insists that "coaches are not quick-fix agents." Conversely, Judge and Cowell (1997) and Sperry (1993) argue that coaching is designed to act in a far shorter timeframe than therapy. For while there are short-term therapy models, such as possibility therapy (O'Hanlon, 1998) and solution-focused therapy (de Shazer, 1988), comparatively speaking, coaching tends to focus "as rapidly as possible on potential solutions that the person can recognize and take personal responsibility for implementing" (Parsloe & Wray, 2000 p. 65).

Coaching paradigms may also differ in how specific are their pre-stated aims. For example, adult-development approaches to coaching (Berger, 2006; Cox, 2006) rarely seek to pre-state specific aims. Brookfield (1986 p. 213) argues that personal learning "cannot be specified in advance in terms of objectives to be obtained." West and Milan (2001) suggest that the role of coaching is to create the psychological space for reflective learning. This is in contrast to the emphasis in some of the coaching literature on a clear goal (e.g. Berg & Szabo, 2005; Greene & Grant, 2003; Whitmore, 2003). These two perspectives on coaching – goal- or development-focused – also differ as to the kind of goals that the coaching typically stimulates. Goals exist at varying levels of abstraction (Locke & Latham, 1990), forming a hierarchal goal structure (Carver & Scheier, 1998). This will be described in more detail in Chapters 8 and 9.

Development-focused or Goal-focused – How Outcome Centric?

- How holistic a strategy must the coach adopt (breadth)?
- To what extent must the coach delve beneath the surface (depth)?
- Is coaching problem- or solution-focused? Is the focus on what is holding the person back or what can help to pull him/her forward?
- Is coaching primarily designed to achieve specific aims, or more general development?
- Is coaching short-term or longer-term?
- Are coaching goals pre-specified?

Therapeutic versus Performance-driven

In contrast to goal-oriented coaching which is designed to stimulate effective action, many coaching approaches are therapeutic in nature (Judge & Cowell, 1997). These therapeutic approaches place heightened emphasis on the practitioner–client relationship (e.g. de Haan, 2008; Flaherty, 2005; Kemp, 2008a), extending the range and depth of issues that are perceived to be crucial to its success, bringing coaching more in line with the therapeutic relationship. Stober (2006) advocates a high degree of empathy and unconditional positive regard and acceptance of the coachee. This, as suggested earlier, may be related to a broader remit such as personal development and affective issues and her emphasis on the relationship reflects a conceptualisation of coaching designed to achieve a more therapeutic aim.

This calls into question the difference between therapy and coaching. Coaching researchers (e.g. Bluckert, 2005; Stober, 2006) claim that there are fundamental differences between theories and practices of therapy and coaching: psychological disciplines are designed to ameliorate dysfunction and address mental health problems, whereas coaching is intended to stimulate growth and development, targeting well-functioning people to enhance their performance or life success (Grant, 2007). Furthermore, Grant (2007 p. 31) argues, based on Fox (1996) and Laungani (1999), that psychology "has not risen to the challenge of meeting the needs of consumers in the normal adult population," and although positive psychology represents a significant effort in this direction, the need is currently being met by coaching.

In reality though, many coaches attempt to identify the profound psychological causes of the coachee's problems and coaches often draw up a psychological profile of their coachee before proceeding with coaching (Gray, 2006). This suggests, as O'Connell and Palmer (2007 p. 286) point out, that many coaches may be struggling to acknowledge the limitations of their approach.

In recent years, several substantial studies have called into question the simplistic and unsubstantiated distinctions drawn between coaching and therapy (Bachkirova & Cox, 2005). The difference between 'therapeutic coaching' and therapy is often exaggerated, with Griffith and Campbell (2008) arguing that there is significant overlap between coaching and counselling in their techniques and sometimes even in their client base. They disagree that the similarities are limited to the most basic outline of the two disciplines, and argue that it extends to the techniques and processes each use.

Given that coaching is designed to address the healthy population, Gray (2006) questions why coaching should necessarily so often adopt a psychotherapeutic approach, as it blurs the line between coaching and therapy. Goodman (2002) likewise insists that coaches who "overemphasise personal enlightenment will ultimately undermine a coaching program" (2002 p. 197). Hodgetts (2002) and Saporito (1996) argue that while psychotherapy focuses on the individual's personal issues and the holistic person, coaching needs to focus on achieving work- or life-related improvements.

Despite the need for differentiation, all coaching models recognize that effective management of the relationship is vital (Whitworth, Kimsey-House & Sandahl, 2007). If coachees feel forced into the relationship, or if they are not convinced it is designed to help them, the coaching is unlikely to be successful (Latham, Almost, Mann & Moore, 2005). However, coaching models vary as to both the degree of importance and the extent of the requisite relationship skills. As a minimum, the coach must display a genuine interest in the coachee, apply effective communication skills such as listening and verbal skills, and needs to provide an encouraging and supportive space within which exploration of the coachee's strengths, weaknesses, hopes and aspirations can occur (Dunbar, 2009; Skiffington & Zeus, 2003; Starr, 2007).

Even with regard to therapy, the client and the client's resources (rather than the client–therapist relationship) are seen as the most critical factor to a successful outcome (Hubble & Miller, 2004; Linley, 2006) and the relationship is likely to be even less salient with most coaching interventions, where the sensitivity of the subject matter is normally far less than in a typical therapy situation. D. B. Peterson (2006) and Grant (2006), for example, argue that in coaching the nature of the relationship is less important, and Cox (2009, p. 162) also confirms that in coaching the relationship plays a less 'curative role'.

Therapeutic and performance coaching may also differ in their approach to raising awareness. The therapeutic approaches encourage self-exploration and enlightenment (Drake, 2008; Spinelli, 2010; Whitmore & Einzig, 2006) and advocate high levels of self-awareness as a therapeutic end in itself (e.g. Yontef, 2005). By contrast, in GFC, awareness refers to attaining a clearer understanding of one's circumstances and is a means towards taking appropriate action (Whitmore, 2003), comparing the way things are with the way they could be (Parsloe & Wray, 2000) and gaining clarity of one's circumstances and options to facilitate effective action (Grant, 2003; Jackson & McKergow, 2008).

Therapeutic versus Performance-driven – How Relationship Centric?

- Is coaching intended to stimulate inner or outer change? Is coaching primarily designed to change feelings or actions, personal growth or improved performance?
- How central is the relationship to the coaching process?
- Is awareness-raising a means or the end?
- What kind of awareness is raised: getting in touch with feeling or attaining a clearer understanding of one's circumstances?
- What is the primary role of feedback: to guide future actions or to act as a learning tool?

Comparative Analysis

As noted earlier, no approach to coaching falls exclusively into one category (e.g. 'directive' or 'non-directive'). Furthermore, the terms used to describe the coaching approaches (such as 'therapeutic') are relative; even among the coaching approaches clustered together by this study there is likely to be considerable variation. Thus there is an inherent danger in clustering approaches. However, for the sake of clarity, it is useful to identify broad tendencies – with the clear understanding that such categorisations are likely to be contentious, fraught and imperfect.

Table 2.2 highlights that it is only goal-oriented approaches to coaching that are strictly non-directive, goal-focused and performance-driven. On this basis, we argue that GFC is distinguished by three key features: (a) non-directive, (b) goal-focused and (c) performance-driven. Goal-oriented approaches to coaching have quite distinct features and theoretical foundations, and diverge from more therapeutic personal development approaches on the issue of what coaching is primarily intended to accomplish.

It can also be seen from Table 2.2 that quite fundamental issues, both theoretical and practical, divide the various approaches to coaching, and that these

Table 2.2 Comparison of Coaching Approaches

Type of coaching	Directive vs. Non-Directive	Solution vs. Development	Therapeutic vs. Performance
Humanist	Non-directive	Development	Therapeutic
Behaviourist	Directive	Solution	Performance
Adult development	Directive	Development	Therapeutic
Cognitive coaching	Directive	Development	Therapeutic
Adult Learning	Non-directive	Development	Therapeutic
Positive psychology	Directive	Development	Therapeutic
Systemic coaching	Non-directive	Development	Therapeutic
Goal-oriented	Non-directive	Solution	Performance

divergent approaches will also be suited to varying situations. By understanding more clearly the nature of the difference between approaches, it is easier to fit a coaching model to specific circumstances, and to clarify the distinctive goal-focused paradigm. However, while these models of coaching are based on differing coaching philosophies and methodologies, they are not mutually exclusive. Rather, each of the various approaches to coaching has unique strengths and is best suited for particular situations.

In reality, no actual approach to coaching stereotypically fits this exact categorisation, nor do any of them conform consistently to this trichotomy, but by thinking in terms of 'ideal types' we can position coaching approaches along a spectrum. For example, all coaching models would regard a totally directive approach as incompatible with coaching, and similarly, all approaches to coaching would consider themselves solution-focused compared with psychoanalysis. However, when these coaching methodologies are compared, meaningful distinctions emerge. We therefore conclude that it is useful to cluster coaching approaches into three main headings: therapeutic, developmental and goal-focused.

Goal-focused Coaching

GFC may be identified as essentially being about raising performance and supporting effective action, rather than addressing feelings and inner thoughts (Grant, 2003). Its primary activity is assisting the coachee to identify and form well-crafted goals and develop an effective action plan (Ives, 2008). GFC then, stimulates what Grant (2006) terms 'purposefulness', an action orientation, a mental type of 'rolling up one's sleeves'. GFC follows the view that the goal of coaching is not psychological change (Cox, 2010) nor is it driven by a desire to eradicate psychological dysfunction (Bachkirova, 2007), but is a tool to improve performance. Thus, coaching focuses mostly on external change. While psychological change may occur, it is a by-product, as we explain in Chapters 3 and 4.

Based upon the foregoing analysis, GFC represents a distinct form of coaching that is non-directive, goal-focused and performance-driven. This type of coaching is referred to as 'process-driven' (Skiffington & Zeus, 2003) and is result, performance and goal-directed (Parsloe & Wray, 2000). Summerfield (2006) and Rogers (2008) both distinguish between acquisitional or transactional (to acquire a new ability) versus transformational (to undergo personal change) coaching, which are dealt with by 'how' and 'who' questions respectively (de Haan, 2008). In the former, the coach helps coachees to help themselves, whereas in the latter the coach helps coachees in ways that they cannot help themselves.

Similar bifurcations can be detected across the coaching literature. GFC can be seen as akin to what Snyder (1995) terms a pragmatic rather than an exploratory style. Hudson (1999 p. 20) similarly separates 'coaching for being' and 'coaching for performance' – inner versus outer work. In the same vein, Brockbank (2008 p. 133) distinguishes between coaching that is functionalist and operational (equilibrium) versus transformative and engagement (disequilibrium). The former seeks "to enhance performance in a given function" rather than seeking to achieve fundamental change. By contrast, 'transformative' coaching involves radical change, which challenges existing power structures, fundamental assumptions and prevailing discourses.

Cavanagh (2006 p. 320) also argues that the purpose of coaching is to push the coachee towards the edge of chaos, towards a controlled and managed instability, a condition in which human growth and change is most likely. Similarly, Gray (2006) advances a 'transformative learning' model that seeks to generate critical reflection and the challenging of assumptions. By contrast, O'Neill (2000) takes a more conservative line, suggesting the coach fosters 'dynamic equilibrium'.

In a not too dissimilar fashion, Moen and Skaalvik (2009 p. 31) separate "those who claim that coaching is everything an executive consultant or coach does to realise the coachee's potential" (Hargrove, 2003; Kinlaw, 1989; Schein, 2006) from those who claim that coaching is a specific method to realise that potential (Downey, 2003; Flaherty, 2005; Whitmore, 2003). The latter approach places greater emphasis on the active participation and responsibility of the coachee in the coaching process.

GFC is presented here as an umbrella term, describing a coaching paradigm that incorporates coaching approaches that are largely goal-directed. We view solution-focused coaching (Grant, 2006; Greene & Grant, 2003; Jackson & McKergow, 2008; O'Connell & Palmer, 2007; Pemberton, 2006) and brief coaching (Berg & Szabo, 2005; Szabo & Meier, 2009) as related to GFC as they are comparatively, although to varying degrees, interventions that are action-oriented and focus on a relatively defined issue or goal, even if they are distinct from each other on some issues. On the basis of the above analysis, we propose the following definition of GFC:

> A systematic and collaborative helping intervention that is non-directive, goal-oriented and performance-driven, intended to facilitate the more effective creation and pursuit of another's goals.

As will be set out in later chapters, the main elements of GFC are goal setting, action planning and bolstering the coachee's motivation and commitment. Skiffington and Zeus (2003 p. 33) disparagingly term this the 'accountability model of coaching' and deride it as a 'quick fix', but indeed accountability and acceptance of responsibility is at the heart of this approach (Whitmore, 2003). In GFC, a key role of the coach is leveraging the coaching relationship to support progress towards the goal. Rogers (2008) claims that performance goals can lead to anxiety that actually interferes with the person's ability to perform. However, not only does she provide little support for this claim, but goal-related activity is a central part of people's lives. Furthermore an appropriate amount of pressure can be a positive thing, as will be explained in forthcoming chapters.

Brockbank (2008 p. 134) is also critical of what she terms 'functionalist coaching' that "focuses on improvement, efficiency and equilibrium," as she claims it maintains the status quo. She condemns this approach, as it "leads coaches to socialize their clients, ensuring the preservation of existing values and norms . . .

tends to reinforce existing power relations and even overtly and/or covertly reproduces social inequalities" (2008 p. 134). This is unnecessarily judgmental, for successful conformity to the system may genuinely be in all parties' interests. Coaching does not need to adopt an emancipation agenda in order to offer benefit to the coachee. Brockbank (2008) further argues that functionalist coaching fails to provide the emotional support that some coachees desire. Indeed, we admit that GFC is not best suited for situations when emotional support is the priority. However, in some situations an intensive form of coaching may prove far too invasive and time-consuming to be organisationally sustainable and may lead to chaos.

Inherent in its goal-focused nature, GFC is driven by the needs of the client's goal. Thus, both the format and the direction of the coaching are adjusted to the contingencies of the goal-activity. As will be explained in Chapter 7, the goals coachees are aiming to pursue may require group cooperation, which could necessitate a change from individual to group coaching. Additionally, the nature of the goals that coachees select may call for the assistance of individuals outside the organisation, so the coaching may need to be adapted to include seeking assistance to facilitate effective goal pursuit. Also, the circumstances within the organisation may be unstable, rendering the coachees' most likely goals impracticable. Thus, GFC needs to be adjusted to incorporate a significant exploration of options, to consider and ensure commitment to realistic if imperfect solutions. Moreover, due to necessity coachees may adopt tasks that under better circumstances they would have been unwilling to consider, but which are necessitated by their goals.

This chapter has provided an overview of the goal-focused approach and has compared it with some other forms of coaching in order to create a specific identity for GFC. To this end, three axes were identified that provided key distinctions in approaches to coaching and these could be used to examine any coaching approach in order to inform practice. The defining features of GFC are summarised below:

Summary of Characteristics of GFC

- Coach as facilitator (not guide);
- Adopts wherever possible an 'ask-not-tell' approach;
- Domain-specific expertise less vital;
- More specific focus (less holistic);
- Tends not to delve beneath the surface;
- Forward and solution-focused;
- Designed to achieve more specific aims;
- Generally a short-term process;
- Goals are established towards the beginning of coaching;
- Intended to stimulate outer (cognitive–behavioural) change;
- Coaching relationship is vital but not central;
- Feedback is for clarifying circumstances (not deep self-awareness).

3 Goal-focused Coaching Theory

Aims

- To set out the role of goals in coaching and explain GFC as a self-regulation tool;
- To examine how by facilitating more effective goals, GFC leads to raised performance that in turn enhances self-efficacy.

In this chapter it is argued that Goal-focused Coaching (GFC), like goal and self-regulation theories, considers human activity as a cyclical process of establishing and pursuing goals that energise and direct people's activities (Pervin, 1982). GFC further conceives of self-regulation as a skill that can be managed and enhanced by the individual (Baumeister & Vohs, 2007), and views goals as actionable and amenable to manipulation (McDowall & Millward, 2009). In addition, understanding the *function* and *process* of self-regulation is vital to a proper conception of the role that coaching can play in fostering effective self-regulation. By 'function' we mean the purpose and role of GFC, and by 'process' we mean the method in which it operates. Coaches need a good grasp of both in order to deploy the power of goal-directed self-regulatory activity in the service of the coachee's success.

In this chapter we suggest that GFC should be viewed as a self-regulation tool that helps people to govern the psychological intersection between their self-beliefs and action-related processes. The chapter therefore deals with a number of propositions:

- engaging with cognitive and conscious self-regulation, as GFC aims to do, is the most effective way of enhancing goal attainment;
- enhancing self-regulation is an effective strategy for raising self-efficacy, and that, as a self-regulatory intervention, coaching is similarly an effective method of raising self-efficacy;
- actual progress towards and attainment of goals leads to enhanced self-efficacy and thus effort and performance;
- a key function of GFC is to help the coachee more effectively allocate regulatory and attentional resources.

The chapter consists of five sections: the role of self-regulation; the intersection between past and future; the role of goals; goal setting and discrepancy management; and goal management.

The Role of Self-regulation

Self-regulation is the process whereby people monitor and regulate their progress towards a desired end (Baumeister, 1998). It involves "monitoring and adjusting responses in the service of the self [. . .] by comparing current states with goals, and engaging control processes when the two are discrepant" (Neal, Wood & Quinn, 2006 p. 200). Effective self-regulatory activity also enhances self-control, task focus and feelings of competence (Schunk, 1991). The main and most immediate method by which a person's self-regulation system controls the discrepancy reduction process is through choice of goals, which then leads a series of actions towards their attainment (Bandura, 2001; Carver & Scheier, 1998). Therefore, we would argue that the type of goals stimulated through the self-regulation mechanism are key regulatory factors.

In the management of action, there are two processes: pre-decisional processes (engagement), i.e., the cognitive process of determining what action to take; and post-decisional processes (execution), ensuring implementation of the goal (Heckhausen, 1991; Kuhl, 1984). These processes manage the selection of goals *and* guide their implementation by maintaining concentration and directing effort (Baumeister & Vohs, 2007; Mischel & Ayduk, 2007). These self-regulatory elements are shown in Figure 3.1, and may be enhanced by coaching, as suggested in the coaching literature (Alexander, 2006; Dembkowski, Eldridge and Hunter, 2006; Whitmore, 2003).

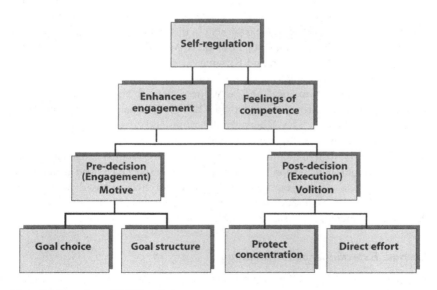

Figure 3.1 Function of Self-Regulation

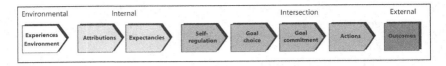

Figure 3.2 Linear View of the Role of Self-Regulation

This formulation of coaching claims that self-regulation serves as a mediator between internal influencers of future actions, and the choices the person makes to direct those actions. Past experiences lead a person to develop perceptions or attributions about his or her abilities and circumstances. These in turn lead to judgements or expectancies about what is likely to occur in the future. These thoughts, appraisals and self-concepts may be collectively termed 'goal cognition' (Karoly, 1993). A person's cognitive choice of actions is largely guided by these expectancies, and unless consciously countervailed will exert overwhelming influence of what goals a person will choose, and thus the consequential actions and outcomes. Self-regulation is therefore a crucial mediating pivot that, if activated, can critique and assess those internal and external influencers, and allow the person to make reasoned decisions about future actions without being imprisoned by the past. This dynamic is captured in Figure 3.2.

Within this theoretical framework, self-regulation is the process that separates environmental antecedents and internal dimensions (attributions and expectancies) from the external outcomes (choices and actions); it therefore moderates between past and future. This juncture will later be described as 'the intersection,' the point at which the locomotive of human activity is given its direction, crossing from the internal, evaluative processes to the more external, action-oriented processes. This idea of an intermediary stage is present in differing forms in many models of motivation (e.g. Deci & Ryan, 2002; Fishbein & Ajzen, 1975). Ommundsen (2006 p. 289), based on Zimmerman and Kitsantas (1996), describes self-regulation as "an important mediator between personal and contextual characteristics and actual achievement and performance" and, as Wolters, Pintrich and Karabenick (2003) assert, it is primarily self-regulatory activities that mediate between the context and the ultimate performance level, between the causes and effects of actions.

This theory further suggests that coaching can play an important role in enhancing self-regulation by fostering optimal choices and actions. We first explain in greater detail the role of self-regulation in mediating between expectancies and attributions, but in order to do so we set out an analysis of how goal choice is based on expectancies (in particular 'self-efficacy'), which in turn are based on attributions (in particular the 'stability dimension'), as suggested by key social cognitive theories.

Internal: Expectancies and Attributions

Expectancies – Early cognitive models of motivation distinguished between beliefs about ability to do the task (expectancy) and the belief in the desirability of the task (value), suggesting that motivation is the result of a combination of the two (Weiner, 1986). Eccles and Wigfield (1993) subdivided these two elements of expectancy and value. Expectancy of success, based on Atkinson's (1964) 'probability for success' (the belief in the likelihood of a positive outcome) is itself comprised of two components: (a) the person's task-specific self-concept, similar to Harter's (1990) 'self-perception of competence' and Bandura's (1986) 'self-efficacy' and (b) their judgement as to task difficulty.

Task value, akin to Atkinson's 'incentive value' and Rotter's (1954) 'reinforcement value,' is the person's level of interest in the outcome. This element also has two components: (a) expectation of outcome, and (b) the desirability thereof. According to expectancy theories, motivation is a combination of these various perceptions, as illustrated in Figure 3.3.

While the self-concept construct in recent expectancy models vary in some respects, they are broadly similar. Harter's (1990) 'self-perception of competence' and Bandura's (1986) 'self-efficacy' are similar to Eccles and Wigfield's (1993) task specific self-concept, and what Ford (1992) terms 'personal agency beliefs.' All focus on the individual's cognitive evaluation of their own ability in a particular domain, rather than on global self-worth or self-esteem. Similarly, Cervone, Mor, Orom, Shadel and Scott (2007 p. 190) emphasise that self-efficacy is not a stable property of the person, but is context-specific; it is a "person-in-context construct – people's thoughts about their capabilities for performance within a particular encounter." Bandura (1997) suggests that self-efficacy is a better predictor of motivation and related behavior than global indices of self-concept.

So, while several expectancies affect motivation, Bandura (1986 p. 393) argues that self-efficacy has the most significant influence: "If you control for how well people judge they can perform, you account for much of the variance in the kinds of outcomes they expect." Thus, of the aforementioned expectancy factors, the most important is the individual's opinion (self-concept) of his or her own competence. In addition to its impact on choice, efficacy beliefs are linked

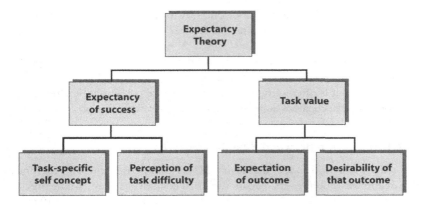

Figure 3.3 Expectancies

to quantity of effort and determination in the face of a difficult task (Bandura & Cervone, 1983; Schunk, 1991), and lead to greater cognitive engagement and a variety of other performance-related skills (Schunk, 1984). Significantly, high self-efficacy is also linked to use of self-regulatory strategies (Linnerbrink & Pintrich, 2002).

Attributions – Self-efficacy and related expectancies are formed through a range of influencers (including social, cultural, environment and disposition), but above all they are created through attributions of the causes of past events, both successes and failures (Bandura, 1997; Williams, S. L. & Cervone, 1998). Weiner (1986) cites extensive empirical evidence that a person's attributions affect his or her expectancies of success and suggests that although attributions are the result of perception, they have very real consequences. For example, C. Peterson, Maier and Seligman (1993) show how professional athletes who make adaptive skill-related attributions of past success or failure go on to do better than those attributing it to luck.

There are three main dimensions to attribution (Weiner, 1986): locus (internal or external), stability (fixed or changeable), and control (degree of influence over outcome). From an attribution theory perspective, where failure lies with personal factors (which are more unstable and controllable), it is maladaptive to attribute them to environmental factors (which are more stable and uncontrollable). The stability dimension is judged to have the greatest influence on the *efficacy* element of expectancy (Weiner, 1986), which, as noted, has the strongest impact on choice of behaviour (while the locus element most influences self-esteem, and the controllability dimension affects guilt and shame).

The antecedents of attributions are the information or perceptions upon which the attributions are based. People organise this information into scripts or schemas that represent consistencies in beliefs about their own competencies. There are two types of antecedent conditions upon which attributions are based:

(1) Environmental factors – information about the material situation and the social conditions (Kelley & Michela, 1980)
(2) Personal factors – beliefs about one's own ability, largely based upon past experiences (Pintrich & Schunk, 1996).

Thus, attribution is the result of inferences that the person makes about prevailing personal and environmental conditions. While it is impossible to reverse past experience and it is often difficult to change external conditions, it is possible to overcome the effects these influencers could have on self-concept.

The Intersection between Past and Future

Key to the theoretical understanding of GFC is the link from action and the choices that determine actions to the person's internal cognitive process. In the previous section we explained a chain running backwards, snaking its way from goal choice to the efficacy dimension of expectancy, tracing its route through to the aptitude/

Figure 3.4 The Goal Choice Chain

stability dimension of attributions and their provenance in the coachee's real-life experience. This conception offers a significant addition to our understanding of GFC, and is summarised in Figure 3.4.

GFC can be viewed as a self-regulatory intervention aimed at helping coachees to assert their conscious decision-making powers and stimulate effective self-regulatory mechanisms. Additionally, helping coachees to achieve goals they have previously failed to meet is a vital method of reversing the effects of negative attributions and expectancies.

At the heart of GFC, then, is the view that by activating conscious self-regulation the person can scrutinise his or her attributions and expectancies to determine firstly whether they are warranted and accurate and, secondly, whether they are conducive to success. Coaching is often used as a method of exploring and assessing the validity and utility of internal psychological processes (Kauffman, 2006; Palmer, 2007). However, the main benefit of GFC is supporting coachees towards taking actions that exceed their current expectancies or attributions. The immediate benefit is increased performance. Nevertheless, as coachees make small steps towards success, the experience of success gives rise to new, more positive attributions. These, in turn, lead to higher expectancies, sustaining the next cycle of growth (Reeves & Allison, 2009), as illustrated in Figure 3.5.

GFC focuses primarily on self-*regulation*, meaning the self's regulation of its actions, rather than regulation of the 'self' (Baumeister & Vohs, 2007). Its primary function is helping the coachee to progress towards his or her self-set task. Any psychological benefits are a consequence, rather than a cause, but in turn they become a cause of subsequent efficacy and increased motivation. Consequently, coaches must focus coachees on those things over which the latter feel they have control and are subject to change, i.e. effort and skills, not aptitude, in order to foster performance-enhancing choices. Supporting this notion, Moen and Skaalvik (2009) found that coaching led to increased attribution to ability and strategy, suggesting that coaching should increase a person's tendency to attribute achievement outcomes to (the more helpful) internal, unstable and controllable factors. Coachees often blame their environment (Dunbar, 2009), but the self-regulatory emphasis in coaching could help coachees to assume responsibility for their own outcomes The most successful way of improving performance is to focus on individuals' situated, immediate, conscious, personal goals rather than their underlying self-concept or psychodynamic causes of behaviour.

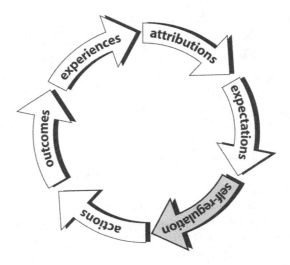

Figure 3.5 Self-Regulation Cycle

Role of Goals

Having explored the particular role of GFC in fostering self-regulation in this intersecting sphere, we now show how goals play a vital role in this process. As Pintrich and Schunk (1996 p. 209) note, "Goals are placed at the *intersection* of the internal and external elements" (emphasis added) and they mediate the effects of expectancy on performance (Latham, 2007).

Most human actions are goal-directed, either to attain valued outcomes or avoid dreaded ones (Bandura, 1986), and are guided by continually adjusting goal-representations. Self-regulation is entirely about the management of the self in reference to a particular task-specific goal (Lewin, Dembo, Festinger & Sears, 1994), which in self-regulation literature is termed the *reference value* (Carver & Scheier, 1998). It is the coachee's system for comparing a desired outcome (the *reference value*, which is the ideal standard that the system aspires to attain) with the current state. If the coachee's self-regulation system detects a discrepancy between those two (referred to as an 'error signal'), much like a thermostat, it triggers actions to reduce the discrepancy and bring the reality closer to the desired state (Carver & Scheier, 1998). This is a circular process, a closed-loop system, whereby the system monitors and detects the environment, which is assessed against the reference value, triggering, where appropriate, behaviour change.

According to goal theories (Locke & Latham, 1990; Ford, 1992), goals are the most vital self-regulation variable, with the influence of attributions and expectancies being primarily mediated by goal selection. Social cognitive theory (Bandura, 1986, 2001) postulates that most human behaviour is purposive and regulated by 'forethought,' which is a person's capability to guide their actions anticipatorily, providing direction, coherence, and meaning to their life (Bandura, 1989). Consciously setting goals stimulates this forethought process, enabling people to plan ahead, select priorities and give structure to their lives (Bandura, 2001). As will be further elaborated, GFC can be deployed as a tool for ferrying the coachee through this 'intersection' by formulating effective goals.

Almost all approaches to coaching emphasise the needs for setting goals (Grant & Stober, 2006) but in GFC the goal is the main means for attaining positive outcomes, and the main aim of the coaching; the key skill of the coach is crafting and constructing the goal. Thus it can be seen that GFC works to achieve positive actions that give rise to and sustain positive attitudes, rather than working on positive attitudes directly.

Goal Setting and Discrepancy Management

Goals, and the self-regulatory system itself, operate as a hierarchy. Abstract goals set the agenda and stimulate more concrete goals that actually attain the desired objectives (Carver, 2007). As long as the self-regulation system is aware of its goal, it will generate a cascading effect of activity, in which the high level, abstract or general goal feeds down the hierarchy, triggering lower level, concrete or specific goals (Carver & Scheier, 1998). Furthermore, it is suggested that if there is no discrepancy between the goal set and what pertains in the real world, there is no goal to reach, and thus no action is triggered. Effective goal setting is therefore about *discrepancy production*. As Locke and Latham (2006 p. 265) remark, "the setting of goals is first and foremost a discrepancy-creating process."

In Figure 3.6 we show this hierarchy in operation. Abstract or values-based goals direct 'intermediate' goals, which in turn drive concrete goals. Figure 3.6 shows that concrete goals, such as getting promotion at work, are merely a means to an end and are driven by the coachee's abstract goals. It also depicts how tensions between concrete goals can emerge. Sometimes there is discord between goals, as shown by the bold dotted line in Figure 3.6, and the coachee experiences a feeling of tension and imbalance until alignment with higher-level goals is achieved.

The higher order levels in the hierarchy thus provide a stabilising influence. Action identification theory (Vallacher & Wenger, 1985) postulates that an abstract goal tends to remain unchanged, so long as the action that it triggered is still being carried out. People are resistant to changing their higher order goals or values, but are willing to change their more concrete plans. This is because, when a discrepancy is detected, the system does not normally suggest a change in reference value, but rather triggers a change in behaviour. Without this quality, Carver and Scheier suggest, "self-regulation would be truly haphazard. Instead of holding on to some reference standard, the system would be all over the place" (1998 p. 25). By contrast, lower level goals and plans are more impulsive, less stable and are vulnerable to being challenged.

Thus, what is a virtue in the lower order is a liability in the higher order, and vice versa. The means of achieving the goal are more amenable to change, as flexibility is required when implementing a task, whereas the key objective tends to remain fixed, providing the motivation and clarity of purpose (Carver & Scheier, 1998). In

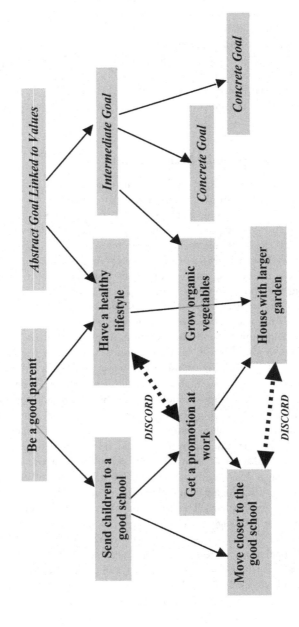

Figure 3.6 Hierarchy of Goal Construction

the self-regulation hierarchy, higher order goals provide the strength and motivation – the 'why' – while the lower order goals convey a sense of 'how' (Powers, 1973).

As will be more fully set out in later chapters, there are two main areas of goal construction: goal setting and action planning. Setting a goal and planning its implementation are two quite separate, even disparate activities. The former is more abstract and conscious, the latter more concrete and automated. The former is principled and rigid, the latter is more flexible. These two activities rely on different 'mindsets' and skill-sets, and are akin to Ford's (1992) distinction between goal content (the objective) and goal processes (operationalisation). The model of action phases (Gollwitzer, 1990; Gollwitzer & Bayer, 1999) argues that the act of setting goals activates cognitive procedures that facilitate decision-making, and the act of planning triggers cognitive processes that support the implementation of goals. GFC recognizes these divergent stages of goal setting and action planning, as two distinct and sequential processes.

However, as suggested in Figure 3.6, for a task to be motivational it must be accepted as a personally valued goal (Ford, 1992; Locke & Latham, 1990; Markus & Ruvolo, 1989). Goal setting, i.e. translating purposeful activities into 'goals', is an important element of self-regulation (Bandura, 1988; Schunk, 1989). It implies discontent with the present condition and a desire to attain an object or outcome. Thus, a goal not only defines the objective, it also creates the motivation by highlighting the gap between the current and desired states (Carver, 2007). Moreover, once in possession of a goal, "people display considerable self-direction in the face of competing influences" (Bandura, 1986 p. 335). Goal setting is an effective method of fostering goal ownership by personalising them to the coachee's needs and circumstances. The act of goal setting combined with action planning contributes toward more effective self-regulation. GFC can therefore assist in facilitating this self-regulatory process, resulting in raised performance and motivation.

Goal Management

While goals are naturally generated in the face of a task, there is a question of their appropriateness (Locke & Latham, 1990). The central function of GFC is to stimulate more adaptive goals than would have been generated spontaneously. Consciously setting a goal stimulates a more rigorous set of activities and focuses the mind towards reaching the goal. Deliberate goal setting is therefore essential to determine the most effective means of completing the task. Thus, goal choice, the outcome the individual decides to pursue, must be supplemented with effective goal construction (Rawsthorne & Elliot, 1999).

Effective goal-management usually involves striking an appropriate balance to suit the prevailing situation and the relevant level in the self-regulation hierarchy. Forming the goal at the right level of discrepancy is vital, for if the discrepancy is too large the person may well despair of achieving it and abandon the goal. However, if the discrepancy is too small the person will feel no need to take action (Carver, 2007). Goal setting could be described as 'defining the discrepancy,' and is therefore also *discrepancy management*, crafting the careful balance that is required to achieve optimum goal-oriented motivation.

Maintaining ongoing goal-directed activity is vital, as reaching a goal may raise self-efficacy but it may also lead to dysphoria and aimlessness (Carver & Scheier, 1998). Pervin (1992) notes how goal attainment inherently contains the seeds of disappointment. It is the gap between the current reality and desired reality that motivates action. Once the discrepancy has been closed, the person will reduce activity towards that goal, what Frijda (1994 p. 113) called 'coasting,' Simon (1953) called 'satisficing' and what Carver and Scheier (1998 p. 131) called acting in 'cruise control.' To avoid a sense of nothingness, there is a need to replace the completed goal with a new one or to extend the original one. Carver and Scheier (1998 p. 155) argue that "success is most likely to lead to sustained positive feelings when the attainment of one goal slides smoothly into a sense of progress towards other goals." Continuously setting new and more challenging targets is necessary to ensure there is always a sufficient discrepancy to motivate action.

In a similar vein, GFC aims to foster stretching goals that stimulate significant efforts. As Cavanagh (2006) argues, coaching should provoke a measure of instability; it should "afflict the comfortable!" It should instigate a healthy disequilibrium, which is essential for change and growth (Duignan, 2007; Reeves & Allison, 2009). That is why goal theorists all agree on the importance of a goal being specific to allow for evaluation of progress, and moderately difficult to maintain a healthy discrepancy. However, goals have a motivational effect only when the person is not already experiencing overload (Brown, Jones & Leigh, 2005). Thus, coaches are encouraged to help coachees to moderate the hardship level of their goals to ensure they are manageable but not boring (Kauffman, 2004).

It is also vital that a goal is set at the right level of proximity. If the goal is not tied to a specific timeframe there can be no self-regulation, for there would be no way to measure and assess behaviour. Disaggregating the main goal through action planning reduces attention overload (Mischel & Ayduk, 2007), lessens depletion of self-regulatory resources (Baumeister & Vohs, 2007) and mitigates impulsive behavior (Gollwitzer, Fujita & Oettingen, 2007). Managing the right balance or combination between proximal (close in time) and distal (longer-term) goals is crucial to the success of goal-related activity (Bandura, 1986).

Similarly, goal orientation, i.e. the source of motivation, is a potentially important factor in the effectiveness of the goal. Whether or not the goal is motivated by intrinsic or extrinsic sources of motivation (Deci & Ryan, 2002), whether or not the goal is concordant with other values (Kasser, 2002; Sheldon, 2002) and whether or not the goal is in keeping with the person's positive or negative regulatory focus (Higgins, 1997, 2000), can all play a part in whether the goal will be motivationally sustainable. If there are tensions, as suggested in the goal hierarchy shown in Figure 3.6, then coaching can help find acceptable alternatives or ways to manage the tension.

On this basis, we would suggest a resolution to Garvey et al.'s (2009) ambivalence about goal-focused activity. They point to studies that suggest that goal pursuit can be destructive (e.g. Kayes, 2006), and cite Hardingham's (2005) anxiety that the goals may turn out to be the wrong ones. On the one hand they acknowledge that studies suggest that goals are effective, but caution that goal activity can sometimes be harmful and destructive. Indeed, goal setting alone can be damaging, but done effectively goals can and do provide the very engine of human performance and provide vital meaning for everyday activities.

Summary

Viewing GFC as a self-regulatory tool helps to clarify the boundaries of GFC and its unique strengths. GFC, unlike many approaches to coaching (e.g. Gray, 2006; Stober, 2006), does not advocate a holistic approach to achieve its purpose, but focuses on stimulating effective action. Additionally, GFC does not focus on stimulating internal change (Hudson, 1999), but works to integrate change processes into daily modes of behaviour. According to this view, the change and learning that occurs in GFC is akin to 'active learning' (Bredo, 2000) where learning progress is closely related to the tasks the new learning seeks to enhance.

In the next chapter we propose that in GFC, the primary way of addressing destructive inhibitions or low self-concept is by helping the coachee to override them. Coaching provides a supportive framework in which the coachee is assisted to set challenging goals despite their reservations, in the view that the self-doubt will be mitigated by the resultant progress.

4 Goal-focused Methodology

Aims

- To explain the two key methodological features of GFC: forward focus and incremental change;
- To describe how GFC is effective in leveraging small concrete actions to support positive change and raise self-efficacy.

As set out in Chapter 2, GFC is defined by three key features: it is non-directive, goal-focused and performance-driven. In this chapter, we explore in greater detail the distinctive methodology of GFC, focusing firstly on its forward focus and secondly on how it stimulates incremental change to raise both performance and self-efficacy. Two examples of models informed by a GFC approach are discussed in detail towards the end of the chapter, and this is followed by a summary of the main features of a GFC methodology.

Forward Focus

Focusing on practical steps to move the coachee forward leads to a reduction of anxiety, makes the task seem more manageable, and enhances buy-in by rendering goals more real, thus energising the coachee. Parker et al. (2008 p. 496) confirm that seeing progress is essential for buy-in: "When coachees experienced the positive learning outcomes of seeing an impact on their professional development from peer coaching, they were more likely to use it later on their own." Practical goals direct attention towards what is attainable and its potential benefit, which renders the coachee more willing to cooperate with others. Similarly, focusing on creating positive change results in an improved coaching climate and enhanced coachee attitude, and contributes towards improved self-efficacy. Our research has found that applying a forward focus through goal setting and action planning engenders acceptance of self-responsibility, encouraging the coachee to focus on trying to improve what he or she can, rather than complaining or making ineffective demands on his or her organisation.

As mentioned in Chapter 2, Grant (2006) captures the essence of this forward-focused approach with the word 'purposefulness,' which indicates an orientation towards action and a mindfulness towards getting things done. Elliot and Harac-kiewicz (1996) confirm a basic principle of this forward focus, that concentrating on the problem exaggerates its impact, whereas a focus on finding solutions reduces the crippling effect of the problem and increases the likelihood of finding a solution. Hudson (1999) similarly urges the coach to remain in the present and future tense and argues that rather than tackle an obstacle, it is best to imagine a way around it. Even when the choices open to the coachee are not ideal, the coaching process helps the coachee to clarify the best available option, which leads to improvement in motivation and performance.

The early stages of coaching, however, suffer from an inherent threat. The initial objective of the coach is to encourage coachees to assume ownership of their own lives, to support the coachees in a more proactive acceptance of responsibility for their own futures. However, until the coaching has reached a practical stage, some coachees may become alarmed by the sense of responsibility, before they have developed the tools to handle it. Coachees may feel overwhelmed by a task they have no idea how to execute. When the coaching still has not got down to details, this can occasionally provide a platform for criticism, resentment and venting, as nothing tangible has happened yet.

This can lead some coachees to remain sceptical of the core principle of coaching, because they may not see how their objectives could be achieved (Reeves & Allison, 2009). In the coaching literature this issue is often addressed by strengthening the coaching relationship (de Haan, 2008) and through encouraging the coachee to adopt a positive attitude (Biswas-Diener & Dean, 2007; Starr, 2007). Following a goal-focused methodology, it is best to deal with negativity by redirecting attention towards something more concrete, focusing on a small, practical desired outcome.

Coachees will become more energised and find the coaching more appealing once it turns practical and starts to focus on concrete issues. These are the comments from some of our coachees:

> In the last few weeks, especially, I have started to work on a couple of things that are useful to me and this has made me feel more positive about my own situation.

> I am much clearer than I was about what I want to get out of my time here – what I am looking to achieve – so staying on longer to learn is about me trying to get that done.

> I think that's right, if I am committed to achieving something, I am doing it for myself, so it is no longer an issue about keeping to just turning up to work.

> Once I got down to doing something that could be useful to me I was much more willing to give the whole thing a go . . . When you started talking about action plans I thought 'what is this guy going on about', but once we got down to discussing real things I could relate to that and understood what you meant.

The coachee will take coaching more seriously if it is seen to lead to more practical implications. A successful method of helping coachees to get over their resentment and disappointment is the act of describing where they want to be, what their aims and ambitions are, and mapping out a path to achievement. The coachee could become negative if the discussion lingers on the problem. However, even when starting from a strongly negative point, the negativity will normally subside if it is replaced with action towards a desired future (Szabo & Meier, 2009). Much of the negativity is overcome not because the problems have been resolved but because the coachee has identified a more compelling alternative.

In conflict-ridden work environments, coachees may sometimes be caught up in hostility towards their superiors and/or colleagues. Coachees may display a vivid sense of grievance toward the organisation, whereas their sense of purpose will typically be much vaguer. The coaching needs to reverse that and make their goals more vivid, which will lead to positive changes. Concrete goals better enable focus on the positive, because they make the objective seem more real, increasing the all-important buy-in. Whereas coachees experience problems as very real, the possible solutions and their potential rewards seem remote. Defining concrete actions has the power to render solutions more immediate, thereby increasing goal salience (Mischel & Ayduk, 2007).

Even just *planning* for action helps coachees to focus on trying to improve what they can, rather than complaining or trying to get the organisation to solve their problems, as this illuminating comment from a coachee demonstrates:

> We have decided to divert our attention towards what we need to do to make the best of the situation. When you first got involved here our main preoccupation was trying to work out why the organisation wasn't doing what it promised and trying to work out how we could get them to do so. This has changed . . . Instead, we are trying to achieve what we need to achieve. Not that we never get frustrated or complain, but this has stopped being such a big deal.

This suggests that if coachees are clear about the goal, they will be focused on the goal and less likely to engage in marginal activities that distract from its attainment.

While coachees may sometimes prefer to express negative goals – what they wish not to have – the general evidence suggests that goals are better if they are positive. Carver and Scheier (1998) argue that there are health benefits in adopting positive goals. Schwartz (1990) suggests that it is easier to pursue a positive goal as all one needs is a single way of achieving it, whereas to avoid an outcome involves avoiding all possible means of being confronted with it. Carver and Scheier (1998 p. 93) conclude that "people dominated by avoidance goals thus have difficult lives." However, studies have shown that some people are naturally oriented to avoidance (negative) goals. Therefore, Grant (2007) argues that coaching needs to be inclusive and use coachee-congruent techniques, as coachees with a defensive pessimism personality style will not respond positively to an over-emphasis on positivity. This is an area of coaching that requires significant further research.

Making Progress

Practical progress, by taking some initial steps towards the goal, however tentative, improves the coaching climate. It is important for the coach to guide the coaching process towards actions that stimulate feelings of empowerment, especially if the context appears to be one of failure and resentment. In therapeutic or developmental types of coaching the coachee may view enlightenment, healing, growth or clarity as evidence of progress, whereas GFC needs to show *practical* results. Actual results raise the confidence the coachee will have in the coaching.

Furthermore, progress in implementing a task is motivational. According to self-regulation theory, a person has a monitoring process that observes the rate of progress made towards narrowing the gap between the current and desired states. Carver and Scheier (1998 p. 121) term this a 'meta-monitoring function' that monitors not only whether progress is being made but the speed or rate of progress, what Carver (2007 p. 17) terms the "psychological analogue of velocity." This process guides the person's level of satisfaction, by noting the rate of progress by comparison to the ideal standard. If the rate of progress towards the goal is satisfactory, the person will experience positive 'affect' or emotion[1]. Good progress towards the goal, even if starting from a very low threshold, has been shown to lead to high levels of satisfaction (Lawrence, Carver & Scheier, 2002).

An additional potential benefit of practical progress is greater willingness on the part of coachees to cooperate with others. When the issue is getting a practical plan worked out, the question of how best to do it will take precedence. Once coachees are focused on getting tasks done, the momentum helps to overcome problems that would otherwise have seemed to be major obstacles. Coachees are willing to forego their own preferences and make significant compromises if they are working towards a recognized goal.

The forward-focus in GFC is not to the total exclusion of considering the past, and looking for solutions is not at the expense of gaining a proper understanding of the problem. Writing in relation to solution-focused coaching, O'Connell and Palmer (2007, p. 280) state that "although we clearly carry our past with us and need to learn from our mistakes and successes, the principal focus in solution-focused work is on the coachee's present and preferred future." Furthermore, they go on to extol the value of learning the lesson from past mistakes! They even argue that not only is it important to learn the lessons of the past, it is also *sometimes* appropriate to analyse the *causes* of the mistakes. Additionally, O'Connell and Palmer (2007) argue that it is sometimes necessary to allow the coachee to get things off his/her chest, which Grant (2006) suggests can be cathartic, although some solution-focused texts, for example Szabo & Meier (2009) seem to reject this completely. Bachkirova (2007 p. 354) astutely points out that "in practice we know that it is impossible to work only with the future and the positive spectrum of client's lives," and that we often require the past to be addressed, at least initially.

Initial Steps towards Self-efficacy

As suggested in Chapter 3, signs of potential progress towards goals can lead to greater motivation. As the coaching begins to produce concrete results, coachees' confidence in the process and in their own ability is likely to grow. It follows therefore that initial action by a coachee, even if small, is necessary to create the platform for progress. Cox (2006 p. 204) similarly argues that "self-efficacy is built upon previous successful experience, which suggests that attention should be paid to goal setting." Earlier, Mathieu and Button (1992) also found that previous performance positively influences subsequent setting of goals.

There are broadly two ways to deal with low self-efficacy (see Margolis & McCabe, 2006; Schunk & Pajares, 2002): one is to build confidence in the relevant ability through self-talk or suchlike. Some motivation theorists advocate using exercises and activities that directly seek to enhance self-concept by ensuring the person has the requisite self-belief. The second way to deal with low self-efficacy is to help people to accomplish actual achievements first, and perceptions of competence will follow. Motivation theorists argue that it is better to encourage actions that begin to prove to the person that he is in fact able. However, Wigfield and Karpathian (1991, p. 256) maintain that "it is relatively fruitless to continue to pursue the general question of which causes which." As Pintrich and Schunk (1996 p. 87) argue, "the relationship is reciprocal; self-concept influences future achievement and actual achievement shapes and constrains self-perceptions of competence."

Goal attainment then is not only the result of enhanced self-efficacy; it is also a key contributor to it (Ford, 1992; Locke & Latham, 1990; Pintrich & Schunk, 1996), because sometimes inhibitions are so strong that the only feasible way is to create facts on the ground, which then feed back into enhanced efficacy (Jackson & McKergow, 2008). As noted, in GFC the role of the coach is not to engage in the personal or psychological development towards long-term attitude change, such as directly attempting to alter efficacy beliefs. Rather, the role of the coach in this form of coaching is to provide the step-by-step structure that enables the coachee to make actual progress, from which raised self-efficacy follows.

Indeed, there is widespread support in the coaching literature for taking small, concrete actions to create positive experiences that ultimately will lead to more positive choices of action. For example, Berg and Szabo (2005) suggest that coaching should aim to secure practical action as soon as possible, which will ultimately alter self-concept. Parsloe and Wray (2000 p. 65) advocate focusing "as rapidly as possible on potential solutions that the person can recognize and take personal responsibility for implementing." Hudson (1999 p. 29) advises: "It is better to evolve brief, small, doable plans than long, huge, impossible ones."

Similarly, Grant (2006 p. 82) advises: "have coachees take small, easily achievable steps that build in time to overall stretching goals, rather than overwhelm them with large initial actions" and Reeves and Allison (2009 p. 148) encourage coaches to "identify high-leverage activities in which a single action by a client will have the greatest probability of yielding the greatest return." Rogers (2008) also argues that quick wins are important in a change process, as they highlight what has changed and what is now starting and, from an education perspective, Pintrich and Schunk (1996 p. 100) write: "Students' perceptions of competence develop not just from accurate feedback from the teacher, but through actual success on academic tasks." Ford (1992) similarly argues that people should focus more on actually engaging in achievement behaviour rather than on preparing the person emotionally and mentally.

These arguments sit well with the theoretical framework of GFC described in Chapter 3, where real-life progress is viewed as an effective method of creating improved attribution and expectancies, which in turn support the selection of challenging goals.

Coaching can impact positively on expectancies in several ways. Coaching has the effect of raising task value, because setting goals raises commitment. Additionally, the coaching improves expectancies and enhances self-concept by helping the coachee to develop adaptive strategies. The development of task strategies may help the coachee to alter his or her perceptions of task difficulty, as will be explained in Chapter 8. The resultant positive outcomes create positive expectancies and thus result in higher future expectations and actual results, creating a virtuous cycle. Indeed, studies have consistently linked positive expectancies to positive outcomes (Pintrich & Schunk, 2003). Thus, coachees' perceptions of progress are 'efficacy cues' that raise motivation as goal attainment enhances self-efficacy (Ford, 1992; Locke & Latham, 1990). In educational terms, Pintrich and Schunk (1996 p. 162) note that, "progress indicators convey that students are capable of learning and performing, which enhances their self-efficacy for further learning."

Sheldon, Kasser, Smith, and Share (2002) also set out some striking evidence that goal attainment not only has numerous positive benefits, such as increases in psychosocial wellbeing, vitality and self-actualisation, but moreover it results in increased self-concordance: people identify more with goals when they enjoy success. Even self-determination theory, which promotes intrinsic motivation, recognizes that goal attainment is a direct contributor to wellbeing (Sheldon & Elliot, 1999). Sheldon et al. (2002) further argue that goal attainment can help someone break out of a deadlock, what they term 'static equilibrium,' demonstrating the benefits of growth.

Thus, coaching enhances self-efficacy and motivation by raising performance (Kauffman, Boniwell & Silberman, 2009) and should encourage the creation of opportunities to experience success at real tasks, which will alter efficacy beliefs. As Pintrich and Schunk (1996 p. 232) explain, "the actual success that comes from learning a specific skill and being able to overcome a problem will provide the direct evidence that the student has learned the appropriate skills and will do much more to increase personal agency than empty platitudes." The relationship between small actions leading to concrete results feeding into enhanced self-efficacy is portrayed in Figure 4.1.

So, rather than trying to alter the coachee's perceptions, GFC recommends that the coach should help the coachee to adopt efficacious goals, which will feed back into more optimistic expectancies thereby creating a cycle of improvement. A further benefit of raising self-efficacy indirectly through helping the coachee to achieve successful outcomes is that it engenders an accurate self-perception based on actual performance results, unlike if self-efficacy is manipulated through motivational prompts, where the efficacy is not substantiated by reality. In fact, exaggerated self-efficacy can actually have negative consequences if it leads to

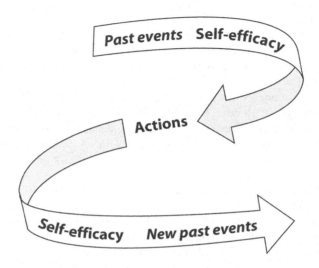

Figure 4.1 Raising Self-Efficacy Through GFC

over-persistence in the face of an unattainable goal (Brandtstädter & Renner, 1990; Janoff-Bulman & Brickman, 1982) or risky endeavours (Haaga & Stewart, 1992).

Increases in self-efficacy also link to concerns about coaching transfer, which has been a preoccupation with organisations in recent years (Spencer, 2011). Stewart, Palmer, Wilkin & Kerrin (2008, p. 32) define successful coaching transfer as the "sustained application of coaching development, specifically the knowledge, skills, attitudes and other qualities acquired during coaching." Spencer similarly concludes her study by suggesting that coaches need to balance their work on beliefs and actions over the period of the coaching in order to make effective contributions to sustained change. However, GFC does not have the transfer of learning as its stated aim (even though that is often a by-product). Rather, its focus is the direct effect during the experience of coaching, even if nothing new is learned: gaining agreements, establishing common understanding, putting forward *modi operandi*, clarifying goals, planning action, and supporting its successful execution, all increase self-efficacy and so indirectly, but significantly, impact transfer.

Change

This section explores issues in relation to the ability of coaching to effect change. Reeves and Alison (2009) have suggested that most personal change initiatives fail. The question, therefore, is how to increase the chances of success. There has been much discussion in the coaching literature about change and development, and many coaching approaches have turned increasingly to personal development, learning or therapeutic interventions, because they believe, as Hudson (1999) cautions, that coaching that exclusively focuses on external change will lack staying power. Similarly, Williams, K., Kiel, Doyle and Sinagra (2002) and Gray (2006) insist that skill-based coaching seldom achieves sustainable change, which they argue requires the individual to recognize the deep-seated and underlying motivators of maladaptive behaviours. For this reason, Skiffington and Zeus (2003, p. 125) assert that change must be "at the heart of any coaching program," and Flaherty (2005, p. 9) insists that the role of coaching is to alter the coachee's "structure of interpretation."

Gray (2006) writes approvingly about a psychotherapeutic approach to coaching that takes a holistic view and incorporates the full range of factors, including family members and friends. Although Gray may well be correct where coaching addresses issues of dysfunction, GFC is not designed to deal with such areas. With GFC, the aim is not to change the way the person is, but the way things are done. It does not attempt to change values or meaning perspectives (Mezirow, 2000); rather it operates by integrating its performance orientation into 'business as usual.' It aims for practical performance instead of personal development.

While developmental and therapeutic coaching styles often work with the coachee on inner change, GFC therefore focuses on achieving *operational* change. D. B. Peterson (2006 p. 53) argues that

> the coach's purpose is not to change a person's motivations or to increase the person's insight into their origin, but to see how the person being coached can most effectively use these motivations to guide, shape, and reinforce desired behaviour.

Hall and Duval (2004), drawing on the work of Argyris and Schön (1974), argue that there are different levels of change: modifying existing skills and behaviour, learning new behaviours and beliefs, changing identity or sense of self, and experiencing a whole new way of living. These 'levels of change' correctly represent the different approaches to change within coaching. GFC operates at the first level of change, whereas developmental coaching helps the person learn new behaviours and beliefs, and therapeutic coaching seeks to engender a change of identity or sense of self. Accordingly, GFC focuses on changing behaviour rather than changing the self. As explained in the previous chapter, GFC fosters regulation *by* the self, as opposed to the regulation *of* the self; it is "a method of facilitating action without changing the self" (Gollwitzer et al., 2007 p. 217). Thus, we see some coaches distinguish between transactional (to acquire a new ability) versus transformational (to undergo personal change) coaching (Rogers, 2008; Summerfield, 2006) and differentiate between pragmatic rather than an exploratory style (Snyder, 1995). GFC concurs with Jackson and McKergow (2008) that it is best not to presuppose that the solution is better sought in 'underlying' rather than 'overlying' issues.

Box 4.1 Summary of GFC Methodology

- Forward focused
- Action-oriented
- Focuses on practical change over personal transformation
- Incremental progress increases buy-in and motivation
- Self-efficacy built via success
- Promotes positive action
- Goal-focus generates cooperation
- Attainment creates positive expectancies

A Brief Look at Two Approaches

The goal-focused methodology as set out in this chapter is reflected, to a greater or lesser degree, in the various approaches to coaching that in our view sit within the goal-focused coaching paradigm. We will briefly highlight two such approaches: solution-focused coaching and the GROW model.

Solution-focused Coaching

Solution-focused coaching has been described as "a collaborative, solution-focused, results-oriented and systematic process in which the coach facilitates the enhancement of life experience and goal attainment in the personal and/or professional life of . . . non-clinical clients" (Grant, 2003 p. 254). According to Grant (2006 p. 73), "coaching is necessarily a solution-focused activity." However, as explained in Chapter 1, not all coaching approaches are equally solution focused.

Akin to appreciative inquiry (Cooperrider & Srivastva, 1987), solution-focused coaching advocates building on what works successfully (Gordon, 2008)[2]. Jackson and McKergow (2007 p. xv) refer to the solution-focused approach as one of 'radical simplicity,' in which the coach avoids searching for the cause of the problem and proceeds straight towards finding a solution.

The solution-focus model as proposed by Jackson and McKergow involves five main elements. 'Platform' is establishing the current position, at this stage it is acceptable to describe the problem and does not need to involve solution-talk, but should set the stage for it by trying to define the problem in terms that are amenable to searching for a solution; 'Future Perfect' refers to the ideal outcome; 'Counters' are already existing part or potential solutions, such as resources, skills, know-how, expertise and cooperation from others that will enable one to achieve the solution; 'Scale' refers to the process of measuring and monitoring progress, placing oneself on the scale implies that some progress has already been made which can be analysed for useful leads; 'Affirm' is the act of reinforcing the positive contributions already being made; 'Small Actions' describes the main method of progress, which consists of repeatedly taking steady actions towards the goal. The importance of these various elements of the model will vary depending on circumstances.

Drawing on O'Connell (2005), Grant (2006) and Jackson and McKergow (2008), we suggest that the following principles characterise solution-focused coaching, and are largely consistent with GFC, although with varying emphases:

- Use of non-pathological framework; problems are seen to stem from a limited repertoire of behaviour. There is no need to complicate things in order to make them better. Attempting to identify *the* cause is futile.
- Future oriented, it focuses on constructing solutions, rather than trying to understand the problem. It regards a detailed understanding of the problem as of little assistance in finding the solution, and it does not assume or seek hidden factors beyond that which is readily apparent. Furthermore, it presupposes that success is inevitable.
- Based on the coachee's own expertise and resources. These resources include the coachee's previous success. Solutions are usually already present in activities that have happened before or are already happening in relation to something else. It finds and builds on what already works well. Inventing solutions takes longer; using preexistent elements gets one closer to the solution.
- Action-oriented; looks to practical solutions instead of addressing issues of 'character,' as the former are easily addressed while the latter are often perceived as intractable. Seeks to change as little as possible, and advocates the path of least resistance. It prefers to focus on the concrete, rather than the abstract.
- Clear and challenging goal setting. Imagining a 'future perfect' is valuable to help make the goal seem less remote. The coach needs to be as clear as possible about what *is* wanted.
- Change can occur over a short period. Small changes are significant and can be amplified to great effect; small incremental actions are easier, require less of an imaginative leap and involve fewer risks.
- Solutions are rarely limited entirely to one person. Seeking solutions requires systems thinking. Solutions therefore need to be co-constructed.

Solution-focused is similarly goal-focused, as O'Connell and Palmer (2007 p. 278) state: "solution focused coaching fits perfectly with the future-focused, goal-directed spirit of coaching." Thus, we would concur with Brockbank (2008 p. 138) that "the benefits of behaviourism in combination with recognition of the cognitive elements in a client's behaviour, can lead to coaching which is problem-solving *and* solution-focused" (emphasis added).

However, in our view solution-focused coaching adopts an overly optimistic view of coaching, and insufficiently acknowledges the challenging realities facing many a coachee. This, as would be expected, can lead to coachees encountering many unanticipated problems. This book argues that coaching needs to recognize and address major barriers to the coaching, which cannot and should not be brushed aside, and needs to focus intensely on effective goal setting and action planning, in order to overcome the real obstacles faced by coachees. Adopting a positive attitude and searching for resourceful solutions is insufficient. O'Connell and Palmer (2007) list numerous reasons why solution-focused coaching may fail, such as coachees being temporarily unable to tap into their resources, looking for a quick fix and unwilling to exert effort, suffering low self-esteem, searching for the roots of their problems, or seeking direction from the coach. However, they provide no solutions to these causes of failure, nor do they consider that these issues reveal an inherent limitation of the solution-focused coaching model.

The GROW Model

The GROW model provides a simple coaching structure for goal setting and problem solving, originally developed by Graham Alexander, who continues to advocate this approach (Alexander, 2006). It was arguably the most popular coaching model in the late 1980s and 1990s, at least in the UK. It was particularly central to the development of executive coaching and was much used in the business arena, and is still popular among many coaches. While the GROW model is forward-focused, it does adopt a problem-solving approach (de Haan, 2008). According to Whitmore (2003), GROW is predicated on the raising of awareness and of stimulating the acceptance of personal responsibility.

GROW is an acronym that is deciphered in a variety of ways. In this brief description we mainly follow Whitmore, whose book *Coaching for Performance* (2003) did more than any other to popularise the approach.

GOAL – The coaching process must be driven by the focus on a specific Goal. The goal needs to be specific and have a date attached to it. It should be clear to both the coach and coachee what criteria would determine that the goal has been reached. Helping the coachee to define a clear and achievable goal is a prerequisite to the coaching process. Whitmore insists on the need to set goals first in order to give purpose to the discussion, and because typically people will set goals on the basis of what has been done before and will make no effort to be creative or to stretch themselves. Setting the goal first by asking 'What would you ideally like to do?', and not censoring the answers due to the possible difficulties faced in reaching the goal, will allow more inspiring and ambitious goals. However, we agree with Dembkowski and Eldridge (2008) that this assumes that the coachee arrives with a clear goal, which is not always possible. However, some coaches use the GROW model as a session planning tool, rather than an overarching coaching methodology. In this case the Goal becomes merely the outcome for the session and could therefore have a legitimate place at the start of any coaching session.

REALITY – In order to be able to understand properly what achieving the specified goal entails, it is necessary for the coachee to clarify the extent of the gap between the present state and the desired future state. Although it is not necessary for the coach to have all the information, it is essential that the coachee has it. This stage has been termed 'gap analysis' because it serves to identify how far coachees have to go to achieve their ultimate aim. The Reality stage needs to elicit factual responses, and should generate descriptive rather than evaluative terminology. The purpose is to get beneath the surface to gain a fuller picture of the situation, as "problems must be solved at the level beneath that at which they show themselves" (Whitmore, 2003 p. 71). This can involve listening for signals from the coachee's mind, body and emotions. Part of this process involves isolating the obstacles that could impede progress towards the goal, as well as identifying the coachee's strengths that may enable the goal to be achieved.

OPTIONS – To begin the process of charting a plan to reach the goal, the coachee needs to open his or her mind to potential solutions. At this point quantity is more important than quality, as the brain stimulating process of gathering the options is as valuable as the options themselves. The coachee needs to brainstorm for creative ways around their obstacles and inventive ways to capitalise on his or her strengths in order to best achieve the goal. At this stage it is necessary to suspend disbelief and assumptions in order to allow for as many possibilities to be considered, as great ideas can arise unexpectedly. A key aim of this stage is to examine how specific challenges may be overcome, by identifying the coachee's own skills and how to access the necessary resources. It may be necessary to analyse the Options on a cost benefit basis to find the most suitable solution.

WILL – Sometimes also referred to as a Way Forward, this stage of the GROW model is about converting the ideas raised during coaching into practical action steps which will lead to the attainment of the goal. Having identified the strategies that are thought most likely to be effective, the coachee can now be helped to develop a detailed, step-by-step action plan along with a specific timeline for each step. At some point during this stage the coach needs to confirm that the coachee is committed to implementing the action plan and to help the coachee overcome any lingering reservations. The coachee can also identify potential risks and plan how to address those.

The two approaches discussed here demonstrate how some of the principles of the goal-focused methodology can be applied, although, as explained, each is to some degree restricted. Later in this book we present a GFC model that demonstrates greater integration and cohesion and so overcomes the limitations of these partial models.

Summary

In this chapter we have looked at the way in which GFC works to provoke change via its focus on future actions. We noted how incremental progress increases 'buy-in' and cooperation and how achieving goals generates self-efficacy and positive expectancy. Figure 4.2 shows the features of GFC that constitute its methodology.

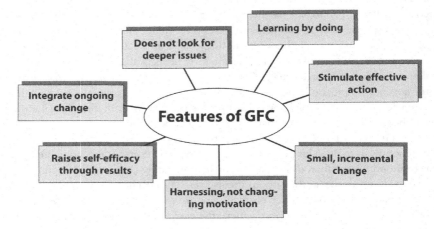

Figure 4.2 Features of GFC

5   Relationship Management in Goal-focused Coaching

Aims

- To explain the role of relationship in a goal-focused coaching alliance, including the importance of relationship with the coaching;
- To explore resistance to coaching;
- To examine some of the barriers to goal-focused coaching, such as indifference and resentment, and how they may be overcome in practice.

This chapter seeks to contribute towards a greater understanding of relationship management in GFC. It explores in depth issues relating to the coaching relationship, and highlights, where appropriate, matters of particular relevance to goal-focused coaching (GFC). Flaherty (2005 p. 41) claims that the relationship aspect of coaching is often "neglected, ignored, or considered to be unnecessary." Indeed, while the relationship is widely noted in the coaching literature, key relationship issues are overlooked when it comes to research.

This chapter reveals that relationship issues are of far greater significance than originally anticipated by many coaches. It will be argued that, although GFC is a goal setting methodology, goal-focused activity requires the wider relationship aspects of the coaching engagement to function properly. Core goal-focused work can only commence when a range of contextual and interpersonal conditions have been met. Sullivan, Skovholt and Jennings (2005) and O'Broin and Palmer (2007) conceive of the coaching intervention as separated into two parts: the safe relationship domain and the challenging relationship domain. The former focuses on building trust, and the latter urges the coachee towards taking action. Before it is possible to extract commitment to action, it is necessary to ensure engagement in the coaching process.

This chapter has three main sections. Section one discusses the coachee's relationship with the coach. Section two explores the coachee's relationship with the *coaching* and section three deals with resistance to coaching. This section examines certain barriers to coaching, such as suspicion, resentment and indifference, and looks at the issue of trust, which can create the 'safe relationship domain' necessary for goal-focused work to begin.

Relationship with the Coach

Empirical research (Cox, 2012a, 2012b; Ives 2010) has confirmed the centrality of the coaching relationship for GFC applications, where the focus is on the goal rather than the coaching process. Coaching works because it is a supportive environment. Thus, the relationship, as many commentators point out, is a central pillar (Peterson, D. B. & Hicks, 1996; Stern, 2004; Wasylyshyn, 2003), and the first stage in the coaching process (Diedrich, 1996; Flaherty, 2005; Harris, 1999). It is also widely accepted that a spirit of openness and trust is an absolute prerequisite for coaching to function properly (O'Broin & Palmer, 2006; Starr, 2007; Whitworth, et al., 2007). The coachee needs to feel that he or she can speak honestly, rather than fear blame or ridicule.

Stober and Grant (2006 p. 360) have also argued that "regardless of preferred theoretical perspective, the foundation of effective coaching is the successful formation of a collaborative relationship." However, in GFC greater emphasis is placed on establishing basic trust and clarity of purpose than on pursuing a particularly high level of rapport, which, as argued in Chapter 1, is more appropriate for therapeutic styles of coaching. We would further argue that relationship requirements vary, depending on the coaching approach. In therapeutic styles of coaching (Stober, 2006), the closeness of the relationship needs to be of a different order to the more pragmatic approach of GFC. Minimal relationship requirements involve respect, courtesy and understanding (Kilburg, 1997), as opposed to the more humanistic aspect of relationships that emphasise empathy, authenticity and unconditional positive regard (Stober, 2006). Bordin (1979) suggests two levels of bond in the therapeutic alliance: a broader, *affective* bond, and a narrower, *work* bond, which is focused on supporting goals and tasks. It could be argued that the latter type of bond is more suited to GFC, where progress is not achieved 'through the relationship' (Stober, 2006 p. 20) but by tailoring the relationship to specific conditions and objectives. Moreover, as O'Broin and Palmer (2009) point out, too much warmth between coach and coachee may undermine the professional effectiveness of the relationship.

Furthermore, as Judge and Cowell (1997) highlight, the coaching process is often a much shorter process than traditional psychotherapy, thus there is often insufficient time to cultivate profound alliance. GFC is a performance-inspiring relationship, not a healing one. Hence, many coaches (Gavin, 2005; Wasylyshyn, 2003; Whitworth, et al., 2007) prefer to describe the coaching relationship as a 'working alliance.'

Regrettably, the importance of the coaching relationship has often been championed without clarification, causing significant confusion. For example, O'Broin and Palmer (2007 p. 296) suggest that the coach–coachee relationship should be compared with its therapeutic equivalent, yet they distinguish the coaching relationship as more collegial, collaborative and egalitarian. No adequate explanation is proffered as to the terms of the comparison, and the authors themselves acknowledge there is little justification for comparing therapy and coaching. Similarly, Fillery-Travis and Lane (2006, p. 66) state that "within all the coaching models in the literature there is clearly an emphasis on the initial stage of the process."

In fact, not all the coaching models that come within the GFC family place equal emphasis on the relationship (e.g. Alexander, 2006; Berg & Szabo, 2005; Szabo & Meier, 2009; Whitmore, 2003).

It is interesting to note that de Haan (2008) and Linley (2006) claim that Rosenzweig's (1936) finding that it was primarily the relationship that accounts for successful therapeutic outcomes, also applies to coaching, and Kemp (2008a, p. 27) further argues that "it is the coaching relationship, rather than any specific coaching model or technique, that is the core determinant and catalyst for client change." However, these authors do not substantiate their claim for transferability of therapeutic requirements to coaching. Indeed, Peterson (2006) argues that although an effective relationship is a prerequisite for coaching, the nature of the relationship is less important. As we will set out, the main relationship objective in GFC is to mitigate the various sources of resistance, such as suspicion, resentment or dependence.

Herzberg's motivation–hygiene theory (Herzberg, 1987) differentiates between factors that prevent dissatisfaction and those that promote satisfaction. Using Hertzberg's theory, we distinguish between the removal of barriers to coaching, which is essential in GFC, and the fostering of a therapeutic relationship, which is not essential in GFC. The suggestion is therefore that in GFC the coaching relationship does not require 'chemistry'; rather it requires the openness, communication, appreciation, fairness, and shared commitment identified by Flaherty (2005).

The core qualities of an effective coaching relationship have been widely addressed in numerous texts, both popular and academic, and will not be explored here in detail. However, in Chapter 11 of this book we discuss questioning and listening skills at some length, with a particular emphasis on their unique role in GFC.

Relationship with the *Coaching*

One of the major challenges facing coaches is establishing buy-in from the coachees, as mentioned in Chapter 4. Our research suggests that it is not the relationship with the *coach*, but with the (need for) *coaching* that makes the difference. The reluctance to engage may be a consequence of hostility toward the coaching process, such as resentment at the time spent engaged in coaching, or the perception that the process is intrusive. Reluctance may also be due to denial that the coachee has a problem (an issue which is the commonly addressed issue in coaching literature, e.g. Grant, 2006; Peltier, 2001), leading to a rejection of the need for coaching. However, we have found that even if the coachee is quite aware that he or she has a problem and may even be keen to resolve it, the challenge may arise whereby the coachee does not view coaching as a potential *solution*. As Flaherty (2005 p. 67) notes, "it's not going to be the event that leads to the potential client being open; it's the interpretation the potential client brings to the event."

So, it is insufficient that coachees are convinced that they have a problem, or even that the problem warrants some intervention; they would also need to think that coaching could be helpful. Our research suggests that those who respond well to the offer of coaching are those who not only recognize the need for coaching but see early on how coaching can address their need, and *accept* that coaching may be a *solution*. Accordingly, then, it is essential, before coaching begins, to establish a relationship not just with the coach but with the *coaching* – for without that, as Flaherty argues, coaching will not proceed.

However, coachees may resist the idea of the coaching as a solution for a number of diverse reasons. They may feel, for example, that work-based problems should be resolved by the leadership of the organisation. Also, the issue being addressed by the coaching may be viewed as irrelevant in comparison to other pressing needs that they or their organisation are facing. Additionally, coachees may initially have difficulty seeing how coaching would lead to practical results. For these and other reasons, securing the coachee's relationship with the coaching – valuing and engaging with the coaching process – is just as important as his or her relationship with the coach. Thus, before goal setting can begin in earnest, it is necessary to address obstacles to the coaching.

As acknowledged in the coaching literature (e.g. Berg & Szabo, 2005), resistance to coaching can consume the largest part of the coaching process. Latham et al. (2005) also warn that coaching is unlikely to succeed if the coachee is not convinced the coaching is designed to help. Zeus and Skiffington (2007 p. 205) further suggest that "the coachee's reluctance can be overcome if the coach can establish and clarify the individual's values and purpose, and generate and encourage commitment and self-responsibility." However, they do not adequately explain how this may be done.

Stober and Grant's 'contextual approach'(2006 p. 361) to coaching successfully captures the underlying structure of coaching in which coaching commences with the stages of collaboration, accountability, awareness, and responsibility. While their model does not adequately explain the process by which coaching leads to actions, it successfully presents the necessary foundations for this process to occur. This aspect of the coaching relationship is rather under-explored and should be the focus of more intensive elucidation. We therefore address some key areas of potential resistance to coaching, and suggestions for how these barriers to successful coaching may be addressed.

Resistance to Coaching

Coaching texts (e.g. Cox et al., 2010; Garvey et al., 2009) warn that resistance may threaten the viability of the coaching process. Resistance can be caused by a wide range of concerns, the most applicable of which will be explored here, namely resistance born out of suspicion and fear, caused by resentment, and resulting from rejection of self-responsibility. The coaching process needs to address these resistances in the order suggested in Figure 5.1, beginning with tackling the maze of suspicion and resentment before addressing issues of self-responsibility and indifference.

However, it is essential to bear in mind that resistance is almost always the direct result of a concern, which to the coachee is very real. Trying to understand what that concern is and how best to address it is the only effective way to address this familiar phenomenon. As long as the coachee is fearful that the coaching is going to work against him or her, there is little chance of progress. Similarly, attempts to provoke in the coachee a greater sense of self-responsibility will be hampered

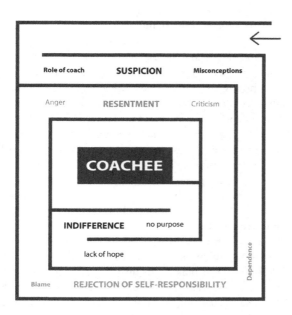

Figure 5.1 The Coaching Maze

if there is strong resentment directed at the leadership of their organisation. Hudson (1999) suggests that resistance is at its strongest in the middle of the coaching process, which fits with the personal change model of coaching on which he focuses. However, in GFC, we suggest that resistance is likely to be strongest at the beginning of the coaching process, primarily around the reluctance to engage in the coaching process. We therefore suggest a basic outline of the early part of the coaching process in Figure 5.2.

Figure 5.2 Addressing Resistance to Coaching

We want to suggest that the three shaded barriers identified in Figure 5.2 can be addressed within a goal-focused orientation, leveraging the goal as a mechanism for raising motivation, inspiring a greater sense of ownership, and fostering collaboration. Without in-depth therapeutic explorations or systematic personal development exercises, even the most reluctant coachees can gradually accept personal responsibility and show willingness to take ownership of the fate of their own work or life. It may legitimately be argued that using a goal orientation, and thus avoiding the more in-depth work, increases the likelihood of regression (Reeves & Allison, 2009). Although therapeutic and developmental approaches to coaching are also not immune to regression, we accept that GFC's practical goal orientation is not best suited where the primary objective is to foster lasting individual change (as discussed in previous chapters). This limitation of GFC is, however, intrinsic to its essence and to what enables it to generate swifter results. Therapeutic approaches also get results but generally take longer. Thus there is a trade-off.

In some instances resistance issues may not arise at all or may require little time, but in others this could turn out to be a significant part of the coaching process (Cavanagh, 2006; Dembkowski & Eldridge, 2008; Flaherty, 2005; Jackson & McKergow, 2008) or even the 'bulk of the time' (Alexander, 2006 p. 63). Furthermore, any explanations the coach may issue before the intervention begins about the nature and purpose of coaching may not be sufficient; misunderstandings may persist until the coaching actually happens. Sometimes, only actual experience of coaching will satisfactorily clarify its nature to a coachee. The coach should therefore realise that however well he or she tries to explain coaching, some people are unlikely to correctly grasp what it is about without some firsthand experience.

Building Trust and Overcoming Suspicion

A prime source of resistance to coaching may arise due to suspicion. This is highly deleterious to coaching, where success is so dependent on trust. Building trust between coach and coachee is a foremost necessity for an effective coaching relationship (Cox, 2012a). Other studies (Luebbe, 2005; Jones & Spooner, 2006) also report that trust is the quality most valued by coachees, and is particularly important for stretching tasks that contain a risk of failure (Hunt & Weintraub, 2007). Trust is a critical element at the early stages of relationship development (Heffernan, 2004) and arises repeatedly in the coaching literature as a vital quality for coaching success (Lowman, 2007; O'Broin & Palmer, 2009). It is the coach's responsibility to ensure that the relationship is capable of supporting the demands of the coaching process.

From the outset, coachees may be suspicious that the coaching is being used, or may be used, as a replacement for the commitments the company or organisation should make, or that the coaching may be used as a way of controlling the coachee. The context in which the coaching takes place may lend itself to such concerns, as the organisation may already have defaulted on promises and assurances of resources for example, thus giving rise to an atmosphere of mistrust. Thus, the coach needs to try to establish that coaching is unlikely to harm the coachee's interests. From the coachee's perspective it can seem highly plausible that the coaching is a ruse to get them to agree to changes that they feel that they have good reason to resist. It can be standard management practice to get things through the 'back door'. Depending on the culture in the industry or organisation there can be an established tendency to transfer responsibilities to employees in the name of personal development.

For this reason, Natale and Diamante (2005 p. 363) note that the coachee "will likely need to determine whether or not this 'positive' service is a ploy." Indeed our research has suggested two likely threats to trust caused by such suspicions: that the organisation leadership may use the coaching to evade their commitments, and that it may be deployed to apply greater pressure on the coachees. For example, coaching can be perceived as an attempt to cut back and transfer additional tasks and responsibilities to workers. Here clarity and factually accurate information, rather than bland reassurances, are required to ensure that suspicion does not envelop the coaching process. Ferrar (2006) highlights how coaches may struggle to gain openness, especially if they have a stake in the outcome. The coachee's suspicion, however, is mitigated when the coach is helping the coachee to develop strategy without being directly involved in the project (Clutterbuck, 2010; Wageman, Nunes, Burruss & Hackman, 2008).

The following comments from participants in Ives' study demonstrate a feeling of being 'let down' by the organisation and that the coaching was a mechanism for 'shoring up' failing management practices:

> Your involvement in no way resolves our issues with the directors and we remain of the view that they have a responsibility to do what they said they would.

> But the directors should not be allowed to get away with this, and it would be completely wrong if the coaching was used to cover up on the broken promises.

> I think they need to know that we don't think the coaching gets them off the hook. It is not a replacement for them doing what they need to do. I think it is important that you don't get sucked into that.

In Cox's (2012a) study the importance of organisational culture on coaching relationships is also recognized. This exploratory research suggests that suspicion regarding management motivations can undermine the real intentions of an organisation. Thus there is a vital need for organisational transparency. One way of achieving this is three-way contracting, where concerns can be brought into the open and suspicion eliminated. Luckily, most organisations with the foresight to commission coaching for their employees also have a good coaching culture in place that involves careful contracting between coachee, coach and the organisation in order to avoid such misunderstandings. In the two studies that Cox (2012a) and Ives (2010) undertook, coaching interventions were introduced into organisations where a coaching culture was not in evidence, and the consequences for coachees and the coaching relationship soon became apparent. In such organisations a coach may confront what Zeus and Skiffington (2007 p. 202) term 'blatant resistance,' with the coachee "displaying evident hostility, mistrust and unwillingness to engage with the coaching in any meaningful way." They suggest that it can take several sessions to overcome such resistance with the right application and patience from the coach. This is confirmed by the research. The coach must ensure that misconceptions are addressed, and should avoid making assumptions about what coachees think is the status of the coach and the purpose of the coaching. De Haan (2008) highlights that the coachee may bring a range of presumptions, and urges the coach to explore the perceived role of the coach.

In some cases the concerns of the coachee may contain a grain of truth, and the coaching is indeed being commissioned because of the failures of senior management. As can be seen from the foregoing quotes, coachees may be eager to alert the coach to this danger and prevent him/her from being part of this perceived injustice. Whether or not coachees then direct their resentment towards the coach or the coaching largely depends on whether they can ultimately make a distinction between the management/organisation and the coaching intervention. The same issues become apparent in remedial coaching, where coachees may not be committed to the coaching process, and have not come to the process voluntarily. Such coachees will show greater willingness to respond to the coaching if it is not seen as serving the agenda of others, but is genuinely about helping them.

In some instances, coachees may display concern that they will end up with additional and unfair pressure imposed upon them, purely because they have received coaching. This is especially true if they already feel aggrieved, as in many remedial cases. For example, coachees may be worried that, having been given the coaching, they would now be expected to be able to do tasks they feel unable to do. One coachee confided: "It would be totally wrong if I was made to feel responsible instead of the directors. I don't want to be put under pressure to be responsible for my own training – that surely is ridiculous." According to this concern, the coach becomes an instrument of their harassment, rather than one of empowerment. This raises an important point: coaching that overemphasises the issue of personal responsibility can backfire if coachees feel that they are being put under pressure.

Coaching in organisations is often an intensely political act. The party that commissions the coaching is often not the object of the intervention. However, in challenging situations the coach needs to recognize that he could lose the goodwill of the coachees if they perceive the coach as cooperating too closely with the directorate. If the coach is receiving payment from one party, it is hard to shake off the impression that he/she is operating according to the organisational agenda. Again, good three-way contracting can alleviate this tension.

The problem of suspicion then is best addressed by everyone being open and honest about their roles and the coaching method expected, as Natale and Diamante (2005) recommend. The coach in particular strengthens the coaching alliance by being honest, insightful and helpful. Effort should be made at the outset to forestall confusion about the role of coaching and to be explicit over what agenda the coaching serves. When the role of the coaching is described abstractly, it may leave the coachee wondering what the coaching is really about, which creates room for suspicion. Clarifying the purpose of the coaching is vital to establishing a platform for trust. Ultimately, suspicion is overcome most effectively by discussing what coaching is and what it is designed to do.

Trust in the coach and the sense that the coachees' concerns are respected are key contributors to the effectiveness of the relationship, as 'trust and mutual respect' are vital to enabling the coach to advocate stretching tasks (Hunt & Weintraub, 2004 p. 42). However, as mentioned earlier, in GFC the emphasis on a trusting relationship is not a key aspect of the coaching itself, but is primarily a prerequisite to the success of the coaching. The relationship may not be the cause of the success, but it is necessary to handle the rigours of the coaching process (Ives, 2008).

Dealing with Resentment

Resentment and anger are problematic for coaching and for GFC more specifically, because they create a tendency to focus on the past, when the coaching requires a forward focus. Some coachees will resort to blame, even though this does not bring them nearer to an acceptable outcome. In fact, quite the reverse happens, as energy is expended on criticism, rather than utilising the opportunities available.

As mentioned, sometimes coachees will blame their organisation for the issue the coaching is intended to address and will take the view that it is the duty of those in charge to address it. In such instances, coachees are likely to view the coaching as underscoring how their organisation is failing them. Here is a sample of comments made by coachees in such a situation:

> I still maintain that this should not really be my problem. It is wrong that we are in this situation.

> I agree that we should not have been in the situation. It is not what I expected when I came here.

> If this was someone else's problem, we wouldn't have to worry about it. We would just turn up to work.

The coach may get caught up in the resentment if coachees accuse the coach of being complicit in the grievances they have with their superiors or their organisation. Where there are funding problems, the coachee may well be resentful that money is being diverted to coaching when what they regard as 'basic needs' are not being met. In Ives' research a coachee implied that had the coach been paid, he would have been annoyed that resources were going to pay the coach rather than provide for more pressing needs. It seems that had the coach been paid, the coachee would have been less willing to accept claims of independence. Coachees may at times harbour profound resentment towards their organisation, and there is a risk of the coaching becoming implicated in this situation, thus putting the coaching intervention at risk.

A state of resentment then is highly destructive for coaching, as "it keeps at a distance everything we encounter, even when it is in close physical proximity" (Flaherty, 2005 p. 27). Resentment at being denied one opportunity blinds the coachee to potential alternatives. However, it is vital that the coach resists the pressure to delve into the problems of the past, and remains steadfast in the resolve to look for solutions in the future. While coaching texts (e.g. Jackson & McKergow, 2008; Rogers, 2008) recognize that it may be necessary to temporarily allow the coachee to vent any anger or express his frustrations, this must be quickly steered towards a positive and constructive discussion about a preferred alternative. By retaining a focus on the positive, the coachee will normally gradually adopt a more constructive approach. We recommend focusing on urging and helping coachees to take practical measures to ameliorate their situation as a means of reducing negativity, rather than addressing the negative issue itself.

Addressing Dependence and Lack of Responsibility

At the heart of coaching, and GFC in particular, is the need for personal responsibility (Whitmore, 2003). This is all the more important in work environments that are highly structured or have top-down leadership, where in the coaching the coachee may need to display greater independence and self-sufficiency than he/she is used to. In these settings, some coachees may perceive that they are participating in a pre-set training programme or playing a clearly defined role and will feel no responsibility to direct their own development. Such a passive stance may result in stagnation or failure; thus, overcoming their rejection of personal responsibility is an essential prerequisite to effective goal-focused coaching.

Furthermore, some of the roles that coachees find themselves in require a degree of leadership, which in reality the organisation may fail to nurture. The upshot is that coachees need to develop their own leadership skills, and coaching is where this growth and development can occur. For example, coaching may help coachees to assume greater responsibility for their own training and development, rather than merely blame the organisation for failing to provide it. Coaching can help coachees focus on what can be done under prevailing conditions, as this comment from one coachee illustrates: "I was just blaming directors and getting more and more upset about it. I was even thinking of leaving. But for the moment I am concentrating on what it may be possible to achieve."

In our experience, there are two distinct types of dependence displayed by coachees. The first type of coachee more or less knows what he/she wants to achieve but expects the organisation to provide it, and then gets frustrated that it is not being provided. The second type of coachee does not know what he/she wants and expects to get direction from 'above,' and looks to others for guidance. Both types are dependent, but they differ as to why they reject personal responsibility: Either because they don't *want* to have to deal with challenges or because they feel they *need* help doing so. The difference is that the former are *unwilling*, while the latter believe they *can't*.

As explained in Chapter 1, GFC is non-directive. The purpose of the coach is not to offer advice, but to support the coachee towards a higher level of achievement. Parsloe and Wray (2000 p. 61) confirm that performance is enhanced when "control and responsibility is transferred from the coach to the learner" and the coach adopts a hand-off approach. Also, in coaching it is the coachee who is supposed to suggest and commit to the goal plan. Unlike mentoring, for example, which is predicated on the superior knowledge or experience of the mentor, the coach is not necessarily an expert or authority but someone who, as Gray suggests (2006 p. 479) "relates to the client in a spirit of partnership and collaboration." It is the coachee who "holds the ultimate responsibility for, and ownership of, the desired outcomes." As Flaherty (2005 p. xviii) puts it, coaching "is not telling people what to do; it's giving them a chance to examine what they are doing in the light of their intentions." In GFC, in particular, the coach is advised to resist pleas for more specific guidance (Berg & Szabo, 2005; Grant, 2006; Whitmore, 2003).

In a survey of coaching practice by Palmer and Whybrow (2007), a comfortable majority of coaches (67.9%) described their approach as 'facilitation' while a small minority (17.4%) described their approach as 'instructional.' Some coaches emphasise, to varying degrees, advice-giving and robust feedback, and Grant (2007) suggests that whether or not to be directive depends on the requirements of the coachee and the nature of the coaching issue. However, in keeping with much of the coaching literature (Jackson & McKergow, 2008; Stober, 2006; Pemberton, 2006), Hudson (1999) suggests that coaches should direct structure and process, but not content or outcome. Rogers (2008) discourages offering advice in case the coachee either mindlessly agrees or flatly rejects it. Overall, advice-giving can undermine and may remove a sense of personal responsibility from the coachees, which is harmful to coaching (Whitmore, 2003). Thus, to foster acceptance of responsibility, it is best to maintain a non-directive approach, which retains the onus of the coaching outcome on the coachee. Additionally, the goal-focused coach should ensure a participatory, collaborative process in which the coachees have maximum involvement and ownership of the process and its outcomes.

Responsibility cannot be imposed or cajoled; it must emerge organically. The coach needs to find ways that help coachees to motivate themselves and to transition from a stance of indifference to one of active concern. Reluctance to assume responsibility is best overcome through cooperation, rather than pressure (Hudson, 1999), as only the coachee can persuade him/herself in the long run (Whitmore, 2003). A solution-focused approach (Berg & Szabo, 2005; Grant, 2006; Greene & Grant, 2003; Jackson & McKergow, 2008) that prompts coachees to describe their preferred alternatives can be an effective method of overcoming rejection of responsibility.

Based on transition theory, Grant (2006) suggests that a person needs to give up on the previous way for the new way to be possible. However, as Reeves and Allison (2009 p. 13) remind us "every change requires dissonance." If there is no cognitive dissonance, either the change is illusory or it is insignificant. Coachees' resistance to a heightened level of responsibility is therefore to be expected. Nevertheless, as coaching progresses coachees will most likely increasingly accept that personal responsibility is a legitimate aim and not merely a necessary response to some problematic situation. Despite initial reluctance, coachees will typically accept that personal responsibility is proper and necessary, independent of external contingencies.

However, personal responsibility can come across as overwhelming instead of empowering, which is the exact opposite of its intention, and coachees often question the extent to which they are able to help themselves. An example would be where a group of workers are informed that due to new technology they will now be undertaking a task on their own that was previously sent to a separate department. Although they are promised training to ensure their familiarity with the new technology, the workers remain nervous about this change and display high levels of resistance to the move.

Before coachees have delineated an action plan for putting their goals into practice, self-responsibility therefore may feel somewhat daunting. Taking practical steps may provide reassurance that goals are attainable. In GFC, it is best to begin some sort of action plan as early as possible. As already mentioned, the achievement of small goals can lead to valuable increases in self-efficacy that will enhance further goal attainment. In keeping with a goal-focused orientation, the 'preferred alternative' should be clearly articulated and should direct attention to practical tasks and outcomes.

Apathy and Indifference

As noted, in order for coachees to view coaching as a solution, they need to be convinced that it can be helpful. Someone without previous positive experience of coaching may well be sceptical about how the coach could help, especially if the coach states explicitly that he or she is not there to provide solutions. The coach asks the coachee to view the coaching as a positive process, even though no solution or advice is being provided. This can be particularly difficult during the early sessions, when goals are often unclear. At the early stages of coaching, the focus is on helping coachees to clarify what they were hoping to achieve, and does not make much progress towards charting a course to its actual achievement. This may mean that coachees have difficulty relating to the coaching as a solution.

Acceptance of coaching as a solution is enhanced when the coachee is clear about the goal and has a method of achieving it. Enthusiasm grows on the basis of the clarity that the coaching brings. In GFC, the more practical the coaching gets the more likely there is to be buy-in, which is why the coaching should set small objectives towards the goal as soon as possible (Berg & Szabo, 2005; Jackson & McKergow, 2008). Commitment to and faith in the coaching process is likely to strengthen as the coaching shows potential for practical improvements.

However, occasionally, apathy results because coachees have other priorities. An example could be where a coach is brought in by a company manager, because tensions were identified within a particular team. However, once coaching begins it emerges that this team have been failing to meet their sales targets for three consecutive quarters and there is a threat that the department may be closed down. While the coaching mandate is to address stress management and team cohesion, the greater and more pressing concern of the team members is keeping their jobs and attracting more business. The coach is genuinely convinced that the high levels of stress are getting in the way of performance and are preventing the success that will save this department. However, under such circumstances it proves difficult to engage the coachees in the coaching process. Furthermore, the team members believe that what they need to succeed are greater resources and more support from the leadership. The coachees are convinced, perhaps rightly, that they have legitimate and real needs that are currently not being met by the organisation.

Thus coachees may identify pressing issues that they consider more critical to satisfying their needs, which could lead them to view the coaching as comparatively unimportant. As Flaherty (2005) suggests, if the coachee's mind is engaged with more pressing matters, coaching cannot function properly. In such instances, the issues intended to be addressed by the coaching will be treated as secondary. Their immediate interest in the coaching will focus on its capacity to lessen their pressing burden.

It is not possible to attempt coaching without clarifying what the needs are, and positioning the coaching in relation to these needs, even if in many instances coaching cannot solve them. The coach needs to recognize the needs and articulate his/her role in relation to those other needs as well, even if the aim is to refrain from trying to address them. The coaching process is acting within this space and cannot expect to be unaffected by major currents in the coachees' context. Ensuring the boundaries of the coaching prevents time being wasted on fending off inappropriate appeals, and frees both parties to focus on charting a path forward.

When there is a link between another unfulfilled need and the object of the coaching, it is necessary to establish how the coaching is going to position itself in relation to this need. Ultimately, the coachee must be satisfied with the focus of the coaching in order to ensure commitment to the coaching process. The coach may be tempted to present coaching as addressing the needs that the coachee finds most important, which would render the coaching of greater utilitarian benefit. However, not only is this sometimes incompatible with the coaching contract, but moreover those other issues may well be beyond the coach's ability to address. Coaching interventions need to acknowledge those realities, for otherwise they lose credibility, and the coachee will lose interest in the coaching.

A key part of managing the coaching relationship is managing expectations (Flaherty, 2005). This usually refers to ensuring the coachee is realistic about the outcomes of the coaching. However, an equally important aspect is ensuring a reasonable correlation between what the coachee and coach think is the purpose of the coaching. For example, this could emerge as a problem if coachees are hoping the coaching will provide training or advice, and they may be surprised that the coach intends to provide strictly non-directive coaching. This exchange between coachees in a focus group undertaken as part of Ives (2010) study, illustrates how coaching may be perceived:

A: I thought for sure you were coming here to tell us what to do . . .

C: And when you didn't tell us what to do, it did seem a little strange . . .

A: I expected you to have some answer or something, but you . . .

G: Yes, I also expected you were going to advise us . . . I guess we are used to people telling us what to do. I imagined you were going to give us some advice about how to cope better or function better – something like that, anyway.

Our research and experience suggests that some coachees will request advice even if the nature of goal-focused coaching was clearly spelled out at the outset. Particularly when dealing with coachees working in inadequate circumstances, the coach may be looked upon as a problem solver even if that is not the stated intention.

Coachees may therefore have their own wishes for the coaching and may confuse that with the declared purpose of coaching, even if the coach has done his/her reasonable best to communicate. The coachee may then be surprised and disappointed when those wishes are not fulfilled. False or unrealistic expectations cannot always be avoided, as some coachees will engage in wishful thinking and ignore early explanations proffered as to the nature of coaching. However, in order to reduce this risk we suggest that the coach should ascertain what the coachees think the coach's role is and what they consider the purpose of the coaching to be, and direct the explanation to address those perceptions. The coach cannot expect that coachees arrive without presumptions, even if they are unfamiliar with coaching. Whatever explanation the coach gives may not be fully internalised unless the coach addresses those conceptions. It is necessary to undo what they already think before the new information can be properly assimilated. The initial communication effort should be as much focused on trying to remove erroneous conceptions as on fostering correct ones.

Summary

This chapter has explored four key areas of resistance that can present formidable barriers to the progress of a coaching intervention: suspicion or lack of trust; resentment; lack of personal responsibility, which can manifest as blame and dependence; and apathy towards the coaching. Table 5.1 sets out the challenges for the coach in addressing these potential barriers to coaching and summarises how they may be addressed within GFC.

Table 5.1 Barriers to Coaching

Barrier to coaching	Solution
Suspicion – Organisational misconceptions – Misunderstanding the role of the coach – Insufficient coach/coachee communication	Factual communication about the role and purpose of the coaching
Resentment – Criticism – Anger	Focus on the positive
Dependence – Blame – Rejection of responsibility	Focus on the practical
Indifference – Despair – Purposelessness	Focus on hope and goals

6   The Coaching Cycle

Aims

- To explain why the start and the end of the process are crucial in GFC;
- To describe what can happen when there are breaks in coaching and how this impacts continuity in relation to goal formation;
- To examine how GFC works with reality to identify the best available option for goal achievement.

The process of coaching follows to a certain extent the cycle of development of any kind of relationship between two people: initially there needs to be a reason for meeting, what Flaherty (2005) calls an 'opening.' Then once the opening is established, an assessment is made, either formally or informally by both parties. In coaching this assessment might take the form of both personal and professional appraisal. The next stage in the process, as rapport begins to build, involves consideration of the direction the alliance will take. This 'direction setting' (Clutterbuck, 2005) is characterised by the identification and clarification of what is possible in relation to goals and the checking of commitment to those goals. Flaherty terms this stage 'enrolment': "making apparent in the coaching relationship the intended outcomes of the programme, the coachee's commitment to the outcomes and the coach's commitment to the same." Thus, planning how to achieve the goals and creating opportunities to implement the goals comes only after a lengthy and important period of needs analysis and motivation checks.

In this chapter we describe how the goal-focused approach impacts and informs different stages in the coaching process. We begin in section one by explaining the importance of the opening before going on, in sections two and three, to examine in more detail the need to explore with coachees their reality and their best available options for making progress. This chapter also discusses in section four how, during the coaching process, the solving of one problem may only result in the emergence of a different, even more complex problem. Later in the chapter, in sections five, six and seven, interruptions in the coaching are also discussed, together with the final two stages of the process: endings and follow-up.

The Opening

As explained at length in Chapter 5, rather than placing exclusive emphasis on the quality of the interpersonal alliance between the coachee and the *coach*, it is equally important that the coachee has an effective relationship with the *coaching*. Even if the coach establishes an excellent relationship with the coachee, the latter must be convinced of the purpose of the coaching; indifference to the intervention will stymie progress. Passmore (2005 p. 6) similarly suggests that before a goal can be set it is necessary to "establish whether there is a need for coaching, to reach agreement that coaching is acceptable as an approach in the eyes of all parties involved."

Coaching needs an 'opening', an occasion that creates the willingness to commit to the process. In fact, according to Flaherty (2005 p. 67) "sometimes coaching fails because the coach has not coordinated the beginning of the effort with an appropriate opening." The majority of people will not be ready for coaching until there is such an opening – something that happens that interrupts their normal pattern of living or working, and for which they currently have no existing coping strategies.

Grant (2006) also argues that for coaching to succeed there needs to be discontent with the present; and that it may be necessary to 'amplify' existing levels of discontent, since otherwise the coachee will be unmotivated to change. We would suggest that once an opening has been discerned, motivation can be raised by focusing on the benefits of the change, as research by Carver and Scheier (1998) suggests that generally positive goals are better than negative ones. Raising hope for a positive outcome has also been identified as helpful for engagement in the coaching process (Green, Oades & Grant, 2006; Pooley, 2006) and is supported by coaches that have adopted an appreciative inquiry approach, where the focus is on how to build on previous positive experiences (Gordon, 2008; Orem, Binkert & Clancy, 2007).

Facing Reality

Coaching often operates in less than ideal conditions. To 'win over' the coachee, it is tempting for the coach to put a positive gloss on a situation, by either playing down the significance of the problem or adopting a highly optimistic outlook (e.g. Jackson & McKergow, 2008). An argument could be made for the coach to build expectancies of the usefulness of the coaching in order obtain full engagement from the coachee (O'Broin & Palmer, 2009). However, the results of Ives' research suggest that overly encouraging optimism is likely to cause distrust of and disbelief in the coaching. More specifically, where the coaching context is struggling with problems, the coach needs to acknowledge their existence and establish the position the coaching takes in relation to them. The coach should acknowledge any deficiencies and not unreasonably raise expectations. Adopting a realistic disposition raises the credibility of the coaching and the confidence of the coachee. Coaches regard addressing reality as a significant dimension of coaching (Cavanagh, 2006; Dembkowski & Eldridge, 2008; Flaherty, 2005), which can take up the "bulk of the time in coaching" (Alexander, 2006 p. 63).

Reeves and Allison (2009 p. 34) claim that "both coach and client must confront reality," and that "coaches must help develop a reality orientation" (p. 81). Furthermore, as Hackman and Wageman (2005) suggest, coaching should only, and can only, address issues that are available and amenable to intervention. If certain tasks are predictable and can only be done a certain way, strategising is pointless and harmful. Similarly, Cocivera and Cronshaw (2004 p. 238) suggest that coaching has to be set in the context of the 'conditions' under which the coaching must operate, namely, "the constraints inherent in the situation over which the actor has no immediate or direct control and which must be considered as givens within the temporal and spatial arrangement." Acknowledging these conditions avoids time-wasting and frustration.

However, facing reality does not mean intense analysis of the past or delving into internal psychological process; rather, GFC is forward-focused and aims to generate practical action, as explained in earlier chapters. Goal-focused coaching approaches divert attention from what cannot be changed and direct efforts towards those improvements that can be made (Jackson & McKergow, 2008; Peltier, 2001; Pemberton, 2006). Therefore, being realistic does not result in disillusionment; rather, the coachee will appreciate the candour and realism. Facing the limitations of reality helps to accelerate the process of setting a practicable goal. Coaching should operate within a culture of honesty that accepts that problems are normal, and GFC in particular should extend beyond obtaining an accurate assessment of the situation to incorporate an assessment of what can be realistically achieved.

The Best Available Option

Helping coachees to become reconciled to the situation as it is and recognising that it may not change is helpful for coaching. There is great emphasis in coaching on looking at how things can change, but this needs to be set against accepting that there are some things that are not susceptible to modification. Otherwise, time and effort is expended wastefully. Accepting the harsh reality helped the coachees in Ives' study to focus on what *could* be done – leading to a better attitude and thus a better performance. Coaching can suffer from excessive expectation, which is as problematic as defeatism. It is as important that the coachee recognizes practical limitations as it is to not exaggerate them. Learning how to cope with a given reality may sometimes be more useful than insisting on replacing it.

Where the problems in the coachee's work environment, for example, are deeply entrenched, accepting that they may not change could actually help him or her to gain perspective. A sense of realism may enable the coachee to overcome disappointment and adopt a constructive approach, as this coachee focus group exchange suggests:

D: It's pretty clear to everyone what kind of state the world is in. The situation for the institutions here has been brutal and devastating. Our organisation is no exception to this rule; it is in a terrible financial mess.

A: Yep, it is in survival mode now. Providing us with proper training is now a low priority. I don't think anyone is under any illusion right now . . .

D: Ironically, as the situation has gotten worse, I have come to expect less.

B: Yes, that's a good way of putting it – the overall situation is deteriorated so much that, like, what are we to do?

D: We are now seeing what is happening around us, guys leaving, people really struggling, organisations are having to consider closing – under such circumstances, what chance is there of improvement here? . . .

C: There is no point complaining when you know how problematic the situation is . . .

For some people, a pessimistic prognosis for change will result in resignation and abandonment. However, sometimes the reverse happens, and coachees recognize that the problems are 'here to stay' and stop battling with their situation. They can then redirect their energies and focus on changing those things over which they have some control.

This approach contrasts with the miracle question, frequently used in solution-focused coaching, (namely, asking the coachee to imagine a miracle has happened, the solution has occurred and to describe what has changed). This question tries to get the coachee to believe that any problem can definitely be overcome (de Shazer, 1988; Grant, 2007; O'Broin & Palmer, 2007). We would argue that there is room for the opposite type of coaching question: *what happens if you woke up one morning and realised that the situation is not going to change, what could you still do to make the best of it?* Coachees will see the benefit of taking ownership of their goals, because they will recognize that they are necessary, even if they continue to blame others for their situation.

Thus, goal-focused approaches should direct efforts towards helping coachees to identify where progress *is* possible. The best solution possible, even if far from ideal, will earn the commitment of the coachee, whereas overly hopeful goals will be rejected. Indeed, goal theories (Locke & Latham, 1990) note that goal attainability is vital to ensure commitment to the goal – a topic explored later in Chapter 8.

In Box 6.1 we describe a scenario where multiple problems existed and where the opening for coaching needed to be carefully managed.

Coaching operates within a context and will be affected by events within that context. It needs therefore to be responsive to these events. GFC, in particular, is sensitive to conditions under which the coachee is forced to operate, as these conditions inform what is possible and what is appropriate in terms of goals.

Box 6.1 Example of Multiple Problems

We were responsible for introducing coaching into a training organisation where problems were readily evident and tension was correspondingly high. A sharp budget cut meant that recruitment was put on hold and key vacant positions were left unfilled. At first, no one knew why this was happening. Later, it began to emerge that there was a serious funding crisis, so plans for development were put on hold. Existing staff tried to carry out work without suitable skills, and the staff's relationship with the managers rapidly deteriorated. The worsening financial situation meant even fewer resources to provide adequate training for the trainees, resulting in a general sense of gloom and deepening dissatisfaction from both the trainees and managers. As a result, one senior manager left the company, leaving it listless and unstable. Moreover, several members of staff were struggling with serious health matters, casting a shadow over the entire organisation. The conditions were poor and the trainees realised that it was likely to remain this way.

With such multiple problems, we were rather apprehensive that the trainees would abandon the coaching, if not the organisation. Additionally, many of them were struggling with feelings of inadequacy, because they had little experience of coping with the challenges the organisation was facing and found the situation both alien and daunting. Nevertheless, the coaching progressed reasonably well. The director decided, as a result of coaching, to alter his communication style and the coachees decided that if they were going to stay they might as well see what they could do to help themselves.

The reports were that the atmosphere at the organisation had improved, and both motivation and performance had risen, as this comment from a coachee suggests:

> We are making good progress. I am in a reasonably good mood; I think the same is true for the others. Our relationship with the director has improved and we are looking forward. But the general situation is terrible. A manager has left, the company is in a financial mess, we live from hand to mouth and we are getting very little help from the company.

The coachees thought, to varying degrees, that the coaching was successful. The action planning was considered a "positive experience," "useful process," and "quite exciting," and the coaching was described as a "worthwhile experience" which led to "concrete results." Furthermore, action plans were adopted without too much struggle, despite them being far removed from what the coachees expected upon joining the organisation.

However, the optimistic conclusion is that challenging circumstances do not necessarily spell disaster for a coaching intervention. Problems within the environment may not pose a major threat within an effective coaching framework. As Bandura (1982) notes, events often *interrupt* people's plans, but whether they *disrupt* these depends on how the person reacts.

Coaching is designed to help coachees to achieve the best possible outcome under prevailing circumstances, not to create the perfect outcome. Coachees can be satisfied with the plan they create, not because it is an ideal result but because they determine that this is the best available option, as this comment from a coachee illustrates:

> Under the circumstances, this is not a bad result . . . So the way things worked out in the end was the way it should have worked out, not because it was the best way, but because it was the only practical way forward.

In certain circumstances, coachees may view coaching as a method of making the best out of a pretty bad situation. Perhaps they will not create an ideal situation, but they may render a bad one a little less bad.

Even if the coaching is judged by the coachees not to have solved most of the problems or the main problems, they may be satisfied with the progress that they now attribute to the coaching. A coachee expects to see progress; he or she does not expect miracles. As long as the coach does not build unrealistic expectations, the coach need not fear that the persistence of some problems – even be they significant – is going to threaten the credibility of the coach or the usefulness of the coaching.

This calls into question terms like 'future perfect' (Jackson & McKergow, 2008) and 'dream goal' (Whitmore, 2003) to describe the goals set in coaching, when much of coaching is working in challenging environments where the most appropriate course of action is probably not the most appealing. The least-worst plan is just as good as the best plan if in each case that is the most appropriate thing to do. While coachees may be far from euphoric about their goal or plan, they can still regard it as a sensible and necessary outcome.

Problems are also Solutions

It is inevitable that as matters develop, new problems will arise; often this illustrates that progress is being made and problems at a new level of activity have now come into view. We therefore question the optimistic tone in some coaching texts in relation to problem-solving, because it is rare that coaching results in the final elimination of problems. The solution-focused coaching literature (e.g. Berg & Szabo, 2005; Greene & Grant, 2003; Jackson & McKergow, 2008) in our view is primarily portrayed as finding a single solution, rather than a process of progressing through a series of problems. Encouraging expectations of one-off solutions is misleading and has the potential to cause disillusionment when a clutch of new problems arise.

Coaching in the real world is a messy affair. Anyone who insists upon working within a predictable linear framework should, we would suggest, avoid practicing coaching. Coaching in challenging environments all the more so is a fraught experience; the coach needs to be flexible and adaptable. Problem solving in coaching should not be viewed as a one-off event, but rather as an ongoing process. In the course of his research, Ives recalls being really downbeat when he realised that despite largely overcoming the original set of issues, a whole set of new ones had emerged, of equal intensity and as potentially damaging. He thought that the coaching assignment was going to struggle and perhaps fail. In reality, problems slowed progress but did not destabilise the coaching process.

Persistence of problems does not necessarily represent a crisis in coaching. On the contrary, coaching is designed to help the coachee navigate through them. Such navigation should be given greater emphasis in coaching texts, which are too often utopian and simplistic. According to D. B. Peterson's (2006) constraint model, development bottlenecks along the pipeline impede progress towards effective implementation. Coaching aims to unblock these constraints, to ensure continuous progress; solving the first level of problems enables the coachee to progress to the next level. Coaching from a goal-focused perspective is about progressing through a self-regulation hierarchy, ranging from the most abstract to the most concrete goals. The challenges at the various levels of abstraction are often divergent, and the coach needs to understand this to guide the coachee through the process.

Progress in GFC, then, does not need to entail moving from a problem to a solution, but may involve progress to a more advanced problem. This may be disconcerting to both coach and coachee, as it may appear that they are just stumbling from one problem to the next. However, progressing to a more advanced level of problem is progress just the same. The original problems may have largely been overcome, but this has moved the discussion onto a new range of issues. This constant dealing with problems can sometimes be perceived as failure to make progress, which is untrue. The coach and coachee need not let them become a source of defeatism. Coaching aims to unblock the constraints to ensure continuous progress; solving the first levels of problems enables the coachee to progress to the next level (Peterson, D. B., 2006), as Figure 6.1, based upon Peterson, illustrates.

Moreover, it seems that some problems may even serve to facilitate greater involvement or commitment in the coaching, as they disabuse the coachees of

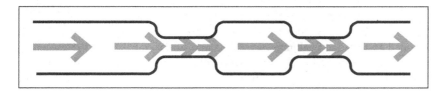

Figure 6.1 Coaching Through Bottlenecks

high expectations from their organisation and lead them to assume greater self-responsibility. Excessive hopefulness can actually get in the way of progress, as the coachee thinks that the situation may improve itself. Under poor conditions coachees may give up expecting their organisation, or other outside influences, to solve their problems and may be more inclined to act themselves. Realisation that the endemic problems at their organisation, for example, are unlikely to be imminently resolved may lead to the departure of some coachees, but for those who remain this realisation may have an energising effect.

Breaks in Coaching

Sometimes in coaching there can be a hiatus for holidays, illness or for internal organisational reasons. Coachee feedback suggests that these breaks can be disruptive. For example, when coaching in Ives' project was interrupted for a three-week period a coachee said: "I didn't like that this coaching cycle had a break in the middle. It set us back almost to the beginning . . . I think you should start and continue without such a big interruption." Another coachee added: "Especially as we were in middle of creating our schedule and then we stopped right in middle, even a week or two later would have been better." If the coaching is in the middle of a process, a break can be particularly disruptive, as after an extended gap it is usually difficult to begin again from where it was left off. Consequently, when the coaching involves a systematic structured element, thought needs to be given to how it is scheduled, with effort made to allow the process to be subject to as little interruption as possible.

However, when the coaching breaks at appropriate junctures, this does not cause disruption. For example, if there is a break between setting the goal and creating the action plan, this may not cause disruption. Conversely, sometimes a break in the coaching allows for any change to settle in and for adjustments to be made following on from the previous coaching sessions. However, some coachees do indicate that they would prefer maintaining occasional contact during the interim periods to address issues as they arise. Although this may not always be possible, it is worth bearing in mind when designing a coaching intervention. We would also suggest that it is best to clarify the breaks if possible before the coaching starts, so as to manage expectations and avoid disappointment or frustration.

Ending

Coaching authors (e.g. Cox 2009; Skiffington & Zeus, 2003) highlight potential difficulties with ending a coaching intervention, and Hodgetts (2002 p. 217) argues that "well-managed endings are just as essential to coaching success as clearly designed and explicit beginnings are." It is part of the coach's role to ensure that the coachee reacts well to the termination of the coaching. Cox (2009) suggests that the non-interpretive approach to coaching, that is to say a non-therapeutic approach, leaves the decision when to end coaching largely up to the coachee, although many coaching interventions will require a specific timeframe. However,

Cox (2009) acknowledges that a time limitation stimulates completion of the work and cites Ledman (2004), stressing that setting a timeframe is a potent coaching tool, as it brings a focus on endings at the outset of the intervention.

Cox (2009) further suggests that an ending can operate as a useful organising principle from the start. A properly planned ending guides and structures the work that will lead up to it. She argues that a clear ending in sight both evokes an energising force for the intervention and provides an overt rite of passage that facilitates an effective transfer to the post-intervention state. Focusing on a defined end enhances goal salience and acts as a motivating force for the goal-driven processes. Figure 6.2 illustrates how the end should influence the beginning and should be firmly in sight when the coaching intervention is established.

It also seems that planning for a post-intervention stage reduces the risk of dependence on the coach and can draw the coach and coachee closer (Garvey et al., 2009). Clutterbuck and Megginson (2004) distinguish between 'winding up' and 'winding down,' with the former being the more proactive approach aiming to ensure that the progress made during the relationship is carried forward. By defining the ending at the beginning, it is possible to set out the indicators that would suggest that the end has indeed been reached and that the coachee is ready for the intervention to conclude. Additionally, by anticipating a positive ending, as Cox (2009) argues, it is more likely for this ending to transpire. Having a defined timeline of the coaching intervention may mitigate feelings of loss, as the coach and coachees are operating with a clear sense of an ending.

Planning an ending is particularly appropriate in GFC, where working towards a clear end-goal is at the heart of the coaching approach and where leveraging a powerful goal is a key tool in driving motivation and performance. In GFC there is less emotional dependency than in therapeutic modes of coaching, and conse-

Figure 6.2 Beginning with the End

quently coachees are less likely to be badly affected by its termination. However, even this type of coaching can create a close bond between the parties to the process, and this is particularly so when they are working together through challenging problems. To some extent, the reaction to ending the coaching will depend on prevailing circumstances. If the climate is highly negative, ending the coaching will be more problematic. Similarly, if the coaching has not reached a productive outcome it may lead to dissatisfaction. If there is an optimistic climate in the coachee's life or organisation, it is likely to render the transition less traumatic.

Follow-up

Even if the coaching ends successfully, there may still be concern as to the sustainability of the action plans. This was expressed by one organisational director as follows:

> The biggest problem is what happens now. Will they actually do it now that you have gone? The situation at the company is still volatile and uncertain. They need someone who can talk to them. My worry is that the whole thing could just grind to a halt.

Therefore, we argue that coaching needs to have a follow-up strategy. This could either take the form of agreeing with management in the organisation to maintain the plans that have been put into place through the coaching or it could involve some minimal follow-up from the coach at set intervals.

The necessity for follow-up varies depending on the nature of the work the coaching sought to address and the outcome of the coaching process itself. If the coaching resulted in structural adjustments, these should sustain the change once the coaching ends. Similarly, if a great deal of the action occurred while the coaching was ongoing, again the need for a follow-up plan will be less. Fundamentally, GFC is introducing a goal-oriented approach to a person's daily work. Its value is greatest when it becomes the method of operation on a daily basis. If the coaching has resulted in successfully imparting this orientation to the coachee, then follow-up may be redundant. This is why involving senior management in the GFC process is generally a successful strategy, as it enables the goal-focused orientation to be embedded in the running of the organisation.

Summary

In this chapter, we have focused on the beginnings and endings of the coaching process.

It was noted that the opening for coaching may involve helping coachees to come to terms with their current reality and identify goals that are practical in the prevailing circumstances. This 'best available option' was contrasted with the miracle question, where the entire problem is deemed to have been solved overnight, and posited as vital for achieving focus and determination against difficult odds. Indeed we have suggested that problems are also solutions in that they arise from previous problems that have seemingly been solved only to reveal more of life's complexities.

We have also considered what may happen to the goal focus if breaks in the process occur. In fact it may be that coachees' goals have shifted in the interim and have to be revisited in order to regain motivation and momentum. Events will have intervened.

7 Team, Group and Peer Coaching with a Goal Focus

Aims

* To emphasise the importance of genuine, shared goals in team coaching situations;
* To discuss the opportunities and risks of team, group and peer coaching using the goal-focused approach.

Coaching in organisations is generally conducted in a dyadic format, involving a professional (often external) coach working with an individual coachee, although there is an emerging shift towards team and group coaching. Evidence-based research relating to group coaching is however, currently very limited. According to Clutterbuck (2010 p. 281) there is "little targeted literature" on the subject, although Brown and Grant (2010) provide an overview of current developments in group coaching. In relation to peer coaching there is rather more research available and in particular Ladyshewsky (2010), working in the field of education, has made a number of useful contributions.

In this chapter, we explore some key issues arising from several of our own recent research projects, which we hope will contribute to greater understanding of these three vital coaching formats and how they relate to GFC. We begin in section one by defining group and team coaching, as there are small but significant differences that impact upon coaching practice. We then discuss the relationship between group and individual coaching, using real scenarios and dialogue to illustrate our points. In section three we examine group relations and note the importance of the coach having effective group management skills. Group goals are explored in section four and a model of group coaching presented in section five. Finally, in section six, issues related to peer coaching are discussed.

Group and Team Coaching – Some Definitions

Team coaching outside of the sports arena is a new phenomenon and moreover the term has multifarious meanings (Clutterbuck, 2007). Clutterbuck (2010 p. 271) defines team coaching thus: "a learning intervention designed to increase collective capability and performance of a group or team, through application of the coaching principles of assisted reflection, analysis and motivation for change." This definition highlights learning and reflection, and views team coaching as facilitating learning rather than having a short-term performance orientation, which we would argue is less relevant to GFC, where the focus is not primarily on learning and reflection. The definition offered by Hackman and Wageman (2005 p. 269) is perhaps more fitting. They suggest that team coaching is a "direct interaction with a team intended to help members make coordinated and task-appropriate use of their collective resources in accomplishing the team's work."

In our view, *group* coaching should be distinguished from *team* coaching. Team coaching is not merely coaching done as a group; rather, it is coaching offered to a group that is structured and is, or is about to be, operating as a team where there are specific joint goals. All definitions of a team centre on this distinction: according to Bloisi, Cook and Hunsaker (2003) the team works together on a clearly defined and mutually accountable goal, and Hackman and Wageman (2005) emphasise that for a team to be effective, participants must share responsibility and accountability. Zeus and Skiffington (2007 p. 130) similarly note that "a group of individuals working together on a project does not necessarily constitute a team."

Katzenbach and Smith (1993) define a team as a small group committed to a common purpose for which they are *mutually accountable*. Likewise, Bandura (2001 p. 7) suggests that "joint activities require commitment to a shared intention and coordination of interdependent plans of action." Effective team or group work, then, must feature a high level of interdependence, and group goals must override the goals of the individual members.

Group Coaching

According to Hackman and Wageman (2005) team coaching has three distinct functions:

(1) It enhances effort – it is motivational
(2) It addresses strategy – it is consultative
(3) It encourages effective sharing of skills and knowledge – it is educational.

We would suggest that group GFC should encompass these three functions as well. Coachees become more motivated by the new horizons that open up as a result of collaboration, they formulate a group action plan and these efforts result in the acquisition of new skills and knowledge.

However, group coaching may not be part of the original intervention plan, but could grow out of a realisation that the kind of tasks the coachees need to undertake cannot be sensibly attained solo. Where the coach is working with more than one person in an organisation, group coaching may be the best option, especially where the goals that the individual coachees wish to fulfil cannot be achieved without what we might call inter-coachee cooperation. Of course, it is not possible in all situations to engage with a coachee's workmates, but where this is an option group coaching may be the best solution.

The case study in Box 7.1 describes a situation where group coaching was seen as a necessary adjunct to one-to-one coaching.

Box 7.1 'Seen Better Times'

Seen Better Times, a large packaging firm, has suffered badly under a recession and commercially is in a holding pattern. The company has sustained heavy losses and has scaled back on investment and any unnecessary expenditure. A key victim of this crisis is the training department, which has been closed down entirely and seemingly for good. Each department is now responsible for organising its own training, within its own budgets. While working one-to-one with individual staff members, it became readily apparent to the coach that the kind of training each person required could not be realistically organised by each coachee. Thus, a consensus soon emerged that individual action plans were not feasible, and that the group needed to convene to work out a way forward. This led to the suggestion that they should collaborate on their action plans, as the following dialogue shows:

> D: I think we should see if there are things that we all want to do and then we can work as a team . . .

> A: That is an excellent suggestion . . .

> D: Let's see where we have the same goals. I am sure that this is often the case. This was certainly the case with my own colleagues . . . Let's work as a team . . . Making a plan should be done in conjunction with others. Instead of having ten different plans, let's work out what we all

---

Thus, at times individual coaching requires expansion to the wider context in order to incorporate the involvement of other key stakeholders. Several coaching authors (Cavanagh, 2006; Peltier, 2001; Starr, 2007) have noted that coaching frequently needs to adopt a holistic or systemic approach, in recognition of the wider issues that impact on the individual.

It is therefore surprising that the coaching literature does not seem to acknowledge adequately that individual coaching may not be able to effectively proceed without group cooperation. Often group action planning and group coaching is the only realistic approach. When the individual goals of members of a single organisation overlap or are intertwined, there is little sense in each planning individually. Similarly, if the most valuable options for each individual are such tasks that are only realistic as a combined effort, group work would seem inevitable. According to Clutterbuck (2010), group coaching is necessary where the wider environment exercises significant influence on the individuals. In these circumstances, individual coaching has limitations, and group coaching may sometimes be the more appropriate coaching format (Hudson, 1999).

However, Ives' study found that when coachees had no previous experience of working as a group, coachees found the process of forming the working alliance fairly challenging. Since prior to the coaching intervention they were not a functioning group, significant time and effort was required to establish group norms. Crucially, the coachees had divergent needs and interests, which added an additional layer of complexity to the task. Coaching a group that did not previously act as a team independent of the coaching is more difficult and needs to be approached with added caution.

Even when a group is well structured as a functioning team, Skiffington and Zeus (2003) claim that this coaching form "requires considerable competence in core facilitation processes," including analysing requirements to satisfy all the stakeholders, designing the structure of the coaching, establishing group roles and norms, managing group dynamics, and introducing appropriate interventions. The skills required for effective team coaching are different and possibly wider than individual coaching (Ashton & Wilkerton, 1996; Clutterbuck, 2010). In fact Brown and Grant (2010 p. 32) argue that a group coach requires "a strong understanding of group dynamics or group-based dialogue processes."

Group coaching can provide several benefits:

Pooling of skills and knowledge – Coachees have different knowledge and skills that collectively enable actions for which individual coachees lack the ability. As one coachee said, "working as a group has been very helpful for me. Between us normally someone had the right idea or the necessary contact."

Pooling of resources – Working as a group makes it possible to pursue goals that would have been rejected as impractical for one person. Individual coachees may not pursue key objectives because they are perceived as impracticable for a single individual.

Mutual responsibility – Working in a group can serve to reinforce mutual responsibility, as each person's contribution affects others. As a coachee explained, "it has been interesting working as a group, where we all have parts to play in a single project. If each of us doesn't do what he promised to do, the whole project won't happen." Group accountability can mitigate a tendency to blame the organisation.

However, although there are several benefits in creating a group action plan, there are also numerous challenges that can sap a great deal of time and energy, especially when there is wrangling over the content of the action plan and dividing up roles (Kets de Vries, 2005). Indeed Ives' research suggests that while group coaching can be successful insofar as the coachees agree on a mostly satisfactory joint action plan, there are several unique difficulties involved in group GFC. Coachees in a group may have conflicting work styles, with some coachees adopting a more aggressive work ethic or a more competitive approach. While some coachees may be ambitious and impatient, others may regard big goals as over-ambitious and unrealistic. These variations require a fair amount of compromise. Coachees in a group may also have conflicting interests and requirements. Coachees may differ in their training needs, their ambitions and their expectations, and not all coachees will be interested in pursuing the same goal. In a group action planning situation, some actions will invariably have to be omitted even though they are of importance to one or more coachee.

Although group coaching can lead to the formulation of a successful action plan, some group members may display dissatisfaction due to contrasting expectations from the process. Some coachees may resent having to deal with issues not directly related to their tasks, while, conversely, others may feel frustrated that the group does not share their concerns. Some coachees may get annoyed that they are being dragged into aspects they feel are of *too* practical a nature, while others may resent that some coachees were unwilling to deal with practicalities. A sense of unfairness risks undermining the trust essential to group coaching. Coachees cannot be forced into group work that is neither practical nor appropriate (Kets de Vries, 2005).

Indeed, some groups consist of several sub-groups which may vary in their needs. In the following extract one coachee raised the concern that the joint plan would not accommodate the needs of each individual coachee:

> C: I have been listening to this whole discussion and D is saying that we should make this a joint plan, but I see things not working. Who says his plan will work for me?

> C: On my plan there are items such as writing and speaking skills. Are you interested in those?

> D: I confess, this is not important to me.

> C: So you accept that we cannot have a joint plan?

> A: Let's not forget how we got to this point. We all recognize that many of the actions in our plan are impractical for each of us to organise individually.

> E: Exactly.

> A: And I would guess that most if not all of these items would appear on everyone's list.

> C: So what happens to those things that are not on everyone's list?

> A: They can still stay on your list.

> C: But D was saying we should have a joint plan?

> D: Okay, so not everything on your plan must be the same as the joint plan...

> A: Each person still has their own plan, but where our plans overlap we will make one plan.

In a group or team situation, an effective use of GFC would be to facilitate coachee-created personalised work or learning schedules. Creating a joint action plan will typically exclude tasks that are only pertinent to a minority of coachees, as a group plan cannot realistically incorporate all the concerns of the group members. Action planning needs to be adjusted to suit the individual coachee's goals. Additionally, coachees may have personal struggles, such as procrastination, lack of self-efficacy or inexperience that are coachee-specific, and cannot be properly addressed in a group plan, as this quote from a group coaching participant reveals:

> We all have different strengths and weaknesses. D and A just wanted the project to happen, without putting in any of the work. B was too pessimistic and negative; to him, no idea was workable. To me, the issue is about getting down to it and not procrastinating. And so on. The group coaching was necessary at this point – we all accepted that in the end – but it left a problem that each person needs to focus on a different issue for them.

In Ives' action research study, it was eventually agreed that coaching would proceed as a group session, and that individual coachees would add to their action plans to fit their requirements, which confirms the judgement that "social groups develop rules about when and how to act for individual benefit and for the wider group benefit" (Clutterbuck, 2008 p. 222). While to some coaches, group coaching may not seem ideal, they may nevertheless regard compromise as inevitable. Those who are reluctant to participate in group coaching may ultimately accept that group coaching is the best option available.

Group coaching often needs to be accompanied by individual coaching to support the implementation of the non-group goals. The individual coaching will ensure, firstly, that coachee-specific goals omitted from the group are not overlooked and, secondly, that the group action plan is personalised for the specific tasks of individual coachees. Hudson (1999 p. 22) similarly states that "coaching goes along faster and more effectively when one-on-one meetings are used in combination with group meetings." Brown and Grant (2010 p. 31) likewise argue "for increased use of group coaching in organisational settings, alongside dyadic coaching," as this combination "better enables performance improvement at the individual, group and organisational levels."

Furthermore, it would seem that group coaching is best suited for a particular stage in the goal setting process. As the goal and self-regulation literature explains, goals proceed through a progression from abstract to concrete (Carver & Scheier, 1998), gradually moving from being general and universal to becoming increasingly specific and individual (Carver, 2007; Locke & Latham, 1990). Thus, the higher the goal is in this hierarchy, the more suited it is as a group goal. As it progresses towards implementation, it requires increasing specificity to meet the contingencies of the specific context, the requirements of the particular circumstances, and individual challenges (see also Figure 3.6). A group action plan, in some instances, will require personalisation to meet the requirements of particular coachees. Moreover, individual coachees need coaching to further break down the group plan into a more detailed and time-specific action plan suited to their specific abilities and situation, as will be explained in Chapter 8.

Group work naturally suffers from the diverse requirements of its members, but simultaneously benefits from their diverse skills. The art of coaching a group is to manage the diverse requirements while building on the diverse abilities. In practice, this is accomplished through focusing on the core objectives and facilitating compromise.

Group Relations

A large part of the work in group coaching relates to managing the group. It is inherent in the coach's role to balance the needs of individuals and the group (Clutterbuck, 2007). Establishing the focus of the group work can be difficult because of key priority differences among group members, which is greatly exacerbated in the absence of a natural core or focus to the group. Without addressing interpersonal relations the group will not function properly. The literature suggests that effective groups are distinguished by mutual trust, openness and respect, but most importantly by a high level of interdependence, and a commitment to group goals over those of individual members (Katzenbach & Smith, 1993).

Hackman and Wageman (2005) also note that original working patterns are often 'imported' into the group and if not addressed early on can be extremely difficult to dislodge. Thus, as Zeus and Skiffington (2007 p. 135) suggest, "one of the major roles of the team coach is to ensure that sufficient individual and/or team time is allocated to establishing the individual's commitments to team goals and dealing with any resistance." Similarly, Hackman and Wageman (2005 p. 275) suggest that when team members come together for the first time, the most pressing piece of business for them is "to get oriented to one another and to the task in preparation of the actual work." Often, the coachees are already oriented with one another, but they need to be oriented towards a mutual task.

However, while good group relations are indispensible, the relationship between group members is less important in purely goal-related or performance-related coaching. Ives' research provided little evidence that the coaching impacted on coachee interrelations, as the coachees only cooperate for utilitarian purposes and do not display increased empathy towards one another. This supports Hackman and Wageman's (2005 p. 273) view that, "the pervasive emphasis on interpersonal processes in the team performance literature reflects a logical fallacy about the role of those processes in shaping performance outcomes." Cox's research (2012b) however suggests that if the individual goals, and indeed group goals, are focused on improving communication skills and emotional awareness, for example, then group coaching in addition to one-to-one support can result in increased interpersonal understanding and improved performance. Furthermore, it may be that even if relationship building is not the immediate focus of the group coaching, better relations manifest as an outcome.

GFC, we would argue, is primarily an individual pursuit and in Ives' study the group coaching was ultimately viewed as a mechanism for each coachee to attain his or her own objectives. Thus, GFC is not overtly a means of team building. Hackman and Wageman (2005 p. 273) similarly restrict coaching to the betterment of task performance, not to the group's or team's interpersonal relationships, which they argue distinguishes their model "from the great majority of writing and practice about team coaching" that prioritises enhancing the quality of the member's interpersonal relationships. Thus, they argue that "coaching interventions that focus specifically on team effort, strategy and knowledge and skill, facilitate team effectiveness more than do interventions that focus on members' interpersonal relationships" (2005 p. 273).

Thus, it is generally better to help the group or team achieve in order ultimately to improve its interpersonal relationships, instead of the reverse, as performance often drives interpersonal processes (Wageman et al. 2008). Clutterbuck (2007) similarly suggests that team coaching interventions focused on raising performance are best when focused on a specific objective or process. Brown and Grant (2010 p. 37) also argue that group coaching is goal focused; thus, in a goal-focused format the work conducted to formulate an actual task becomes the primary contributor towards greater inter-group cooperation.

Group Goals

As already seen, the coaching literature recognizes the challenge of facilitating group coaching. However, goal-focused group coaching faces particular difficulties. Firstly, there is a strong possibility that the group members will have diverse interests and conflicting needs, obstructing the formation of group goals. Secondly, with group goals, there will often be the need to balance the needs of the group and individual. The group coach must therefore be more proactive in managing the coaching process, and must have "the flexibility to facilitate or be directive as the situation demands" (Zeus & Skiffington 2007 p. 138).

With group work, Ives found that there is a tendency for some coachees to shirk responsibility by free-riding on the backs of others willing to assume responsibility. This may result in passivity on the part of some coachees and resentment on the part of others. The more ambitious coachees may feel resentful that they are carrying most of the load, while the others show little willingness to share in the burden. The latter coachees may conveniently portray themselves as clueless in the expectation that the former will take control. Here are the words of one coachee, who expressed his resentment that some participants attempted to evade a fair workload:

> I think that all participants need to understand what is expected of them. I don't know what D was thinking, to be honest. Who exactly did he think was going to do everything? And so we ended up wasting I don't know how much time till he got the obvious and started to cooperate. Also I think that all participants should know that they need to be reasonable. It was amazing how selfish some of the coachees were.

It is well know that the presence of others can reduce performance. Social loafing refers to work done in (large) groups, whereby lack of evaluation anxiety results in reduced effort (Rothwell, 2004). Group coaching needs to address the issue of effort "to minimize free riding or 'social loafing' and to build shared commitment to the group and its work" (Hackman & Wageman, 2005 p. 273). Conversely, however, once a group goal is set, group members are likely to feel a degree of responsibility to the group, as the group goal adds an additional dimension of motivation. This has been described as a 'coaction effect,' whereby people model each other's behaviour (Zajonc, 1965). Reeves and Allison (2009 p. 123) confirm that the 'greater good' provides an imperative that drives coachees to action: "It is not unusual for clients to feel quite uncomfortable when they don't follow through on actions they know are needed to move their project forward."

Work in groups can be highly beneficial providing that: (1) there is an incentive structure and (2) the individual is accountable to the group (Slavin, 1990). Johnson and Johnson (1991) argue in relation to group learning that positive interdependence requires that coachees have mutually reinforcing goals. Positive interdependence is only present when "coachees perceive that they can reach their learning goals if and only if the other coachees in the learning group reach their goals" (Johnson, Johnson & Smith, 1998 p. 6). Cooperative goal setting is effective, they say, providing that the coachees accept that "the only way to achieve their personal goal is to ensure that the group achieves its goal."

Thus, it is necessary for each group member to have a clearly defined role and task, such that the group goals depend on the involvement of the entire group, and that individuals feel accountable to the group. Additionally, it is vital that group members clearly understand the nature of group work and are prepared for and committed to it. Otherwise, in place of social facilitation, what may result is social loafing.

Based on these discussions, we argue that the requirements for group coaching involve the following six elements:

(1)   Incentive structure
(2)   Interdependent goals
(3)   Clear group tasks
(4)   Sharing of tasks across groups
(5)   Group trust and team spirit
(6)   High competence of coach.

Group Coaching Model

Brown and Grant (2010) propose a group coaching model called GROUP, based on the GROW model of coaching (described in Chapter 4). Beginning with Goal (determine focus of the coaching), Reality (raise awareness of prevailing conditions) and Options (explore and evaluate alternatives), it then contains Understand others and Perform. These latter stages are designed to facilitate 'transformative learning, 'changing a way of being,' and 'challenging underlying assumptions.' More specifically, in Brown and Grant's model, 'Understand others' aims to "foster a shift in individual and groups awareness, which then enables generative solutions at a systemic level" (p. 39), and 'Perform' refers to "an ongoing iterative learning process" (p. 40) involving triple loop learning.

While such a transformative learning approach may be suited for developmental forms of coaching and may be appropriate for *team* coaching where the group is an integral unit, we suggest that this is not suited to *group* coaching, which needs to be goal-focused (Hackman & Wageman, 2005). Rather, a goal-focused group coaching approach prioritises ensuring that group members meet their group and individual goals through developing the necessary action plans. Therefore, we propose a different group coaching model, also called GROUP and based upon the initial three stages of GROW. However, our model recognizes, as explored earlier, that once the Options are clarified, it will often emerge that some of the needs of individual group members will not be met by the joint group goal. It will therefore be necessary to 'Unpick' which needs, excluded from the group goal, still need to be met and ensure that these are addressed outside the group work in individual coaching. It will also be necessary for each group member to 'Personalise' their part of the group action plan, as it will often be inappropriate in group sessions for individuals to create action plans for their specific tasks in the group plan. The model is set out in Table 7.1.

Table 7.1 The Goal-Focused GROUP Model

Acronym	Definition	Sample Questions
Goal	Establish the purpose of the group coaching and clarify what is to be its focus. Ensure the goal is clear and positive.	• What would you like to achieve? • What is the timeline for this goal? • How will achievement be measured? • What motivates you about this goal?
Reality	Explore the conditions that gave rise to the group coaching, and raise awareness of challenges and opportunities.	• What are the factors in this situation? • What progress have you made so far? • What has been successful in the past? • What is missing at the moment? • What are the challenges? • What resources are available to you?
Options	Group brainstorming for ideas and solutions, and carefully assessing their respective merits, based on a realistic acceptance of what is possible under the circumstances.	• What are the different ways you could approach this issue? • What could you do to move yourself forward just one step right now? • What are the pluses and minuses of each option? • Who do you know who is already doing this? • Which of the above options would give you the best result?
Unpick	Clarify the group goal, but also acknowledge necessary individual goals to be addressed outside the group.	• Which of your needs are being addressed by the group goal? • How can you meet those other needs outside the group work? • Who can help you to meet these needs? • What are your priorities?
Personalise	Ensure that the tasks individual group members accept as part of the group goal are personalised to suit their abilities and circumstances.	• What tasks are you contributing to the group goal? • In which order do these tasks need to be completed? • What skills do you require to complete these tasks?

We concur with Brown and Grant's RE-GROUP structure, whereby progress is Reviewed and Evaluated, so these two steps should also be added. They reflect the iterative nature of coaching, in which the coach and coachee are involved in a cyclical process of action and reflection, as we set out in detail when discussing the role of feedback in GFC (see Chapter 8).

Summary of Team and Group Coaching Issues

In our studies, although coachees varied in their attitudes towards coaching, overall group coaching was less popular and was regarded as less rewarding than individual coaching. Many coachees in Ives' research found the group coaching 'excruciating' and 'stressful' or were generally unenthusiastic. One coachee thought it struggled "because we had different points of view. Some of the guys were not very cooperative. It took a long time to get them to accept that things weren't going to go exactly the way they wanted it." Another coachee asserted that "a lot of stuff was raised by some of the guys that were not at all important for me. In the group coaching, this became a real problem." Coachees may find the experience of working in a group unappealing. They may consider the efforts required to establish a group dynamic and engage in negotiations to be frustrating. In Cox's study (2012b), similar comments were made about the difficulty of focusing on individual concerns. Despite their recognition of the usefulness of the group work, workers in that study expressed concerns that in the groups they had to generalise. As one worker confirmed: "we can't say what's really bothering us 'cus we work together."

Consequently, some coachees may resent what they consider 'time wasting' due to the difficulty of gaining cooperation and establishing consensus. The inevitable extra time that group coaching requires due to its complexity can lead to impatience with the coaching process. Group coaching is a challenging task which calls for specialised skills and is subject to a high risk of failure (King & Eaton, 1999).

Peer Coaching

Slater and Simmons describe peer coaching as a confidential process through which colleagues work together to "reflect on current practices; expand, refine, and build new skills; share ideas and solve problems in the workplace" (2001 p.68). According to Parker et al. (2008 p. 488) peer coaching is more focused than general peer learning insofar as it is designed to help individuals achieve their career objectives. Peer coaching is mostly reported in education, where it is used by teachers to improve classroom skills (Buzbee Little, 2005; Smith, Hofer, Gillespie, Solomon & Rowe, 2006), but it is otherwise rare. It highlights the centrality of relationships, and acknowledges multiple viewpoints and the personal construction of meaning. It is established on the idea that mutual and meaningful relationships are a key facilitator of successful learning as they provide for greater vision and self-understanding (Walsh, Bartunek & Lacey, 1998). It also has an affiliative emphasis, akin to communities of practice (Lave & Wenger, 1991), which encourages learning through social activity and promotes social structures that support ongoing development. Writers on peer coaching (e.g. Parker et al., 2008; Showers & Joyce, 1996) tend to agree that trust and support are the most crucial requirements for an effective peer relationship. However, with a goal-focused approach to coaching, as explained earlier, relationship issues could be considered less central.

Notably, peer coaching usually involves persons of broadly equal experience and status, which removes the power dimension from the relationship (Siegel, 2000; Waddell & Dunn, 2005) and indeed Truijen and Van Woerkom (2008) demonstrate how the coaching of employees by senior colleagues mostly fails due to the asymmetrical nature of the relationship, and conclude that "models of reciprocal peer coaching may be more appropriate for realizing open dialogue in academic settings" (p. 325). Peer coaching of coachees of equal standing has the potential to enhance the learning performance of both parties.

Parker et al. (2008) further suggest that coachees should be given the opportunity to select their own peer, as this leads to the satisfaction and success of the coaching. Even though the actual choice is not a significant factor, the act of choosing is. Evidence from mentoring suggests that social similarity (homophily) of the partners, defined as similarity in attitudes, values, background and appearance (McCroskey, Richmond & Daly, 1974) would enhance coaching success. However, similar attitudes and values, contribute more to the success of the coaching relationship than a shared background does (Nielson & Eisenbach, 2003).

The frequency of the interaction and the duration of the relationship are also marginally beneficial factors in peer coaching (Chao, Lee & Jeng, 1992), as they are thought to build trust and intimacy. These factors add to the quality of the relationship, although they do not necessarily render it more productive. However, in Ives' research, peer coaching struggled despite high frequency of interaction and social similarity, which suggests that even effective peer relations are insufficient for the generation of successful peer coaching.

At the outset of Ives' study, peer coaching was the preferred approach, as he wished to explore how a brief form of coaching may be adopted by the coachees themselves. However, the situation at the institution in question was quite problematic and it was therefore concluded that, at least initially, the coaching would need to be conducted personally, as the complexity of the situation rendered peer coaching unsuitable. Towards the end of the coaching intervention, however, it was considered possible and desirable to attempt peer coaching, since it is "grounded in the assumption that interaction with others is a critical resource for learning" (Parker et al., 2008 p. 488). According to Skiffington and Zeus (2003 p.11), peer coaching is typically a less structured and informal approach, although no reason or evidence is provided in support of this claim. Effective peer relationships can provide a useful horizontal communication link (Siegel, 2000). Ives therefore considered this approach suited to the circumstance at the institution where vertical communication was weak and the horizontal communication, namely coachee mutual support, would be particularly helpful.

Ives had intended for the coachees to work as dyads to map out a plan for all their tasks. In reality, the peers limited their collaboration to creating a joint learning schedule to prepare for a forthcoming seminar. The peer coaching worked effectively as a method of helping the coachees to manage their study workload, but it failed when it came to planning other tasks, as the following comments demonstrate:

> A: It was strange and neither of us really knew what to do. It just never really took off.

> C: I won't even claim to have tried to do anything else. It just didn't happen.

> D: I think you know what happened; it didn't really get off the ground in the way you wanted.

It emerged that the coachees did not feel capable of coaching each other, even after several months' experience as coachees, and despite detailed instruction. Research into the peer coaching literature and close examination of the coachee responses led to some far-reaching conclusions regarding the viability and appropriateness of peer coaching. Comments from the coachees made it clear that they did not think the peer coaching model *could* work beyond the very limited role of planning mutual tasks. The coachees were only interested in collaboration for tasks relevant to both parties, and were not confident to coach another on their own tasks. They were acting as study partners, rather than as peer coaches. In Ives' study it only resulted in a more structured approach to organising their learning mutual tasks, and this can hardly be called coaching.

Limitations of Peer Coaching

The poor result of the peer coaching in Ives' study leads us to consider strict criteria for effective peer coaching. Although the peer-study partners did formulate learning plans, which they credited with improving their ability to manage their workload and minimise procrastination, they refused to assist each other in planning tasks with which they were not directly involved. They were learning peers, not coaches. It is therefore concluded that (1) peer coaching, even of a goal-focused nature, requires significant training and support; (2) it only works if embraced by participants; and (3) it should be restricted to goal-focused issues. We will now briefly comment on these points.

(1) Requires significant training and ongoing support – Surprisingly, the coachees did not feel confident to coach one another, despite having some months of experience as part of a coaching programme. Most striking was the fact that these coachees had years of peer learning experience, which it might have been presumed would have equipped them with the requisite skills and attitudes for peer coaching. The reluctance and resistance towards peer coaching led to the conclusion that for peer coaching to succeed it requires thorough training in coaching skills and preparation for a coaching orientation – even for a limited GFC approach. Coaching is an intricate and complex task, and must be of a high quality to succeed. For this reason, Truijen and Van Woerkom (2008) and Moen and Skaalvik (2009) argue that it is preferable to use a professional external coach to ensure the quality of

the intervention. Furthermore, the more complex the tasks, the more likely that professional coaches will be required. Similarly, Parker et al. (2008 p. 500) found that "peer coaching does not always work" and will only succeed with the requisite training and education.

(2) Must be embraced by participants – The coachees viewed peer coaching only as a method of achieving their personal aims, and not as a genuinely mutual activity. Indeed, the peer coaching literature (Lam, S. Yim & Lam, T., 2002) reports that rejection of peer coaching is not uncommon. We therefore conclude that peer coaching can only succeed if the coachees embrace the process and enter into the coaching relationship willingly (Waddell & Dunn, 2005). Hargreaves and Dawe (1990) show how teachers tend to distance themselves from peer coaching that is perceived as contrived, inauthentic and mandated. Similarly, Lam et al. (2002) insist that peer coaching must emerge bottom up and cannot be imposed. Levene and Frank (1993 p. 36) argue that "the process must be voluntary. The voluntary nature encourages participants to own the process." Cox's (2012a) research also confirms the importance of the voluntary aspect of peer coaching, as the quotes from one of her peer dyad interviews highlights.

> G: It's one thing to trust another person but I think when it's an institutional initiative, such as this is, at the back of your mind you do have concerns as to whether or not there is going to be a requirement at some point to formalise and send in a formal account of the process which from my perspective I think would kill it.

> H: We'd just be subversive wouldn't we, we wouldn't do it! (Laughs)

Hargreaves (1994) has distinguished between contrived collegiality and genuinely collaborative cultures that are sustained by the coachees themselves and that are marked by a high level of spontaneity and authenticity. Lam et al. (2002 p. 183) also argue that people will resist 'contrived collegiality' as an administratively imposed form of collaboration. However, as Grimmett and Crehan (1992) point out, organisationally induced collegiality retains the potential to evolve into some-thing authentic, but will only succeed if the participants embrace it. This seems to have been confirmed in Ives' study, as the group coaching which was suggested by the coachees was successful, whereas the peer coaching that was advocated by the coach largely failed.

(3) Limit to goal-oriented issues – Feedback from coachees suggests that they did not think the peer coaching model *could* work beyond the very limited task of planning their joint learning tasks. The coachees used peer coaching as a specific self-regula-tion tactic, rather than as a self-regulation strategy (Lenz, Ellis & Scanlon, 1996). It was therefore concluded that, even with adequate training, peer coaching should be restricted to minimalist goal setting and action planning, as the training require-ments for more reflective approaches to coaching would render it impractical in most instances. In our view, therapeutic or developmental approaches to coach-ing (discussed in Chapter 1) would be unsuited to peer coaching, unless extensive training and expert facilitation was put in place.

Summary

In this chapter, we have looked at three formats of coaching: team coaching, group coaching and peer coaching, and have discussed some of the issues that arise in using a goal-focused approach in these settings.

In relation to team and group coaching, we concurred with the sparse literature available that for any team or group coaching to work there should be a mutually agreed and preferably jointly accountable goal. In the case of Ives' study, this was not readily available and the group work was challenging. In Cox's (2012b) research with retail support workers, although each member of the group worked on similar individual goals connected with strengthening their emotional awareness, and the group coaching was designed to meet those individual needs, there was also a mutually accountable goal. The organisation had commissioned the coaching to try and improve group effectiveness, so the goal was directly linked to that effectiveness and to reporting improvement to the firm.

Social loafing was also identified as an issue for some teams, but we would argue that a combination of goal focused one-to-one and team or group coaching can overcome this tendency by some team members. In fact, both studies (Cox, 2012b; Ives, 2010) confirm the notion that in many settings individual coaching interventions can be strengthened by a group or team coaching component and vice versa.

In our discussion of peer coaching we asserted an element of voluntariness is also essential. Indeed in Cox's study of peer coaching (2012a) findings suggest that relationships held together by a voluntary bond are stronger and so potentially more productive than those held together by some form of control. The voluntary nature of the scheme described in that study was felt by participants to be vital. Another major claim in relation to peer coaching was that peers should be given adequate and appropriate training. The absence of such training could account for the failure of peer coaching schemes identified earlier. Finally, we argue that given the challenges inherent in peer coaching, where the coaching is not provided by a professional, GFC is in fact the only realistic coaching paradigm. In a work context, at least, more exploratory or reflective styles of coaching may gain little traction and are likely to provoke resistance or apathy from both members of the dyad.

8 Goal Setting

Aims

- To explain how optimal goal setting is vital to GFC;
- To analyse three key elements in effective goal setting: clarity, specificity, proximity and difficulty;
- To examine the role of feedback in achieving set goals.

A central tenet of goal-focused coaching is the importance of constructing the goal effectively. Goals are a key means of self-regulation, and the directional variables (the specific characteristics of the goal that are manipulated) play a crucial role in governing behaviour and influencing motivation. We propose that there are three main aspects of goal construction, goal setting, action planning and motivation – which we term the '3Ws': what (goal setting), when and how (action planning), and why (motivation and commitment). In GFC setting clear goals, planning and then securing commitment and motivation, are central to coaching success. In this chapter and in Chapters 9 and 10 we examine these aspects in detail. In this chapter we focus on the first 'W', goal setting. In section one of this chapter the three main components of goal setting will be explored: goal specificity, goal proximity and goal difficulty (Cantor & Fleeson, 1991), while the role of feedback in the goal setting process is discussed in section two.

Getting to Goal Setting

Some coachees will be unable to state a clear goal at the outset of the coaching intervention and will have only a vague idea of their achievement goal. Goal setting is part of an iterative and multi-layered process (Skiffington & Zeus, 2003), and should therefore be treated as a graduated procedure in which the activity of setting the goal contributes to the ultimate achievement of the goal.

Principally, there are two levels of goal clarification, and effective goal setting can only occur at the second level. The initial level is where the coachee has a general idea of what he or she wishes to accomplish, and the object at this point is to solidify that vision.

The first level of clarification is the most general and relates to the coachee establishing what he or she is hoping to *become* or arrive at (a high level goal). This is akin to the meta goals described in Carver and Scheier (1998). The second level relates to defining the goal in operational terms, what the coachee wants to *do* (a lower level goal). For example, a coachee may want to change career, and coming to this decision may itself be a major decision-making process, but this decision adds little clarity to the kind of alternative career the coachee may consider. Or a coachee may decide that in order to reduce stress she will take up a hobby, which is a general goal, but she will now need to decide which hobby it will be.

These goal clarification levels also differ in their level of flexibility. A higher level goal will typically remain the same, unless there are drastic changes to the coachee's circumstances. By contrast, the more specific, lower level goal will change more easily, and needs to be replaced if it is no longer suited to the coachee's needs. In the career change example, it is far more likely that the coachee will change his or her mind about the kind of career change than about the overall decision to make the change. Similarly, it is more common that the coachee will alter his or her choice of hobby, rather than decide that reducing stress is unimportant or can be approached in a different way. So, the more concrete the goal, the more subject it will be to alteration.

An additional distinction between these two levels of goals is their relationship to time. Many coaching websites quote the aphorism: 'a goal is a dream with a date on it,' suggesting that only by committing to a specific timeframe will the goal have any chance of being reached. While this is ultimately correct, it is not so when it comes to setting a high level goal. At the highest level of goal setting, the issue is about establishing the principle; it is not essential that it has an explicit timeframe, for its main purpose is to set out a vision and basic direction. By contrast, lower level goals require a timeframe to be effective, as will be explained in detail in the next chapter. According to Carver and Sheier (1998), motivation is a product of progress measured against time. However, while this is the case with regard to specific goals, at the higher level the motivation derives from a dream or vision.

While some coaches (Alexander, 2006; Whitmore, 2003) advocate starting the coaching process by setting a specific goal, Dembkowski and Eldridge (2008) correctly note that such an approach is often unsuitable, as it assumes that the coachee arrives with a clear higher level goal in mind. Similarly, Pemberton (2006 p. 36) argues that "goals are outputs, not the starting point," and cautions against premature goal setting, suggesting that setting a specific goal is only appropriate once the coachee is clear what he or she wants to achieve. Thus, Pemberton (2006 p. 67) advocates beginning with 'fuzzy vision' (based on Greene & Grant, 2003), which "validates people for not knowing precisely what they want by encouraging them to talk about how they would like things to be different, rather than setting a precise outcome." Rogers (2008) similarly argues that it is the coach's job to help the coachee form and structure the goal; the coachee is not expected to present a ready-formed goal.

Thus, the goal setting activity, before reaching the second stage of defining a more action-oriented goal, may need to clarify a general high level goal, what has been termed a 'dream goal' (Whitmore, 2003) or the 'future perfect' (Jackson & McKergow, 2008). This level of goal abstraction is akin to the constructs of 'current concern' (Klinger, 1975), 'personal project' (Little, 1993), 'personal striving' (Emmons, 1986) and 'life task' (Cantor & Khilstrom, 1987). It is not appropriate to begin working with concrete, lower level goals, such as specific skill-sets or personal competencies, without first securely establishing a more abstract goal (where one doesn't already exist). Thus, a high level goal is a prerequisite to an action-oriented goal, even though it is at the lower level where the substance of goal setting actually occurs.

Coachees vary regarding their initial level of goal clarity. Some are clear about their objective, but lack clarity about what that goal means in practice. Some start out unclear about both, and others come to coaching with a highly developed goal in mind. Although it is unusual for the coachee not to present at least a general objective, many a coach will recall sitting with people who had little idea of what they wanted the outcome of the coaching to be. In practice, we would recommend asking the coachee at the beginning *whether* he or she has a clear goal, rather than asking them *what* it is. Once the fuzzy vision or vague goal has been replaced with a clear focus, it is possible to proceed to goal setting: narrowing the goal to specific targets, and an action plan, as Figure 8.1 illustrates.

In forming a clear goal, there are three main factors for which it is essential to strike the right balance: goal proximity, goal specificity and goal difficulty. As each coachee and each situation is unique, there can be no absolute formula for determining the optimal level of proximity, specificity or difficulty. What can be

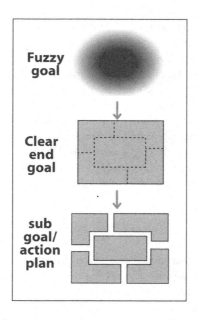

Figure 8.1 Clarifying Goals

said is that rarely, if ever, would an extreme be appropriate. Thus, the work of goal setting is matching the prevailing circumstances to the characteristics of the individual coachee and ensuring that the goal set is the most capable of leading to high performance. There is, in fact, a fourth key factor in goal setting: goal concordance, which we discuss in Chapter 10. The three main factors are now described in more detail.

Goal Specificity

As already intimated, coachees may have a problem relating to the coaching in the absence of concrete goals, and their support of the coaching intervention and the tasks it seeks to address is likely to grow as the goals become ever more concrete and specific. Goal specificity (Locke & Latham, 1990) or goal clarity (Moen & Skaalvik, 2009) enables a clear standard against which to measure attainment. Research (Latham, 2007) suggests that being told to just 'do your best' or having no goals allows the person to settle for the lowest standard with no price to pay in terms of self-concept. Bandura (2001 p. 8) likewise suggests that "general goals are too indefinite and non-committing to serve as guides and incentives." We therefore concur with Rubin (2002) that the 'S' in SMART goals should stand for 'specific,' and not 'simple,' 'sensible' or 'significant,' as some have suggested.

Additionally, goal clarity enhances task focus, rendering the coachee less likely to engage in marginal activities. Clarity enhances goal salience, making the goal seem more real and impactful. Mischel and Ayduk (2007 p. 111) argue that the delay of gratification required for successful goal pursuit is enhanced when the mental image of the goal is made more salient. Finally, Cervone (1989) states that clear goals seem more manageable and thus raise self-efficacy, a key factor in goal attainment.

Thus, goal specificity is a vital ingredient in GFC. Goal theories suggest that designated outcomes must be observable and measurable (Bandura, 2001). Coaches similarly suggest that "the outcomes must be stated in sufficient clarity that both parties will be able to recognize them as occurring or not and also be able to discern what progress has been made toward them" (Flaherty, 2005 p. 119). We have found the precision tool advocated by Alexander and Renshaw (2005) and Alexander (2006) to be useful. It asks coachees to define their words more precisely: what exactly do they mean, in comparison to what, and so forth. A recent study (Moen & Skaalvik, 2009) similarly found that goal specificity increased through coaching.

Goal Proximity

As suggested earlier, goal setting and action planning are two separate stages in goal activity: goal setting refers to setting distal (long-term) goals, whereas the setting of proximal (short-term) goals is part of the action planning stage, which will be addressed in the next chapter. Proximal goals need to be accompanied by distal goals, although the distal goal may itself consist of two stages, as has been explained. In this section we explain that the effective pursuit of goals requires both proximal and distal goals, but that focusing too soon on proximal goals clouds or confuses the distal vision, and that action planning, which is about setting out proximal goals, is best done once the distal goal is firmly in place. Moreover, proximal goals generally emerge over time, unlike distal goals that are typically set in place at the outset and remain so unless there is a significant change in circumstances. Distal goals need to be in concordance with the coachee's values and aspirations; by contrast, proximal goals may be more instrumental, aimed at simply getting a job done.

Goal theory literature deals at length with the relative merits of proximal and distal goals, what Miller and Brickman (2004) refer to as future versus immediate goals, and Bandura (1986) calls end goals and subgoals. In coaching, these are sometimes termed end versus performance goals (Whitmore, 2003). Most studies seem to focus on the regulation (Husman & Lens, 1999; Miller & Brickman, 2004) and the benefits (e.g. Ames, 1992; Bandura, 1986) of short-term goals, since distal goals are too remote: "Distal goals alone set the general course of pursuits but are far too removed in time to provide effective incentives and guides to present action, given inviting competing activities at hand" (Bandura, 2001 p. 8).

Proximal goals generate more detailed action plans and infuse immediate tasks with relevance (Manderlink & Harackiewicz, 1984; Miller & Brickman, 2004). They also provide more immediate evidence of progress, thereby raising self-efficacy (Bandura & Cervone, 1983), and creating criteria to monitor for self-evaluation, thus enabling more effective feedback (Bandura, 1991; Locke & Latham, 1990). They are more effective in defining the person's intended performance target (Bandura, 1991), and feel more psychologically 'real' (Bandura, 1986). Additionally, goal theory postulates that the self-regulative effectiveness of a goal wanes as it is projected further into the future, whereas proximal goals, given their immediacy, are more effective at mobilising self-influencers (Latham, 2007).

Based on self-regulation studies, we would further suggest that proximal goals assist with the challenge posed by delay of gratification. Such temporal discounting is a phenomenon found in all animal species, according to which the perceived value of a reward decreases in accordance with the expected delay in its arrival (Mischel, 1996). A more distant goal may result in discounting the value of a positive outcome, whereas immediate goals provide instant satisfaction and thus motivation. To overcome this, Mischel and Ayduk (2007) argue that the delay of gratification required for successful goal pursuit is enhanced when the mental image of the goal is made more salient, which it may be argued is rendered more salient by proximal goals.

However, long-term, distal goals, which Miller and Brickman (2004 p. 15) term 'personally valued future goals,' are also of great importance. Long-term goals, they suggest, are objectives where success in performing the current task does not usually produce the desired end result (Miller & Brickman, 2004). It has been suggested that it is the initial commitment to a valued distal goal that instigates the process of developing proximal goals (Nuttin, 1984) and the progress towards reaching the distal goal that is the most motivational reward of subgoal achieve-

Table 8.1 Distal vs. Proximal Goals

Distal Goals	*Proximate Goals*
More suitable for long-term planning	Generate more detailed act on plans
Have high motivational value	Infuse immediate tasks with relevance
Instigates initial action	Better at defining performance target
Allow for greater flexibility	Feel more psychologically real
Enables strategic and orderly thinking	Provide more frequent feedback
Less interfering	More immediate impact on self-efficacy
	Produce more effective short-term incentives

ment (Carver, 2007; Miller & Brickman, 2004). Only tasks that are instrumental to future achievement endeavours arouse motivation (Raynor & Entin, 1982). In real life, people do not normally strive for proximal goals that are not tied to a longer-term objective (Miller & Brickman, 2004).

Additionally, recognition of distal goals allows for greater flexibility in developing action planning strategies (Khan & Quaddus, 2004), because the person's actions are being guided by an overarching principle. According to Arriaga & Rusbult (1998 p. 928), focusing on a long-term objective or goal enables effective self-regulation, as "immediate, self-interested preferences are replaced by preferences that take into account broader concerns, including considerations to some degree that transcend the immediate situation." Moreover, Vallacher and Kauffman (1996) suggest that people who construe their actions solely in low-order goals are in effect in a state of relative disorder, guided by short-term considerations that are quite restricted in scope and transitory in application. Locke and Latham (1990 p. 59) further argue that "it is likely that goals that are too proximal or frequent will be viewed as intrusive, distracting, and annoying and thus will be rejected."

The various strengths of distal and proximal goals are summarised in Table 8.1.

Due to the different strengths of distal and proximal goals, goal theorists (e.g. Bandura, 2001; Locke & Latham, 1990; Pintrich & Schunk, 1996) advocate setting both proximal and distal goals, as linking the two appear to serve personal development better. Combining both goal types in the coaching process enhances strategy and improves performance (Weldon & Yun, 2000). Several studies (DeBacker & Nelson, 1999; Miller, Green, Montalvo, Ravindran & Nichols, 1996) confirm the association between coachees' proximal learning goals and their 'personally valued future goals.' For this reason, coaches should help coachees link short-term strategies to long-term goals (Scamardo & Harnden, 2007; Skiffington & Zeus, 2003).

GFC therefore includes a goal setting stage that aims to generate a clear and highly motivational distal goal, and an action planning stage that focuses on ensuring proximal goals.

Goal Difficulty

Progress is primarily made when coachees assume challenging tasks. A recent study of coaching (Moen & Skaalvik, 2009) found that goal difficulty increased through coaching, which was also borne out by Ives' research. However, challenging tasks are only effective if the coachees genuinely accept the task, which in turn is dependent on them considering the goals to be realistic. Thus, it is essential that coachees consider tasks attainable.

Goal theory (Locke & Latham, 1990) highlights goal difficulty as a significant variable in goal setting. Difficulty is not an objective measure against a universal standard, but refers to the judgment of the individual in question – namely at the limit or close to the limit of the person's capabilities (Bandura, 1986). Difficulty includes a wide range of challenging aspects of a task, including complexity and time constraints. The main purpose of the goal setting stage is to ensure that the person maintains goal difficultly at an optimal discrepancy level – wide enough to motivate action, but sufficiently narrow to be considered attainable. If the goal is too easy, there is insufficient discrepancy between the current reality and the desired change to stimulate action, whereas if it is too difficult there is too much discrepancy and it will lead to inaction. Ford (1992) calls this 'the optimal challenge principle.' In Box 8.1 an example is given of how the motivation to attend to a mundane task can vary depending on the perceived difficulty of the task.

Box 8.1 Example of the Optimal Challenge Principle

Jane is a successful maintenance services sales person and normally completes ten contracts a week. This week a few family issues arose and on Thursday morning Jane notes that she has fallen behind by her normally high standards.

If she has already completed six contracts, she may feel that she is not far off from her target and there is no reason to make any special effort. By contrast, if Jane has only secured three contracts, she is likely to feel that 'something has to be done' and will start to devise a plan to dramatically increase her sales. Similarly, if Jane decides next month to alter her target to eleven contracts, this may not be sufficient to stimulate a change in performance activity, whereas if the target was increased to fifteen contracts, she would likely be motivated to make some significant change.

Brown et al. (2005) found that goals only had a motivational effect when the person was not already experiencing overload. Thus, motivation will be highest when tasks are at an intermediary level (Pintrich & Schunk, 1996) to ensure they are manageable but not boring (Kauffman, 2004; Nakamura & Csikszentmihalyi, 2002). Coachees will be reluctant about setting challenging goals and will be resistant to committing to tasks that they perceive as too difficult. They will use their anxiety levels as a guide for moderating the ambitiousness of their goals.

Reaching the goal also leads to a drop-off or even cessation of activity. Self-regulation theory suggests that closing the discrepancy between the goal and its attainment reduces activity towards that goal. Frijda (1994 p. 113) calls this 'coasting.' Rather than optimising performance on the current goal, the person will 'satisfice'

(Simon, 1953), that is, only do enough to maintain the status quo, in relation to the current task, and may divert attention towards another goal. The previous goal will then be put into 'cruise control' (Carver & Scheier, 1998 p. 133). In addition, overshooting a goal will register as an 'error' and will result in switching off efforts (Carver & Scheier, 1998). So, for example, if on Thursday morning Jane discovers that she has already reached her target of ten contracts, she is very likely to 'take her foot off the pedal' and relax, because her goal has already been reached, unless she immediately sets herself a harder goal. For this reason, there is a need for continual setting of new and more challenging targets to reduce the likelihood of satisficing.

Completing a task and reaching the goal, can also produce dysphoria, leaving the person aimless (Pervin, 1992). To avoid a sense of nothingness, there is a need to replace the completed goal with a new one and the goal setting process begins again. Carver and Scheier (1998 p. 155) argue that "success is most likely to lead to sustained positive feelings when the attainment of one goal slides smoothly into a sense of progress towards other goals."

Goal setting is thus a motivating activity. Goals do not motivate directly, but rather through the self-engagement with the task that they engender (Bandura, 2001). However, the self-engagement value of easy goals is negligible, as they have no significant impact on motivation or performance. Conversely, difficult goals create satisfaction contingent on a high performance level, generating an incentive to persist towards greater achievement (Latham, 2007). Engagement, therefore, is a core concept in GFC, because around this concept revolves most of the key features of goal-driven activity.

Despite this emphasis on difficulty, the goal must not be so difficult that the coachee doubts his or her capacity to achieve it. If a goal is perceived as unattainable, there is similarly a risk of disengagement. Coachees are generally willing to set challenging goals, but they are likely to become alarmed if they sense that they are putting themselves under excessive pressure, as "high commitment is attained when the goal is perceived as being *attainable*" (Grant, 2006 p. 158). In our view, there is an important distinction between attainment and attainability. Attaining a goal is not in itself motivational, but the attainability of a goal certainly is. Carver (2007) argues that goals that are perceived as unattainable are usually downgraded or abandoned: "Sufficient doubt about goal attainment results in an impetus to disengage from efforts to reach the goal and even to disengage from the goal itself" (Carver, 2007 p. 28). If the discrepancy is too great, rather than leading to efforts to reduce the gap, it results in loss of will.

In the example above, if Jane realised on Thursday morning that she had only secured three of her normal ten contracts, she may conclude that she is simply unable to reach her target and may abandon any attempt at doing so. On the other hand, she may decide that, under the circumstances, a revised target of eight is still possible and become motivated to pursue her new, more realistic goal. Thus coachees will have a different emotional response to the discrepancy depending on whether goals are perceived to be attainable.

Several coaching texts (Cox, 2009; Cox & Jackson, 2010; Kemp, 2006) present the role of coaching as stretching the coachee to spur both learning and growth.

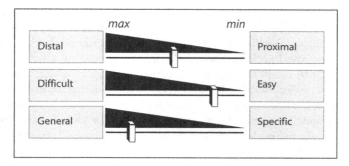

Figure 8.2 Striking a Balance in Goal Setting

As mentioned earlier, Cavanagh (2006) states that "coaching seeks to help the person and organization maintain themselves at the border between chaos and sameness – a place complexity theory calls the 'edge of chaos'." Coaching, then, seeks a 'sustainable instability' or a 'dynamic equilibrium' (Haines, 1998; Stacey, 2000), a 'bounded instability' that seeks sufficient flexibility to sustain growth and change, while preventing breakdown and chaos (Cavanagh, 2006 p. 319). GFC, in particular, stretches the coachee by encouraging the setting of appropriately difficult goals.

Figure 8.2 illustrates the three spectra along which the coachee needs to position his or her goal. It is the task of coaching to help the coachee strike a suitable balance between the extremes of proximity, difficulty and specificity, in accordance with the needs of the situation, the characteristics of the coachee, and the stage in the goal setting process.

Feedback

This section discusses the specific role that feedback plays in GFC, suggesting that feedback from the coach, as well as feedback in the form of coachee self-awareness, are only effective to the extent that they feed into more effective goal-setting. The role of praise is also examined, together with the importance of monitoring progress.

There are two main types of feedback, both involving the collation and analysis of knowledge. Long-term feedback is the linking together of information that informs the person as to the likely consequences of actions and this knowledge becomes a guide to inform action under similar conditions. This process is called 'learning' (Carver & Scheier, 1998). Short-term feedback is the immediate feedback from actions that inform the person whether or not to alter the course of action. Short-term feedback emerges from the task itself, as "performance itself is feedback" (McDowall & Millward, 2009 p. 61).

Feedback, with the monitoring and evaluation that it enables, is cited as central to coaching (Grant, 2006). It is also important in peer coaching (Lam et al., 2002; Parker et al., 2008), group coaching (Hackman & Wageman, 2005) and in executive coaching, where it is often a key part of the process (Gregory, Beck & Carr, 2011; Thompson, Purdy & Summers, 2008). Parsloe and Wray (2000 p. 123) even suggest that "it is not an exaggeration to describe feedback as 'the fuel that drives improved performance'." Indeed, a recent study of coaching (Moen & Skaalvik, 2009) found that feedback increased through coaching, in a kind of virtuous circle, thus confirming Hudson's (1999) assertion that feedback from the coach both facilitates communication and adds to the coachee's awareness.

Feedback and the associated self-awareness that it engenders, is therefore seen as crucial for effective goal-focused coaching. However, these two constructs have a particular meaning in relation to GFC, as they are conceived in a more minimalistic sense than in therapeutic and developmental coaching. Within GFC, their main benefit is their ability to guide the selection and implementation of more effective goals.

Feedback is vital to inform coachees how closely their performance approximates or deviates from the intended task and to ensure accurate information is available upon which to base decisions (Locke & Latham, 2002). In fact, self-regulation theories view the person as an organism that is constantly monitoring and evaluating itself and proposes a course of action consistent with its assessment (Carver & Scheier, 1998), and Gregory et al. (2011) propose that a simplified control loop might be usefully applied to provide structure for feedback in executive coaching. They describe how "control loops require feedback to function" and suggest that in order for a coachee to "initiate and sustain behavioural change, it is imperative that he or she received information that the goal has not yet been reached" (Gregory et al., p. 32).

In addition, the more specific the feedback, the more useful it will be. Specific information provides a feedback loop that can aid learning and development, whereas general information is insufficient to guide action. Both goal setting and action planning are most effective when there is feedback showing progress, and when they incorporate some means of monitoring and evaluating performance (Grant, 2006). Grant (2006, p. 154) interprets this demand as a need "to ensure that action plans focus on observable concrete behaviours that are clearly discernable to the coachee." In our view, monitoring and evaluation should be part of the essence of GFC, by virtue of the whole coaching strategy revolving around clearly defined and time-specific goals.

The coaching process can be viewed as a recursive, cyclical process in which coachees monitor the effectiveness of their strategies, which, where necessary, generates a goal that directs future action (Zimmerman, 2000). Goal-related activity, therefore, is a constant cycle of self-management based upon assessment of performance to date compared with the goals set. On the basis of the outcome of that analysis, coachees decide what new goal to set next and the process begins anew. Accurate feedback is thus empowering, as the coachee has reliable information on which to base effective decisions, rather than groping in the dark.

Evidence about the effects of feedback is mixed (McDowall & Millward, 2009). While there are many who argue that feedback impacts positively on performance, Kluger and DeNisi (1996) and Smither, London and Reilly (2005) question the value of feedback, as studies show that performance improvement resulting from feedback is overall rather modest, and even drops for some. Crucially, it has been noted that it is the lack of concrete actions from feedback that is the main reason that feedback sometimes fails to produce positive results (London, Smither & Adsit, 1997), suggesting the main goal of feedback should be to guide more effective future actions. It is therefore right that GFC looks to feedback primarily to facilitate the coachees' handling of his or her immediate goals, as feedback is most powerful when it leads to concrete and future-directed goals (McDowall and Millward, 2009). GFC uses feedback as a means of ensuring that the coachee has the necessary information to guide future actions. Where the coach does provide feedback, it would be non-evaluative (Chase & Wolfe, 1989). The most useful form of feedback provided by the coach in GFC is paraphrasing and clarifying the coachee's own words, because in addition to the raised attention that this achieves, "coachees receive a boost when they hear their own words coming from someone else" (Bresser & Wilson, 2006 p. 20).

Awareness

The term awareness can have varying interpretations, and in the GFC paradigm it has a particular meaning. Awareness here is minimalist, referring to cognisance of a person's current state or progress towards a goal, rather than the more 'psychological' meaning of the term implying deeper self-understanding. Awareness is the product of focused attention, concentration and clarity. In a physical sense it is alertness to what is heard, seen, and so forth. In a mental sense it means obtaining an accurate and full picture of reality, including a person's own emotions and feelings (Whitmore, 2003). Increased attention to the task gives greater clarity of perception.

Based upon Schön's (1983) distinction between reflection in action and reflection on action, we suggest that in coaching too there is a distinction between the attention drawn to the task as part of the execution of the task, and the attention drawn to learn broader lessons subsequent to the task. The former is done simultaneously with the doing, whereas the latter is more meditative and more conscious. The attention devoted to a task-in-action helps coachees to complete tasks effectively. It enables coachees to adjust activities to overcome any hurdles or take advantage of sudden fortuitous opportunities *while* working on the task. Paying close attention to a task generates data upon which to base a viable solution. By contrast, attention separate from the task is a more formal process of data collection and analysis, and is designed to bring critical thinking to the question of whether the coachee's assumptions about the task were correct. It is the former type of attention that is the dominant one in GFC.

The primary function of awareness in GFC is monitoring progress towards goal attainment to ensure that the circumstances have not changed, requiring remedial goal-directed action, or that the actions are having the desired effect (Carver & Scheier, 1998). GFC provides a framework for raising the requisite awareness and facilitating ongoing monitoring. Awareness in GFC is primarily about obtaining accurate data (feedback) and meticulously comparing this information against a goal. In this way, "increases in *self-focus* can promote increases in *task-focus*" (Carver & Scheier, 1998 p. 34). In Ives' research, coachees' clarity about their situation and their options led to greater willingness to address training needs. Attention to the practical limitations along with clarification of the realistic options resulted in a better attitude and thus improved performance.

Reeves and Allison (2009 p. 32) state that "the primary obligation of the coach is to speak the truth, even when clients are reluctant to hear it," including feedback on the coachee's comments during sessions, observable behaviours, external realities, and so forth. Similarly, Hudson (1999 p. 22) claims that the coach needs to "offer tough love – confrontation, blunt feedback [. . .] insistence that certain habits change," although it is hard to see how this sentiment is reconciled with his contention (p. 21) that coaches are not supposed to be directive or control the content of the coaching.

However, while feedback can be proffered by the coach, especially when the manager is also the coach as in many organisations, in GFC the most important feedback is that which coachees give to themselves. Many coaching approaches advocate a specific feedback stage (e.g. Tracy, Thompson & Purdy, 2008) or encourage the coach to provide critical feedback (Thach & Heinselman, 1999). However, in GFC feedback is not a separate stage but is a continuous process derived from raised attention and heightened focus of the consequences of a coachee's activities. Indeed, feedback is best drawn from all relevant sources, by being aware of the wide range of factors that may impact on a person's choices: a systemic approach to coaching points to the diverse influencers and seeks feedback from these multifarious sources (Cavanagh, 2006).

According to Bandura (1986), self-management has three components: (1) self-observation or monitoring of behaviour; (2) evaluation of progress or self-judgement; (3) self-reaction, consisting of consequential responses that provide incentives and disincentives based on goal-related achievement (Miller & Brickman, 2004). Thus, self-management relies on accurate feedback that is supplied through attentive awareness of one's environment. Awareness and feedback, then, are two sides of the same coin. Awareness produces useful feedback, while getting feedback raises awareness. This cycle is shown in Figure 8.3.

Accurate Feedback and Praise

Not all feedback is good, however. Feedback must be accurate, as in the long run it facilitates accurate attributions and expectancies, rather than trying to boost self-esteem by giving exaggerated praise (Blumenfeld, Pintrich, Meece & Wessels, 1982). Where there is a lack of skills, coachees should be helped to understand this (Pintrich & Schunk, 1996). Following Linnerbrink and Pintrich (2002 p. 316), we argue that self-efficacy beliefs should not be so overly positive that the coachee "attempts a climb that is well beyond his capabilities." To be most effective, self-efficacy beliefs should be adjusted to the real abilities of the individual (Bandura, 1997), through careful action planning. Invalid praise or

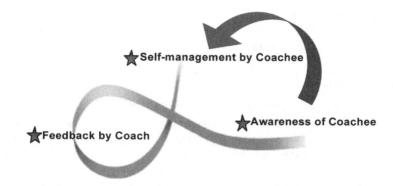

Figure 8.3 The Feedback Cycle

inaccurate feedback only leads to the fostering of unrealistic feelings of efficacy (Pintrich & Schunk, 2003).

Somewhat controversially, Costa and Garmston (2002 p. 101) eschew the use of praise, as they believe it "interferes with thinking," and "communicates a value judgement about another person or the person's performance." Deci (1995) further argues that praise may serve to merely reinforce conventional solutions and diminishes the willingness to experiment, while Kegan and Lahey (2001) claim that praise should be replaced by genuine feedback. By contrast, Herzberg (1959) argues that recognition, praise and acknowledgement of achievement are powerful motivators and Fournies (2000) writes that the coach should recognize routine progress as much as outstanding achievement.

Generally, the coaching literature is supportive of the coach deploying targeted praise as a source of positive feedback. However, praise needs to be informative, providing concrete feedback on people's qualities, skills and achievements that the coach has directly observed (Jackson & McKergow, 2008), while the lavish heaping of compliments is likely to come across as patronising. Research within positive psychology has shown that too much positivity, exclusive praise with no critical feedback, actually results in reduced performance (Fredrickson & Losada, 2005). The purpose of feedback is to guide future actions. If the feedback is unrealistically positive, it will produce unrealistic future expectations which may result in the setting of inappropriate goals and ultimate failure – so that any short-term positive effect will be more than undone by the long-term negative consequences. Furthermore, when positive feedback is never moderated with constructive criticism, the praise ceases to be believed; consequently, the coachee will not attribute the praise to his/her actions, breaking down the attribution process that is so important to expectancies and self-efficacy. As Linnenbrink and Pintrich (2002, p.316) point out: "self-efficacy is not fostered by providing inaccurate or effusive praise [. . .] in the absence of specific task accomplishments. This type of praise is meaningless and invalid and may foster inaccurate beliefs."

By contrast, accurate positive reinforcement creates the self-confidence that generates task interest and thus performance (Bandura, 1986; Deci & Ryan, 1985). Above all, a realistic assessment, even if negative, will better lead to enhanced focus and greater effort, than misleading or erroneously optimistic perceptions.

Feedback Process

To have a clearer understanding of the role of feedback in coaching, we contextualise feedback within a framework of self-regulation. A fundament of all self-regulation theories is the idea that the person is an organism that is constantly monitoring and evaluating itself and proposes a course of action consistent with its assessment (Baumeister & Vohs, 2007). A person's self-regulation of activity is based around an assessment of the need for action by comparison to an existing normative standard. It involves a four-part structure which operates much like a room thermostat (Carver, 2007):

(1) Input function, which acts as a sensor to assess the current situation;
(2) Reference value, which is the ideal standard that the system aspires to attain;
(3) Comparator, which is the capacity to compare the first two elements in order to detect a discrepancy;
(4) An output function, which acts to trigger such course of action that may work to bring the system in alignment with its goal.

This self-regulatory structure is a circular process, a closed-loop system, whereby the output function creates changes that are detected by the input function and assessed by the comparator function against the reference value, resulting in an updated analysis and possible changes in behaviour. Of course, in the real world other activities besides those directly prompted by the output function may occur, and those too will feed into the system via the input function. Thus, coachees need to be cognisant of what is going on in their environment in order to assess as fully as possible whether any action is required. Where the system is an open system, with the output not feeding back into the system, it is normally dysfunctional, unless under circumstances where the output is so rapid that there is no time for feedback.

Having set out the coaching structure, we now briefly explain the process through which the self-regulatory system determines whether action is necessary. This too involves a four-part process called TOTE (Carver & Scheier, 1998):

Test – Tests one's current state in a given area compared to a desired standard;
Operate – Activates change to close the gap between the current and desire states;
Test – Progress to this effect is monitored;
Exit – If found satisfactory, the process is terminated; otherwise the process continues with 'Operate'.

The successful functionality of all aspects of both the structure and process of self-regulatory feedback determines the effectiveness of a person's self-regulation.

For example, the system's capacity for detecting errors and making accurate judgements is critical to the analyses it generates and the action generated thereby (Carver & Scheier, 1998).

Thus, 'self-awareness,' drawing attention to one or more aspect of a person's self-regulation, triggers the feedback system and decisions about appropriate action. It initiates a 'study' of the current state of play and a comparison between what is and what is aimed for. If there is a significant discrepancy, a motion towards action is normally instigated. Self-attention manifests itself in slightly varying ways depending on what aspect of the feedback loop is being discussed. It is helpful to think of the way in which the stages of the feedback loop are activated using attenuated terminology: the input function is activated by 'self-consciousness,' the reference value is activated by 'self-focus' and the comparator and output function is activated by 'self-awareness.'

As explained, the self-regulatory system depends on regularly updated information to enable an accurate assessment and effective choices. Normally attention is intermittently drawn to various aspects of the feedback loop, however for various reasons this may not happen. If the self-regulation system operates too intermittently and does not check often enough, a coachee could have gone a long way down a particular path without noticing that the action is leading increasingly further from the goal or desired state. For this reason, integrating feedback into a coachee's self-management is vital. A coachee pursuing a goal needs to inculcate or formalise the habit of continuously checking on the effects of his/her behaviour and ensure that those assessments are accurate. Coaching should contribute towards this end by encouraging self-awareness. As Parsloe and Wray (2000 p. 44) state, coaching can help coachees to raise their awareness by "analysing their current performance and comparing it to the level that they would like to move towards."

Monitoring Progress

In GFC, feedback is not only in the form of reports on consequences of action, but it also involves the monitoring of progress. Self-regulation theory conceives of a meta-feedback loop that is time-sensitive; it picks up on the need for change more quickly than the core feedback loop. Awareness and feedback inform coachees about whether they are progressing towards the goal (not just whether the action was successfully completed) and significantly whether the rate of progress is satisfactory. Even if progress is being made, if it is happening too slowly the feedback would trigger a reaction to apply more effort or to reconsider the effectiveness of the existing strategy (Carver & Scheier, 1998). Feedback that shows a positive rate of progress will motivate the coachee, and feedback that shows that a gap remains between the current state and the desired state will similarly urge on the coachee to persist with his or her efforts towards goal attainment.

The meta-feedback loop works through monitoring 'affect' or the level of satisfaction a person feels about how things are going. Put simply, the feedback system checks for 'velocity,' the speed at which progress is being made (Carver, 2007). An accurate assessment is only possible through continuous monitoring of progress along the way, which is why it is necessary to have subgoals that act as landmarks towards achievement of the end goal. For this reason it is necessary to set both proximal and distal goals, as explained earlier.

Summary

The coach would need to discuss each aspect of goal setting with the coachee to ensure the goal is set to optimum effectiveness. Coachees can come to coaching without a clear goal and may be highly dependent on their organisation to guide their tasks, thus limiting their self-directedness. By contrast, goal setting taps goal-directedness, which is a key attribute of human behaviour (Lee, Locke & Latham, 1989). Setting and clarifying goals has an enabling and motivating effect that helps coachees to focus on a clear objective that could then be acted upon.

We have noted how GFC requires accurate task-related feedback and how the coachee's resulting awareness enables him/her to pursue the goal in a functional manner. We further discussed that every aspect of goal setting depends on heightened attention to the task and accurate and timely feedback. It is the role of the coach to understand the role of both feedback and awareness and to foster these orientations with the coachee to raise his or her focus, motivation and performance.

9 Action Planning

Aims

- To explain the benefits of action planning and how developing task strategies promotes attainment of goals;
- To examine concepts such as automatic goals and structural tension in relation to goal attainment;
- To present an action planning model.

Action planning has been described as "the process of developing a systematic means of attaining goals" (Grant, 2006 p. 159) and as a central aspect of coaching (Spence & Grant, 2007). Breaking down a goal helps coachees to feel more confident about their ability to complete tasks, thereby raising task-related self-efficacy. However, planning can only occur after goal setting and the basic embracing of the goal has been made, for, as Miller and Brickman (2004 p. 15) note, "it is unlikely that careful analysis of the steps occurs prior to some initial commitment to a goal."

Coaching texts often emphasise the value of planning. For example, Hunt and Weintraub (2007 p. 52) cite "helping the individual being coached to articulate a personal learning agenda" as a key to coaching success. Reeves and Allison (2009 p. 147) similarly suggest that formulating a work plan "is the very spine of the work coaches do with clients." However, while action planning is mentioned as important to coaching (e.g. Bachkirova et al., 2010; Greene & Grant, 2003), it is an area that has received little theoretical attention. In this chapter we explore practical and theoretical aspects of the action planning process and address the implications of self-regulated learning to GFC. The chapter is divided into seven sections. Section one discusses the purpose of action planning, section two explores the considering of 'options' while section three discusses the need for strategy and appropriate skills in relation to goals, and section four discusses self-efficacy. In section five, the need to seek help as part of the planning process is examined and in section six, we look at two recent theories that influence traditional approaches to action planning: structural tension and automatic versus conscious goals. In the final section, flexibility and timing are considered. The chapter summary presents a model of action planning for GFC.

The Purpose of Action Planning

Most goals can sustain a variety of options and do not therefore provide a clear guide to action on their own. The purpose of planning is to reduce the options to a single action plan. In a study by Gollwitzer and Bransdstatter (1997) participants who specified a time and place for implementing a writing project were more likely to complete the project than those who had not, as "planning the when, where, and how of initiating goal-directed behaviours furthers goal attainment" (Gollwitzer & Schaal, 1998 p. 124). McDowall and Millward (2009 p. 74) similarly advise that the goal should be "unpacked into a hierarchy of concrete criterion-based sub-goals against which shorter timescales could be mapped."

As explained in Chapter 8, effective goal pursuit involves a combination of distal and proximal goals, the latter of which are formulated through action planning. Short-term planning is essential to ensure proximal goals are appropriate to prevailing circumstances (Baumeister & Vohs, 2007), whereas distal goals provide consistency and orderliness. Higher order goals focus on the long term, whereas lower order goals are transitory in nature (Carver, 2007). Lower order goals, in fact, need to be considered much closer to their actual execution: "thus, it makes sense to plan in general terms, chart a few steps, get there, reassess, and plan the next bits" (Carver & Scheier, 1998 p. 256).

In our experience, as goals are reduced into manageable tasks and resources and strategies are identified, coachees begin to show greater confidence and willingness to work towards their goal. Thus, the long-term goal, while high in motivation, is low in volition (Achtziger & Gollwitzer, 2008) and the action phase is stimulated more when coachees set short-term goals. Furthermore, detailed work plans lessen the degree of procrastination and enable more effective implementation.

Whereas previously they had remained sceptical, the action planning in Ives' study helped the coachees to perceive how their goals could be realised, which in turn enhanced their commitment. In fact, the 'Rubicon' model of action phases (Gollwitzer, 1996; Heckhausen & Gollwitzer, 1987) suggests that there will be a rise in a person's goal commitment in the transition from a 'deliberative' to an 'implementation' mindset, whereby the careful examination of competing options gives way to a determined focus on implementing a chosen course of action. Other research (Achtziger & Gollwitzer, 2008) shows that considering how a goal may be translated into action can speed up the decision-making process, which also suggests that action planning leads to commitment. Thus, at this planning stage it is necessary to specify "when, where, and how goal-directed behaviour is to be performed" (Achtziger & Gollwitzer, 2008 p. 274).

Planning is akin to Newell and Simon's (1972) 'means-end analysis,' dividing a problem into components from the most abstract to the more concrete. Setting out a plan helps to reduce attention overload (Mischel & Ayduk, 2007), reduces depletion of self-regulatory resources (Baumeister & Vohs, 2007) and can prevent impulsive behaviour (Gollwitzer et al., 2007). Disaggregating the goal makes it feel more attainable, thus raising motivation and preventing disengagement.

Although coachees may prepare a long-term action plan, in practice many coachees will tend to focus on short-term actions, primarily preparing for the next major target, to the exclusion of attending to more distant tasks. This is to be expected, as action planning retains a shorter term focus than goal setting. At the goal setting stage, coachees are in a more reflective, contemplative mode and are inclined to look into the horizon. By contrast, at the implementation stage, they typically get down to the more immediate tasks. In fact, goal setting theory suggests that short-term goals cannot be planned too far in advance as the chances of change are too great. The lower down the goal hierarchy an action is, the more there is a need for greater detail; thus detailed planning is best restricted to short-term goals (Carver & Scheier, 1998).

Options

Given many coachees' inexperience in some of the tasks they may need to undertake in pursuance of their goals, they may need to generate new options that are not part of their normal repertoire of activities. That is why some coaching texts promote the use of brainstorming and the creative pursuit of solutions in order to ensure that positive action is not hindered by an absence of ideas (Rogers, 2008; Whitworth et al., 2007). Dembkowski and Eldridge (2008 p. 202) similarly advocate that the coach helps the coachee to "develop a wider range of ways of achieving the goal," as with only one or two options there is a higher risk that the plan will run into obstacles.

In addition, helping coachees review their options enhances their commitment to the planning process, by clarifying that their strategy is sound. It also helps them to recognize the unsuitability of some options, which results in greater confidence in their ultimate choice. As Achtziger and Gollwitzer (2008 p. 274) argue, the more thoroughly an individual has weighted the consequences of their choices, "the closer he or she comes to the belief of having exhausted all possible routes."

Within goal-focused approaches, reviewing options takes the form of thinking up as many specific ideas for every given issue as possible. However, brainstorming in this way can lead to ideas that are impractical, requiring a refinement process to distinguish between suggestions that are genuinely unsuited, and those that, although beyond their current level of experience, present a growth opportunity (Dembkowski et al., 2006; Wasik, 1984). For this purpose, coaches need to create a supportive environment in which old notions can be rejected and new ideas can be considered without fear of ridicule (Whitmore, 2003). In challenging coaching contexts, in particular, it is necessary to thoroughly review the coachee's options to ensure that the coachee selects the one that is the most viable, rather than the one considered most desirable.

Miller and Brickman (2004) argue that the choice of subgoals is partly determined by whether a particular action is perceived as possible. The problem is that some coachees will perceive certain actions as beyond their ability largely due to lack of previous experience. However, reviewing options helps to explore those possibilities. Giving thought to various options raises them from oblivion to conscious thought, mitigating the tendency to reject tasks merely due to unfamiliarity. In this way, surprising ideas are give fair consideration and are not rejected out of hand. In our view, extremely brief coaching (Szabo & Meier, 2009) that does not incorporate an analysis of options is only suitable where circumstances are relatively uncomplicated.

Strategy and Skills

Action planning however goes beyond the subdivision of coachees' goals and an exploration of options. The action planning process involves identifying strategies for achieving their tasks. For example, coachees may need to devise new methods of operation and cooperation in order to attain their goals. Kanfer and Ackerman (1989) showed that without the requisite skills and knowledge, setting difficult goals can have a deleterious effect, which Mone and Shalley (1995) suggest is due to an absence of strategy. Goal theories are in agreement that the stimulus to carry out a goal is not solely reliant on the correct intention, but depends on the goal-setter having the necessary ability to carry it out. Latham (2007 p. 68) explains that "goal attainment on tasks that are complex for people requires that problems associated with getting started and persisting until the goal is reached are effectively solved."

The implication for GFC is that action planning for complex tasks will require developing strategies. Moen and Skaalvik (2009 p. 34) similarly emphasise that

> as the complexity of the tasks needed to achieve a particular goal increases, the individual's capability to possess and effectively implement efficient and effective goal attainment strategies is essential [. . .] Task strategies are therefore an important moderating variable related to goal setting and performance.

It is through such strategies that the coachee is enabled "to recognize, direct and modulate her or his own behaviour" (Skiffington & Zeus, 2003 p. 87).

If there are gaps in knowledge or ability, it is necessary to first search for and pursue an effective strategy for attaining those skills or knowledge. Putting oneself or others under pressure to meet a challenging goal when there is a deficiency in ability to attain it is courting failure. Focusing on high achievement is pointless without the all-important search for effective strategies (Mone & Shalley, 1995). When a coachee is under pressure to achieve a demanding goal without having an effective strategy, it triggers a mindless trialling of strategies, instead of systematically searching for ones that are effective (Latham, 2007).

High performance, then, is not merely about expending effort or displaying persistence; rather, it is the consequence of a cognitive understanding of the task and an effective plan for achievement (Frese & Zapf, 1994). For example, if a coachee sets a goal to write a book, it is insufficient that the coachee plans the workload unless the coachee has considered what skills and knowledge need to first be in place for the writing to proceed apace. The coach should be asking the coachee, "what do you need in place to be able to write this book?" and then "which of these do you already have?" It is essential that the coachee has carefully considered what skills might be missing *before* launching into the project. Of course, the coachee can learn the hard way, but this is highly inefficient and may lead to loss of motivation. It is the task of the coach to ensure that the coachee either plans to acquire the requisite skills and knowledge or adjusts the task so that they are no longer required. A plan without skills is arguably worse than no plan at all. Thus, it is necessary to set a clear and systematic strategy for goal attainment, as all goal effects are mediated by an ability to perform the task (Latham, 2007).

Self-efficacy

Many coaches, however, will view the tasks required to implement their action plan as daunting and beyond their current skill and experience level. This may provoke feelings of discomfort, as coachees are confronted with challenges for which they feel unprepared. Progress on developing an action plan may therefore paradoxically give rise to apprehension about implementing it. The action plan is intended to be empowering and motivating, but in practice it could have the opposite effect, as the coachee comes face to face with the full force of their challenge.

The coaching may reach a point where the coachee is not disputing the need, in principle, to accept responsibility or to take action; rather, the issue becomes their technical ability to carry out specific functions. In such instances, lack of experience at doing something can easily be perceived as inability, merely by virtue of the fact that this ability has never been confirmed. In our experience, a coachee may drop a vital task because it appears too daunting, which in GFC represents a major problem. This response is primarily related to low self-efficacy, defined as "beliefs in one's capabilities to organize and execute the course of action required to produce given attainments" (Bandura, 1997 p. 3). As one coachee explained:

> [It is] not necessarily that the tasks are difficult, because perhaps for some people this may be simple enough. I am saying that for a 23-year-old guy who has not ever done this sort of thing before, yes it is a bit daunting.

Thus, an action plan needs to be created in such a way that it contributes to raised self-efficacy, and does not do violence to it.

In keeping with the GFC methodology, as explained at length in Chapter 4, self-efficacy is addressed by supporting the coachees in effective action planning so that tasks are broken down into manageable chunks, and resources and strategies are arranged to enhance the coachees' confidence about the task (Pintrich & Schunk, 2003). Self-efficacy is diminished if the person lacks clarity about how they will achieve their goal, whereas a clear plan raises self-efficacy (Cervone, 1989).

Action planning with enhanced self-efficacy leads to less criticism and blaming by employees, for example, and less complaining about the failures of their organisation. Criticism is often the only route employees feel they have, when they perceive their situation as being subject to forces beyond their control. Conversely, coaching aims to restore as much control as possible back to the individual. Thus, the focus shifts from finding others to attribute problems to and focuses instead on identifying solutions. Additionally, having accepted a measure of responsibility for their own destiny, employees would feel under some obligation to themselves to achieve their own goals. As another coachee said, "when someone doesn't do what they say they will it is natural to criticise, but when you are the one who undertook to do it, who do you criticise then?"

While complaining and criticising may seem a form of self-assertiveness, they are actually the product of powerlessness. Reduction in complaining results from acceptance that coachees can help themselves and that their future is their own responsibility. As the aforementioned coachee added, "we are now working on an action plan and this has focused us on doing things, rather than waiting for someone else to do it for us."

Seeking Help

Quite often however, the planning process may reveal that a coachee cannot meet his or her objectives alone, but that it may be possible to proceed by getting assistance from others. Indeed, the coachee's ability to seek help is often a central element in action planning. An action plan may therefore need to take account of this even though, for some, it may be a source of consternation. There is literature that suggests that men in particular have difficulty requesting assistance (Addis & Mahalik, 2003). They may be greatly reluctant to seek help, even though doing so may be essential for a successful outcome.

Some coachees will be reticent about seeking assistance, because they feel embarrassed to be asking for help. Additionally, they may wish to rely on their organisation to achieve their work or learning goals, which may not be a realistic strategy. These are the thoughts of one (male) coachee:

> Many of the tasks we have to carry out involved asking for favours, which I don't feel comfortable with . . . No, I'm not shy, but I don't like asking for favours. The people I am asking owe me nothing and it is uncomfortable asking them to put themselves out for us . . . I guess it is an embarrassment.

The coach, then, needs to encourage identification of necessary assistance and who to approach to obtain it. The issue of seeking help should be an explicit element in goal-oriented, performance-driven coaching, as many goals cannot be achieved in a social vacuum. Some coaching models give excessive emphasis to internal resources and self-sufficiency (e.g. Szabo & Meier, 2009), whereas other approaches to coaching do emphasise the interrelatedness of the coaching context. For example, Peltier (2001) highlights how family therapy can be relevant to coaching for this very reason and systems thinking has become an increasing influence on approaches to coaching (Cavanagh, 2006; Jackson & McKergow, 2008). Furthermore, as noted in Chapter 7 in relation to group goals, the coach should query whether the goals are entirely in the hands of the coachee.

Newman (1998) argues that what he terms 'adaptive help-seeking' when facing a difficult challenge is an effective and healthy self-regulation strategy. Some coaching texts (e.g. Libri, 2004; Whitmore, 2003) also recognize that seeking help is actually vital. Jackson and McKergow (2008) suggest that it is often quicker and easier to get someone else to handle that at which one has poor ability, rather than trying to become better at it oneself, and that this can be seen as a strategic decision and an effective use of available resources, rather than as a weakness.

Although one of the aims of coaching is to ensure that coachees assume maximum responsibility for their goals (Whitmore, 2003), encouraging help-seeking where required is a necessary GFC methodology. It is important to recognize that goal pursuit may require assistance from others – a point insufficiently emphasised in the coaching literature to date.

Creating Structural Tension

An additional benefit of action planning, we suggest, is that coachees can rely on the pre-existing plan, which allows the mind to focus on carrying out the task rather than consciously reflecting on planning (Fitzsimons & Bargh, 2007; Gollwitzer et al., 2007; Mone and Shalley, 1995). Action planning allows coachees to focus on long-term attainment, rather than be focused too closely on the means of achievement (Cropanzano, Kacmar & Bozeman, 1995). Making decisions at each juncture is thought to cause disruption, as attention is diverted to decision-making rather than implementation. Additionally, making conscious decisions risks leaving coachees depleted, as it consumes both regulatory and attentional resources (Schmeichel & Baumeister, 2007).

Fritz (1984 p. 54) introduces the concept of 'structural tension' to describe a subconscious force that can be mobilised to achieve results, in order to avoid such depletion. He argues that there are two parts to this tension: the first is having a vision, and the second is knowing the current reality. Once these two are known, it sets up a tension between the two that generates an internal quest for resolution. Fritz goes on to explain how the structural tension can be reduced in one of two ways: either there is a change in the current reality to come closer to the vision or else there is a change in the vision to meet the current reality. Fritz's point is that this subconscious action planning activity tends towards a 'path of least resistance' and that the tolerance for any discrepancy between reality and vision varies from person to person, resulting in varying degrees of frustration and anxiety. Interestingly, as Fritz (1984 p. 56) also warns: weakening the structural tension will 'temporarily and superficially' relieve the discomfort of any discrepancy, but may also set up a pattern of powerlessness and a low threshold of tolerance.

The concept of structural tension is rooted in the theory of automaticity. We will now spend some time discussing the role of both automatic and conscious goals, since the theory underpinning these ideas is central to action planning in the goal-focused context.

An individual has both a quick, reflexive, impulsive mode, which is capable of responding quickly to immediate situations, and a slow, contemplative, rational mode that is best at handling strategic decisions (Mischel & Ayduk, 2007). GFC is based on the view that consciously reflecting on choices and carefully selecting goals results in improved effectiveness and thus greater success (Whitmore, 2003). Goal theories (Ford, 1992; Locke & Latham, 1990) similarly suggest that perform-ance is optimal when goals are consciously selected through deliberate choice and guidance. This view is also shared by the social cognitive literature (Bandura, 1986) and is supported more broadly by cognitive theories in psychology.

However, several researchers (Fitzsimons & Bargh, 2007; Gollwitzer, 1996; Mischel & Ayduk, 2007) have begun to question this premise, arguing that uncon-scious influencers on behaviour are highly significant and suggest that goal activa-tion can become automatic. They have issued progressively more strident claims for the non-conscious regulation of behaviour, claiming that "the cognitive revo-lution is now in trouble" (Mischel & Ayduk, 2007 p. 106). They argue that their research makes a strong case for the power of the situation to elicit responses without higher order mediation or consciousness. According to this critique, the emphasis within coaching on self-awareness and conscious processes is neither necessary nor effective.

Thus, opinion is divided within the self-regulation literature as to whether to foreground conscious, deliberative self-regulation or unconscious, automated self-regulation. Some (e.g. Baumeister, Schmeichel & H. Vohs 2007) view self-regulation as a limited resource that becomes depleted upon intensive use, but after a period of rest is restored to its original capacity. To supporters of this view, self-regulation depletion impairs physical endurance, persistence and emotion regulation (Muraven, Tice & Baumeister, 1998), and reduces ability at high-level cognitive operations (Schmeichel, Vohs & Baumeister, 2003). Even controlling thoughts has a negative effect on subsequent persistence and further attempts to control emotions (Muraven et al., 1998). Reduction in self-regulation resources impairs the executive functioning of the self and renders the individual more prone to failure.

In contrast, others, like Shah, view self-regulation as a largely unconscious process, suggesting that conscious self-regulation is neither necessary nor typical:

> The process of adopting and pursuing goals has often been construed as a very purposeful affair in which goals are carefully chosen on the basis of the factors such as their perceived value and difficulty and deliberatively pursued through the use of the best possible means. Certainly, many goals are pursued in such an intentional fashion, but a growing body of research suggests that goals may often be initiated and pursued automatically
>
> (Shah, 2005 p. 10).

The argument is that acting on the basis of a conscious intention can be less effi-cient than reacting by instinct, as it can take longer to form the intention than actually carry out the action itself (Kelso, 1995). Despite the acknowledged com-plexity of self-regulatory activity, "accumulating evidence indicates that the role of conscious processes in these operations is considerably less than previously thought" (Fitzsimons & Bargh, 2007 p. 152). These researchers posit an auto-motive model of self-regulation (Bargh, 1990; Bargh & Gollwitzer, 1994) which successfully functions outside of conscious awareness and guidance. It is asserted that without the need for intentional intervention, the person can adapt thought, emotion or behaviour to meet the demands of the current situation or goals (Fitzsimons & Bargh, 2007) and that nonconscious goal-pursuit possesses the same features as if done consciously.

This body of research further argues that a key method of delegating execution to the unconscious is through implementation intentions, whereby "the person strategically decides to delegate control over his goal-directed behaviours to anticipated critical situational cues" (Gollwitzer & Schaal, 1998 p. 134). Gollwitzer and Schaal (1998) suggest that designating a specific 'if–then' contingency between a situational cue and a desired reaction will result in a speedier and more efficient enactment of the desired behaviour. For example, a coachee might plan for a specific event by stipulating a specific response. Jane might say, "If family matters interfere with me getting ten contracts next week, I will ask my husband to take care of them." Consequently, "goal-directed behaviour becomes triggered by the presence of the critical situational cue, without the need for further conscious intent" (Gollwitzer et al., 2007 p. 213). Implementation intentions are thought to facilitate goal attainment by heightening the accessibility of both the forthcoming critical situation and the desired response, and lead to quicker responses and to higher rates of goal attainment (Gollwitzer & Sheeran, 2006). They are particularly useful when dealing with actions that are unpleasant or easy to forget (Gollwitzer et al.).

This new research casts doubt on whether there is in fact benefit in cognitively controlling actions through conscious goal setting, or whether self-regulation is automatic and does not require conscious activation. This is an issue of central concern to GFC.

However, while some human behaviour occurs automatically, in particular as a result of habit, in our analysis there are strict limits on automaticity. There are stages in the hierarchy of self-regulation when automaticity is neither possible nor appropriate, and only some goals and some situations are suited for automation. Furthermore, the evidence suggests that some conditions that are too challenging or volatile for automaticity and relegating behaviour to the unconscious would be damaging. The three main issues are summarised below.

(1) Awareness – Automaticity is by no means the main method by which people can or will regulate the more meaningful decisions of their daily life (Cervone et al., 2007). Key processes vital for effective goal pursuit do not always occur automatically, and so conscious self-reflection on goal-related choice is important for success. For example, the goal setting literature argues for the need to consciously reflect on priorities to ensure they reflect needs and best interests (Carver & Scheier, 1998). Optimal goal pursuit requires that the person calibrates goals with available resources (Freund & Baltes, 2002). Goals are often competing with each other, and self-regulation functions to ensure that less dominant but more adaptive responses are not ignored (Mischel & Ayduk, 2007).

(2) Implementation intentions - Designating a specific 'if–then' contingency results from an initial act of cognition; ultimately they "are conscious mental acts" (Gollwitzer & Schaal, 1998 p. 128). The effect of the implementation intention is

affected by the strength of the goal intention, which requires time and concentration (Bayer, Jaudas & Gollwitzer, 2002; Orbell, Hodgkins & Sheeran, 1997). Implementation intentions are referred to as 'strategic automaticity,' originating in a "conscious act of will" (Gollwitzer & Schaal, 1998 p. 124). The effect of the implementation intention is affected by the strength of the goal intention, which requires time and concentration (Bayer et al., 2002; Orbell et al., 1997). Furthermore, it is often necessary to consciously ensure that the goals set are attainable. Moreover, a person may not automatically disengage from implementation intentions if they should become dysfunctional (Gollwitzer & Schaal, 1998). Additionally, it is often difficult to predict future circumstances, in which case "people need to resort to the strategy of planning out goal pursuit in advance" (Gollwitzer et al., 2007 p. 218).

(3) Suitable conditions – Successful automation requires well entrenched pre-existing patterns and mechanisms. Thus "a goal cannot be nonconsciously activated, unless it already exists in the mind of the individual" (Fitzsimons & Bargh, 2007 p. 161). Left to automatic responses, the person will often incline towards smaller targets (Carver, 2007). Additionally, under stress the rational faculties automatically shut down, allowing the impulsive faculties to run amuck, inhibiting decision-making capacity and triggering poor goals. By contrast, focusing on long-term objectives helps the person rise beyond their immediate concerns and take in the broader picture and transcend their immediate considerations (Arriaga & Rusbult, 1998).

Indeed, Ives' research suggests that it would have been inappropriate to leave his coachees' decisions to automatic responses, as they would almost certainly have failed to take the necessary actions. By reflecting on their goals, the coachees were able to formulate effective action plans. By contrast, once the action plans were put into place, coachees were able to focus on their tasks instead of regularly having to determine what actions were required. This tentatively suggests that coaching should moderate between where there is a need for deliberative reflection and where it would be best to rely on automaticity. This tension is summarised in Figure 9.1.

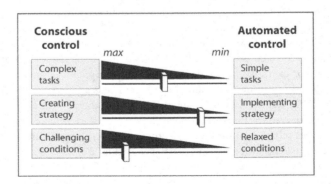

Figure 9.1 Moderating Between Automaticity and Conscious Self-Regulation

The appropriateness of conscious and automatic goal setting varies and GFC should help to manage these processes.

Implementation

Theories in cognitive and social psychology, such as Holyoak & Spellman (1993), Sloman (1996) and Smolensky (1998) view the mind's operation as two divergent processes: controlled and automatic. We now present the argument that these processes are activated depending on the relevant goal activity and circumstances and conclude with implications of this discussion for GFC.

Deliberate or considered actions are caused by controlled processes, whereas habitual actions are the result of automatic processes. According to Smolensky (1998) a conscious cognitive processor handles effortful reasoning and pro-grammes of instruction, while an intuitive processor handles automatic activities. The conscious processor involves self-*control*, and as a limited resource is subject to depletion, whereas the automatic processor acts like cognitive *ability*, which cannot be depleted. The first involves regulation *of* the self; the latter involves regulation *by* the self. Effectiveness of conscious self-regulation is the ability to overcome obstacles and focus on tasks using proactive and deliberative self-management (Schmeichel & Baumeister 2007). By contrast, effectiveness of automatic self-reg-ulation is measured by its efficiency and speed, and its ability to function without active or conscious intervention (Carver, 2007).

The suitability of conscious or automatic goal pursuit depends on the level in a self-regulatory hierarchy. Each level of the self-regulatory system manages its own process without having to be directly controlled from the top (Carver & Scheier, 1998). At the lower levels, behavioural sequences are so well learned that it is possible for actions to be triggered and executed automatically. Once this self-regulation process is triggered, the higher levels are free to turn their atten-tion towards other matters. By virtue of repetition, behaviours can become trans-ferred outside of consciousness. According to this view, familiar actions occur more smoothly and efficiently, but the reverse is true for relatively unfamiliar actions (Vallacher, Wegner, McMahan, Cotter & Larsen, 1992; Vallacher, Wegner & Somoza, 1989).

As a goal filters down the hierarchy, it becomes more concrete and specific, and it is normal and appropriate for self-regulation to become increasingly automatic. Whereas goal setting requires conscious planning for forthcoming contingencies, implementation can and should occur as non-consciously as possible. Long-term, strategic goals are best made deliberately and after careful consideration, whereas short-term, tactical goals are best relegated to automatic processes. Similarly, the purpose and nature of feedback, so crucial for successful self-regulation, varies depending on its level in the regulatory hierarchy. At the higher levels, it is a con-scious process of review and analysis that takes place *after* the event to reflect on the results and consider how to proceed; at the lower levels, it involves awareness *during* the event of the immediate environment. Optimally, initial decision-making is a conscious act, intense in its consumption of attentional resources and high in self-awareness, while the implementation of the decision is rendered as automatic as possible to free up attentional and regulatory resources.

The Rubicon model of action phases, which was mentioned earlier, posits that whereas goal setting and planning is a largely conscious affair, implementation is often enacted below consciousness. The work by Gollwitzer et al. (2007) shows that short-term planning may occur on an unconscious level. Similarly, Carver and Scheier (1998) theorise that once the regulatory responsibility is transferred to lower levels of self-regulation, the superordinate levels disengage and become freed up for other matters. Consequently, "effects on high level discrepancies caused by behaviour guided from a low level wouldn't be noted until attention is redirected to the higher level" (Carver & Scheier, 1998 p. 88). Thus, it is vital to formulate an effective plan, as implementation may occur largely outside of consciousness. The coaching literature regrettably has mostly overlooked the issue of automaticity.

Successful self-regulation, and thus optimal performance, depends on the person's ability to allocate and manage regulatory resources, so that high awareness and consciousness prevails when making key decisions, but quickly switches to automaticity when possible to conserve resources (see Carver & Scheier, 1998). Newly-learned responses may need to be guided consciously, whereas well-learned responses can be effectively handled automatically.

In summary, self-regulation includes both conscious and automatic processes, and seamlessly switches between the two as the situation requires. However, the decision as to whether self-regulation should be automated ultimately can and must be a conscious decision (MacCoon, Wallace & Newman, 2007). The various conditions that warrant either automatic or conscious goals are set out in Table 9.1. A key function of GFC should be to foster a healthy balance between active control and automation. Successful performance is largely the result of getting that balance right.

As noted, delegating implementation to the non-conscious mode enhances self-control in the face of distractions and temptations by making the desired response automatic, thus helping the person resist temptation and distraction (Gollwitzer, 1996). Therefore action plans can survive problems at the organisational or personal level, as once the coachees have set their minds to particular tasks they become less vulnerable to environmental turbulence.

However, as explained earlier, implementation intentions are only beneficial for a difficult task (Gollwitzer & Bransdstatter, 1997) and presuppose that the

Table 9.1 Conditions Requiring Conscious vs. Automatic Self-Regulation

Conscious	Automatic
High in hierarchy: goal setting	Low in hiersrchy: goal implementation
Long term decisions	Short-term decisions
Post-activity feedback loop	Inter-activity feedback loop
Complex issues	Simple issues
'Cool', low stress situations	'Hot', high stress situations
Newly learned responses	Well-learned responses
Implementation intentions	Primed reactions

coachee can predict the situation, which is often impossible. In such instances, the intended response may turn out to be useless, impractical or beyond the coachee's control (Gollwitzer et al., 2007). Thus, implementation intentions are only appropriate where the desired outcome can be specified with a high degree of certainty. Additionally, unconditional reliance on unconscious process is misguided, as feedback needs to be reviewed on an ongoing basis to ensure that the current course of action is still appropriate (Carver & Scheier, 1998).

Flexibility and Timing in Action Planning

In a situation marked by uncertainty or instability, action planning presents unique challenges as it has a tendency to complicate long-term planning. If a particular situation improves, the coachees are likely to judge that some tasks are no longer required; conversely, if the situation worsens coachees may abandon the task or even the organisation. In Ives' study the unfolding changes in circumstances at the organisation or in the lives of coachees led them to contemplate changes to their action plans, both when the situation deteriorated and when it had improved. In the words of one coachee: "whether or not I end up doing all my tasks, who knows? Perhaps it won't even be necessary, if things improve here. And if it gets worse, I probably will have to leave."

Thus, while an action plan must be flexible (Carver & Scheier, 1998; de Haan, 2008; King & Eaton, 1999), it may become overwhelmed by radical rupture. As, Carver and Scheier (1998) confirm, it is neither possible nor appropriate to plan in great detail too far into the future, as circumstances are liable to change. Bandura (2001 p. 6) likewise noted that "future-directed plans are rarely specified in full detail at the outset. It would require omniscience to anticipate every situational detail."

However, even in conditions of uncertainty this need not stop the coach and coachee from formulating plans. Action planning is a flexible process and can be made even more flexible if conditions warrant this. While undoubtedly some coachees will lose interest in creating an action plan if the future is unpredictable, from our research and experience, if the coachee has bought into the idea of coaching, these problems will in most instances not prevent the action planning from proceeding. As the aforementioned coachee also commented: "we don't really know what's happening. It could get better, it could get worse – who knows? So we are just getting on with it."

Irrespective of the fate of specific projects or actions, the clarity of thought and values attained through the action planning process will remain, even though GFC's main objective is practical actions and not internal growth. As one coachee confirmed:

> the action planning has been a useful process for me, whether or not I end up putting my plan into action. I am much clearer about what I want out of my studies and I am clearer about the kinds of skills that I am looking to acquire.

Most coaching books emphasise the importance of relating goals to a specified timeframe. Helping coachees to create work or learning schedules will better enable them to organise and focus themselves, as schedules are an effective time-keeping tool and planning device. A detailed time-plan can help to mitigate the tendency to procrastinate, as the following quotes from two coachees in Ives' research suggest:

> Having a schedule is helpful, because at least that way you don't get caught out in the end when you are left with a short time to complete the material – which then becomes an impossible task.

> Setting out a timeframe from the very beginning meant that I had to face reality early on. I knew precisely what was involved and how much I would have to cover each week; at least now there are fewer surprises . . . It forces a certain discipline.

Coachees also identified a variety of benefits. For one coachee, the action plan enabled him to calculate the real time that was required, rather than underestimating the amount of work involved. Another said the benefit was in getting him to focus on the essential elements and leave out those tasks that were not as important. For others still, the action plan resulted in clarification of what elements they would do themselves and what elements they would delegate to work colleagues. These are essential skills for successful goal-focused activity, for if the person cannot be realistic or stay on track, all the action planning in the world will not work. Additionally, we have noted that the motivation generated by goal pursuit is related to the progress made against an expected timeframe. Even if the coachee is achieving a great deal, if he or she is not operating against a desired timeline it may not feel progress is being made. Thus, progress along a clear work plan will provide encouraging evidence of success.

Our experience of GFC suggests that people have different preferences when it comes to action planning. Some feel that a daily schedule works better than a weekly one, as they struggle to accurately assess how long tasks might take, and others prefer the flexibility of a weekly schedule. The optimal design of the timeframe for proximal goals varies from person to person. Of course, some people naturally work in a goal-focused manner, or have learned to do so before the coaching, so not every coachee will need to be introduced to this method of working. However, for those who are not already goal-focused, there are numerous potential benefits from systematic action planning.

Summary

Miller and Brickman (2004 p. 16) argue that "individuals lacking either the relevant sociocultural knowledge or the cognitive strategies for problem-solving may fail to develop a system of subgoals for attaining the future goals they desire." Cruelly therefore, potential coachees most in need of planning are often those least able to achieve it, meaning that their prospect of failure is doubly increased. For these reasons, GFC should incorporate planning into an integrated self-regulation strategy.

In this chapter we have presented a case for action planning in coaching, which by breaking down the goal makes it seem more attainable and enables its smooth implementation. We also suggested that developing a detailed action plan allows for a goal to be pursued below consciousness, which helps to conserve attentional and regulatory resources.

Figure (9.2) summarises the action planning process in GFC as discussed in this chapter. Before settling on an action plan, the coachee should be assisted to brainstorm as many options as possible, which then need to be carefully reviewed to enable the selection of the most suitable path to success. The selected options need to be developed into an action plan, which must consider the skills and knowledge required and must identify what assistance may be necessary for the goal to be successfully attained. Thereafter, a detailed action plan along with a specific timeframe needs to be elaborated. Key decisions and complex tasks should be identified for future consideration; simpler tasks should be set in motion to be managed automatically, allowing the mind to be freed to focus on taking action. The figure concludes with the need for this process to feed into the coachee's self-regulatory monitoring system.

Table 9.2 summarises the benefits of action planning, as suggested by the foregoing discussion:

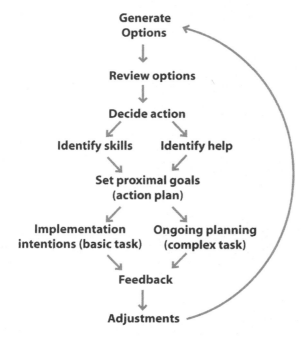

Figure 9.2 Action Planning Model

Table 9.2 Benefits of Action Planning

Benefits of action planning

(1)   Aids focus
(2)   Aid timekeeping
(3)   Increases task confidence
(4)   Raises motivation
(5)   Provides a clear guide to acton
(6)   Facilitates smooth implementation
(7)   Helps to conserve regulatory and attentional resources

10 Commitment in Goal-focused Coaching

Aims

- To examine factors that underpin motivation, such as self-concordance and self-set goals;
- To consider questions that promote motivation and raise commitment to the goal;
- To explore the notion of intrinsic motivation and present a new model of stages in motivation for GFC.

Coaching texts frequently mention motivation as a useful adjunct to the coaching process (e.g. Peltier, 2001; Skiffington and Zeus, 2003). However, perhaps because goals are not the main focus of their activity, most coaching models fail adequately to address motivational issues. Conversely, motivation and commitment need to be overt concerns of GFC, especially since it is vital in the achievement of performance goals.

According to Hollenbeck, Brief, Whitener and Pauli (1988), performance is the interaction between cognitive ability and motivation. Unlike cognition, however, motivation is identified as relatively inconsistent and unstable (Kanfer & Ackerman, 1989). Thus, ongoing management of motivation can be seen as a key requirement for raising performance (Bandura, 1982).

Goal theories distinguish between factors relating to goal choice and factors relating to goal commitment (Locke & Latham, 1990), which, it could be argued, mirror pre-decisional and post-decisional processes (Pintrich & Schunk, 1996). Research into volition has also drawn a distinction between goal setting and goal striving (Achtziger & Gollwitzer, 2008). Similarly Cervone et al. (2007) distinguish between quantitative and qualitative aspects of goals, according to which goal difficulty, specificity and proximity are quantitative aspects (discussed in Chapters 8 and 9), whereas intrinsic motivation, concordance, and commitment are qualitative issues. This latter group of issues we collectively term 'motivation,' meaning "the process whereby goal-directed activity is instigated and sustained" (Pintrich & Schunk, 1996 p. 4).

This chapter explores four key issues: motivational questions; intrinsic motivation; concordance and self-set goals. The chapter argues that motivational needs vary depending on the stage of the goal process, and on this basis, section five proposes a stage model of motivation providing a more nuanced understanding of the coaching process.

Motivational Questions

Although the GFC paradigm foregrounds goal setting and action planning, in our view it should also include an explicit emphasis on motivation, albeit built upon the goal itself. Following Whitmore (2003), two foci for the motivation element of a GFC coaching model are: (1) identifying the benefits of achieving the goal through benefits questions; (2) ensuring commitment through commitment questions.

(1) Benefits questions – Benefits questions involve using a motivational interviewing approach to asking questions (see Miller & Rollnick, 2002) that brings into awareness the benefits of change and verbalise how change could be beneficial to raising motivation (Passmore & Whybrow, 2007). Passmore (2007) argues that in behaviour-oriented approaches to coaching, commitment is engendered by asking coachees to tease out the benefits to them from a particular behaviour or course of action. Coaching texts suggest that motivation is engendered by asking the coachees to articulate the benefits of achieving their goal. Indeed, Ford (1992) argues that aligning a performance target with a benefit reinforces the goal through a synergistic effect. Although identifying benefits could be helpful during any part of coaching, we generally think of securing commitment as the third stage of coaching (after goal setting and action planning), and therefore as occurring near the end of the coaching cycle.

This approach to raising motivation is particularly suited to GFC, for while some coaching styles work with the coachee on inner change, GFC is primarily focused on achieving behavioural change. D. B. Peterson (2006 p. 53) argues that "the coach's purpose is not to change a person's motivations or to increase the person's insight into their origin, but to see how the person being coached can most effectively use these [existing] motivations to guide, shape, and reinforce desired behaviour." Pemberton (2006 p. 9) similarly argues that motivation does not need to take the form of some external threat or incentive, but rather "the challenge is to unearth what the other's motivations are, and then to use them to lever the performance you need." Bandura (2001) uses the term "valued futures" to capture the sense that a goal needs to embody a person's powerful aspirations.

Sieler (2010) reminds us that the words we use influence a person's motivation. Arguing against change reduces the likelihood of it occurring (Miller, Benefield & Tonigan, 1993), whereas advancing reasons for a course of action increases its likelihood. For this reason, it is motivational for the coachee to articulate the specific benefits he or she hopes will accrue from attaining the goal. For example, a coachee may be motivated by saying:

> If I finally complete this course, it will give me a much better chance of gaining a promotion. Gaining a promotion is now really important for me, as I am at a stage in my career where it is crucial that I make some move.

Similarly, Burns (1990) advises that the coachee conducts a cost benefit analysis, as commitment to the goal is more likely if benefits are then found to be important (Allan & Whybrow, 2007; Locke, 1996).

As with goal setting and action planning, in relation to motivation, the key is striking the right balance. As mentioned in the previous chapter on action planning, a person's self-regulatory system is comprised of two modes: the first is a quick reflexive and impulsive mode that is capable of responding quickly to immediate situations. Mischel and Ayduk (2007 p. 109) refer to this as the 'hot system.' The second mode is a slow, contemplative and rational mode that is best at handling strategic decisions, which Mischel and Ayduk call the 'cool system.' While the cool system is reflective and premeditative, the hot system is "an essentially automatic system, governed by stimulus–response reactions, which unless interrupted, preclude effortful control." When the hot system is operating, it is very difficult for the person to exert willpower and to maintain control, whereas the cool system introduces a measure of reflection and calmness. The cool nodes run parallel to the hot spots, as Mischel & Ayduk (2007 p. 109) describe: "Effortful control and willpower become possible to the extent that the cooling strategies generated by the cognitive cool system circumvents hot system activation through such inter-system connections that link hot spots to cool nodes."

Thus, the person's capacity for self-control is influenced, if not entirely determined, by the availability of representations that facilitate the cooling of emotion. Focusing on a long-term objective enables cooling to occur as "immediate, self-interested preferences are replaced by preferences that take into account broader concerns, including considerations to some degree that transcend the immediate situation" (Arriaga & Rusbult, 1998 p. 928). Adopting an exclusively impulsive short-term attitude encourages myopic or erratic behaviour that is deleterious to the kind of long-term goal pursuit necessary for significant achievement. For this reason, working to a clear long-term goal can minimise the likelihood of the coachee overreacting to the immediate situation in a manner that could risk long-term potential. The impulsive reaction is moderated by a rational and considered view of the coachee's goals. However, an overly rational and considered approach depending too heavily on the 'cool' system may result in a loss of enthusiasm. Thus, effective motivation is about striking the right balance.

The cool/hot theory suggests that optimal functioning is the result of a successful balance between the excitable hot system and the reasoned cool system. Too much emphasis on the cool system and the motivation dissipates; too much emphasis on the hot system and the person becomes overexcited resulting in self-regulation failure. Rewards are motivational and can usefully arouse the hot system, but must be kept to a limited degree so as not to cause overheating. In their research, Mischel and Ayduk (2007 p. 114) suggest that the delay in gratification that is vital for self-regulation is facilitated most when attention is intermittently shifted onto rewards

> but then quickly shifted away to prevent arousal from becoming excessive [. . .]
> It is the balanced interaction between the hot and cool system that sustains

delay of gratification and effortful control, as they exert their motivating and cooling effects in tandem.

(2007 p. 114)

Gollwitzer and Schaal (1998 p. 131) similarly caution against over-motivation; the focus should be on planning and implementing the task, they say, not on the reward. Effective self-regulation, they argue, "seems more closely associated with 'cold' skilful cognitive strategies than with the 'hot' determined energization and mobilization of effort." The foregoing discussion therefore suggests that helping the coachee to periodically divert attention to the rewards resulting from goal attainment ensures that motivation remains alert and active, but then the focus needs to revert towards the task at hand. The purpose of asking the 'benefit question' is, then, to draw appropriate attention to the potential reward.

However, when considering deploying a benefit question as a means of raising motivation, it is worth noting that this may be alien to the coachee. In our experience, coachees have at times found such questions disconcerting and some have even been unwilling to cooperate. Despite this, most coachees tend to consider the questions motivational, as these quotes from Ives' study illustrate:

> [It's] kind of weird, you know. It isn't the kind of thing I am used to. But it does kind of motivate in its own way. It becomes clearer why it must get done. When you asked me about the benefits of arranging the seminar, which I wasn't really interested in doing, reminding myself of the reason for doing so did help me not to get too discouraged.

> when you don't really want to do something and you would much prefer not to, then a reminder of why it is important gives a bit of a boost. When I had to research for a book about writing I wasn't really interested in doing this and didn't really know what I am looking for and so on, so I was just pushing it off and was not up for the task. So when I explained why that was important for my role, it got me to decide to do the research.

Asking coachees to specify benefits moderately raises motivation in most coachees. However, the motivational effect of identifying benefits is of short duration; it is only sufficient to gain the coachee's temporary cooperation. It is a useful technique to get over a blockage or overcome a bout of laziness, but it is less likely to have an impact several days later. Thus, ongoing moderate reference to the rewards during the implementation of the action plan is necessary to help to ensure optimal goal-focused motivation.

(2) Commitment questions – Goal commitment refers to the strength of the individual's endorsement of his/her goal and is critical to high performance (Locke & Latham, 1990). The linear relationship between the goal setting variables and performance must pass through goal commitment for the higher performance associated with these variables to be realised (Seijts & Latham, 2001). This is particularly so for goals perceived as difficult (Klein, Wesson, Hollenbeck & Alge, 1999).

A technique which is successfully incorporated into GFC is to ask the coachee to rate from 1 to 10 'their intention to carry out' their stated actions (see Whitmore,

2003), whereby securing a verbal commitment is claimed to increase the likelihood of it being carried out. This approach is widely used in coaching and is recommended in several coaching books (e.g. Dunbar, 2009; Spence, 2007), but surprisingly many others do not mention it despite it being a highly effective coaching tool.

In Ives' study, coachees that gave a rating of seven or below were asked to explain 'what was preventing it from being a 10?' The coachees were then asked to consider what adjustments could be made to the goal or the action plan to raise the commitment level. However, coachees were sometimes 'unenthusiastic' about this exercise, as these comments express:

> I didn't enjoy being asked these types of questions. I suppose to some extent it did [influence fulfilment of my plan], because having so clearly stated that I was going to do it, it made it harder for me not to.

> It wasn't a question I enjoyed being asked. But I could see why you asked it. When you asked me about the research into writing the book, I think I only gave it a six, so I suppose it showed that I wasn't that serious about it.

> I understood why you did this and I think you needed to push me to really commit to certain tasks, because I wasn't that enthusiastic. To be honest, I wasn't so excited about answering this question, but I can see that you didn't want to take the risk that I would agree to do something and then it wouldn't happen. Your job was to make sure that the plan was actually put into effect.

Some coachees may initially be reluctant to confront the question, but from our experience, they will acknowledge some benefit from going through the exercise. This exercise exposes reservations or blockages, is effective in securing commitment to unpopular tasks, and gets the coachee to take action that otherwise may not happen. Asking for commitment can raise the prospects of the coachee implementing their declared goal. From the perspective of the Rubicon model of action phases (Achtziger & Gollwitzer, 2008) it would seem that the motivation and commitment questions add volitional strength, which stimulates the fiat tendency that generates the will and determination to execute the goal. A recent study of coaching (Moen & Skaalvik, 2009) did not find that goal commitment automatically increased through coaching, which seems to confirm our view that securing commitment to the goal needs to be given explicit attention.

Intrinsic and Extrinsic Motivation

Central to goal-related motivation is goal orientation – here intended to mean 'the motivational provenance of the goal.' According to many motivation theories (e.g. Ames, 1992; Deci & Ryan, 2002) a defining issue for goal orientation is whether the goal is intrinsically motivated, which, it is claimed, enhances wellbeing and is more motivational, especially in the long-term. Similarly, concordance theory emphasises the importance of adopting goals that are congruent with the person's values and personality (Kasser, 2002; Sheldon, 2002). Goals that suffer from an internal conflict result in poor motivation and impede wellbeing. We will therefore briefly explore these issues in relation to GFC.

The value of intrinsic motivation is highlighted by several coaching writers (Allan & Whybrow, 2007; Grant, 2006; Moen & Skaalvik, 2009; Passmore & Whybrow, 2007; Rogers, 2008) as necessary for lasting change and optimal motivation. It is therefore surprising that, as Skiffington and Zeus (2003) confirm, the coaching literature focuses so little on examining this key issue in detail.

Ives' research found that even if coachees lacked intrinsic motivation for many of their tasks, they were willing to carry them out for utilitarian reasons. However, as would be expected in such cases, their motivation plummeted where it was possible for the task to be achieved without them doing it. One coachee compared carrying out tasks to going to dentist; he would only do tasks if he had no alternative. Thus, motivation and persistence was weaker where there was an absence of intrinsic motivation. This seems to echo the claims of self-determination theory (Deci & Ryan, 2002) that goals should be intrinsically motivated, driven by the person's autonomous interest in the goal, rather than extrinsically motivated, driven by the pursuit of some external benefit. According to self-determination theory, personality development, wellbeing and performance are enhanced through experiencing autonomy, with individuals perceiving themselves to be the origin of their own behaviour. Although Locke and Latham (1990 p. 58) state that "little can be concluded about the effects of goals on intrinsic motivation," subsequent research suggests that intrinsic motivation results in greater persistence, better social relations, more effective performance and improved health and wellbeing (Kasser and Ryan, 1996; Sheldon & Elliot, 1999).

However, extrinsic goals can also be effective at raising performance, as the coachee decides to adopt tasks that they are reluctant about, or even resentful of, because they are necessary for attainment of their objectives. Indeed, research suggests that pure intrinsic motivation is not always essential (Elliot & Church, 1997; Harackiewicz, Barron, Carter, Lehto & Elliot, 1997; Wong & Csikszentmihalyi, 1991). Self-determination theory suggests that people integrate within themselves what were initially externally instigated objectives (Deci & Ryan, 1985), and may take greater ownership of a task over time (Rothman, Baldwin & Hertel, 2007). If a person finds personal meaning in an activity and synthesises its objectives with other aspects of his psychic makeup, the person may be said to 'identify' with the activity. Whereas intrinsic motivation gains its power from 'supported autonomy' (primarily, the freedom to make choices), identified motivation gains its power from 'structured autonomy,' understanding the reasons that a task is important and meaningful (Grolnick & Ryan, 1989; Reeve, 2002). Furthermore, goal attainment is a direct contributor to wellbeing (Sheldon, 2002; Sheldon & Elliot, 1999) and goals also become intrinsically motivating when made more interesting (Wild & Enzle, 2002).

Thus, the key issue is not how free the coachee is to choose the goal, but whether the coachee can find value in pursuing it. For example, a coachee may have little natural interest in playing golf, but close examination of career issues during coaching may reveal taking up golf to be an important social networking opportunity in the coachee's work environment. Despite previous diffidence towards the sport, the coachee may come to view this pastime as a valuable means of befriending work colleagues. As a sport, the coachee may be indifferent to golf, but as a social activity may view it positively. In our view, coaching should be seen as a process that facilitates internalisation and gives rise to structured autonomy.

Additionally, there may be some advantages to extrinsic motivation, as studies suggest that it can help maintain long-term commitment when intrinsic interest starts to wane (Koestner & Losier 1996; Sheldon & Elliot, 1998). Additionally, in an educational context, it was found that judging the goal as valuable is more important than perceiving it as interesting (Hodgins & Knee, 2002; Koestner, Losier, Fichman & Mallet, 2002).

Concordance

Ives' research suggests that coachees are likely to display resistance to tasks that they feel are inappropriate for them and will typically only be willing to adopt tasks that are consistent with their self-perception and do not arouse psychic resistance. For example, they will resist tasks they perceive as being entirely the responsibility of the organisation. Depending on their level of responsibility in the organisation, the fact that they could benefit from carrying out a task may not be sufficient for some coachees to overcome their resistance to the 'iniquity' of the organisation assigning them tasks that they believe the organisation should be doing. Similarly, a goal that the coachee feels is a waste of time will not draw out the kind of effort required to be successful. As Zeus and Skiffington (2007) point out, individuals may perceive their role to be incompatible with that expected within the team.

It is axiomatic to coaching that goals must be in synchrony with a person's values, meaning and purpose (Palmer & Whybrow, 2007; Pemberton, 2006), and congruity between internal processes and external demands enhances effectiveness. Coaching should work to balance the coachee's agenda with their vision and values (Natale & Diamante, 2005; Kauffman, 2006). From a goal theory perspective, Locke (1996 p. 119) argues that high commitment to the goal is achieved when the person is "convinced that the goal is important." According to Bresser and Wilson (2006 p. 20), for a goal to be effective it must "resonate and be congruent with the coachee's values and personal culture." The coach has a role to facilitate the coachee to pursue goals that fulfil longer-term satisfaction, as goals aligned with the person's core interests and values are associated with greater goal attainment and satisfaction (Waring, 2008).

Grant (2006) identifies self-concordance theory (Sheldon & Elliot, 1998) as a useful framework for relating goals to values. Self-concordance theory (Sheldon, 2002), which emerged from self-determination theory, recognizes that many goals are inconsistent with the person's real objectives or true condition. Self-concordance goals, on the other hand, are those that are genuinely inspired by and work to actualise the person's core life aims (Gruber & Wallace, 1999) and deeply felt core values (Little, 1993), and are motivated by lasting rather than transient impulses and aspirations. Self-concordance goals are more likely to be fulfilled, as they tap into the person's enduring sources of energy, and because they have the person's full emotional backing and volitional support (Hodgins & Knee, 2002; Sheldon & Elliot, 1998; Sheldon & Kasser, 1998). Coaching aims to align goals and strategy and draws together intention, commitment and motivation (Williams, K. et al. 2002). Burke and Linley (2007) found that both self-concordance and commitment significantly increased after just one coaching session, although little empirical evidence has been advanced to support the claim.

Achieving congruence and concordance is a key aspect of goal construction and is a more important factor than intrinsic motivation. Furthermore, concordance should guide the selection and shaping of the goal. Whereas issues of motivation and commitment can be set aside until the action plan has been created, goal concordance needs to be addressed at the earliest stages of the goal setting, to ensure that the goal is appropriate.

Despite the importance of goal congruence, Nadler and Tushman (1989 p. 195) caution that it can be a double-edged sword: "A system with high congruence however, can be resistant to change. It develops ways of insulating itself from outside influences and may be unable to respond to new situations." The coach needs to ensure that the goals selected and pursued are not in internal conflict with their coachees' life goals, while fostering flexibility so that vital tasks are undertaken where intrinsic motivation is low.

Self-set Goals

Goal congruence and concordance can be a tricky issue, however. While on the one hand much coaching occurs in situations where the goals are set by a company or institution, and over which the coachee often has little influence, on the other hand coaching is about restoring ownership to the coachee. It may not always be possible or proper for the coachee to set the goal, and in such situations, as Skiffington and Zeus (2003) suggest, the coachee will accept the goal if it is legitimate. This is consistent with significant research into goal setting (see a comprehensive review by Latham, 2007) suggesting that assigned goals can still be motivational. However, where the coachee is not fully accepting of the goal, he or she may well reject the idea of the organisation assigning goals. When Ives interviewed coachees about how they would have reacted to having their tasks assigned to them, their responses were unequivocal:

> You must be joking. I would never have agreed to such a thing.

> What would have been the point in us carrying out the tasks, but they tell us what to do?

> Nothing would have happened.

Indeed, several goal and learning theories (Ford, 1992; Knowles, 1975), and the general trends in the coaching literature, lean towards self-selection of goals. Hunt and Weintraub (2004) state that coachees will learn more when pursuing a goal they have selected and defined, and that self-directed learning results in better outcomes than those emerging from demands for compliance. Thus, many coaching texts present motivation as the natural effect of handing ownership to the coachee, and encourage self-governance in order to foster self-responsibility (Parsloe & Wray, 2000; Pemberton, 2006; Whitmore, 2003).

As Grant notes (2006 p. 158), high commitment is attained when "the individual participates in determining outcomes." Coaching advocates a decision-making process that allows for those affected by a decision to contribute to shaping it (Hudson, 1999). Furthermore, participation in setting goals is a potentially significant influence on commitment. While the research on this topic is mixed (Locke & Latham, 1990), studies suggest that participation results in higher individual performance (Locke, Alavi, & Wagner, 1997), as it leads to higher quality decisions and can improve goal setting (Latham, 2007; Wagner, 1994). In particular, Latham, Winters and Locke (1994) found that participation in formulating goal strategies is related to improved performance and raised self-efficacy, although properly assigned goals are no barrier to commitment (Latham, Erez, & Locke, 1988; Skiffington & Zeus, 2003). Facilitation, rather than control, is the more effective form of goal-related motivation (Ford, 1992).

Locke and Latham (1990) argue that a task can be assigned, but that a goal must be accepted for it to exist. Commitment is related to acceptance of responsibility, which is enhanced when people take their own decisions. As Whitmore (2003) points out, in a coaching context it is only when people assume responsibility that real learning or performance occurs. It is not only in a goal-focused setting that self-set goals are important. Constructive–developmental approaches to learning (Kegan, 1982) regard adult learning and development as based upon an active participant. Thus, adult development approaches to coaching (e.g. Berger, 2006; Cox, 2006) also strongly emphasise the need for voluntary enrolment.

Furthermore, the self-selection of goals aids coachees in the vital personalisation of their goals. Coachees, even in a team or group, and even if part of an organisational programme, have distinctive aims and seek divergent outcomes and concerns, as well as varying notions of their likely career path. Self-setting goals enables coachees to adjust their goal and direct their action plan to meet their own specific requirements and to address their particular areas of weakness. Ford (1992) asserts what he calls the 'principle of unitary functioning,' which states that, given the complex range of influences on the individual, motivation must be tailored to the individual. For example, coachees with low self-efficacy require easier targets to enable them to experience success, which leads to motivation, whereas high self-efficacy coachees are more motivated by the challenge (Pintrich & Schunk, 2003). To account for this diversity, GFC aims as much as possible to enable coachees to set their own goals.

Some coachees may well prefer choices being made for them, and this may be because choice-making is a taxing activity. Baumeister, Bratslavsky, Muraven and Tice (1998) found that exercising choice leads to depletion of regulatory resources and subsequent reduced effectiveness. As explained in the previous chapter, goal setting is a form of conscious self-regulation that consumes mental energy, which is why the coachee may seem happy to accept assigned goals. However, if the choice relates to the person's own task, we would argue that the low level of depletion is far outweighed by the benefits. It is necessary to secure a sense of ownership from the coachee for the goal-related activity to function effectively.

Stages in Motivation

Motivation-related activity in GFC is not a specific stage in a highly structured process, but an iterative and fluid element of the coaching, which may need to be revisited at various points. Crucially, we believe that this foregrounds the role and the person of the coach, as it is he or she who needs to continually assess and respond to the motivation needs of the coachee. Nevertheless, based on the foregoing discussion, we conclude that there are five main stages in the goal process in relation to motivation, which we briefly describe and which are also summarised in Table 10.1. Each stage has a different motivational requirement, which the coach needs to understand to effectively address the motivational needs of the coachee:

Opening – Before goal-focused activity can begin in earnest, the coaching relationship must be firmly established. In GFC, the priority is to establish the coachee's relationship with the coaching itself; the coachee must accept the need for coaching, be willing to address this need, and moreover must consider that coaching may be helpful (Flaherty, 2005). Initial commitment is a prerequisite for establishing the need for and the focus of the coaching (Alexander, 2006; Starr, 2007).

Goal setting – The way the goal is constructed is directly related to motivation. If the coachee sets his or her goals at an optimal level of proximity, difficulty and specificity, the goal itself will act as a source of motivation (Bandura, 1986; Locke & Latham, 1990). Similarly, it is vital at this stage to ensure that the goal is concordant with the values and aims of the coachee (Sheldon, 2002). Where possible, the

Table 10.1 Stages in Motivation

Coaching stage	Source of motivation
Opening	Establish need for coaching
	Establish the potential benefit of coaching
	Secure initial commitment to coaching
Goal setting	Ensure an effective goal balance
	Ensure goal concordance
	Facilitate self-selection of goals
Action planning	Break down goal
	Facilitate concrete actions
Securing commitment	Coachee to identify benefits of attainment
	Coachee to verbalise commitment
Implementation	Maintain goal salience
	Progress towards goal

coachee should be involved in the selecting of goals, as this enhances goal commitment (Ford, 1992; Grant, 2006).

Action planning – At the action planning stage, motivation stems from enhanced self-efficacy that comes from breaking down the goal into manageable chunks, and from developing task-related strategies (Parker et al., 2008). When the coachee sees how the goal can be made a reality, it raises self-efficacy, which provides motivation for pursuing the goal (Cox, 2006). Applying attention to devising methods of attaining the goal add to the volitional strength to persist with its implementation (Achtziger & Gollwitzer, 2008).

Securing commitment – Once the plan or the first phase of the plan is created, the coach needs to ensure commitment to the implementation, which comes from identifying the benefits of a valued goal and from articulating commitment to the plan (Burns, 1990). In our view, motivation and commitment questions could come after the goal setting or action planning stage but not before, as the coachee can only properly commit to a clearly defined goal (Berg & Szabo, 2005; Whitmore, 2003).

Implementation – In implementation, awareness of the discrepancy provides the motivation for continued effort. Motivation also comes from the satisfaction of progress towards the ultimate goal (Miller & Brickman, 2004), resulting in raised self-efficacy. When randomly asked to describe what they were doing, high-level strivers cited abstract goals, whereas low-level strivers cite concrete goals (Emmons, 1992). Thus, continuous reference should be made to the end goal, as it provides the 'why' for the subgoals (Carver & Scheier, 1998).

Summary

This chapter has described how raising motivation and securing commitment should not be left to chance, and that it cannot be assumed that these factors will be taken care of automatically through core goal-related activity, such as goal setting and action planning. We therefore argue that urging the coachee to articulate the hoped-for benefits of reaching the goal, and asking for specific commitment to pursuing the goal are necessary and helpful facets of GFC. It could also be argued that recognition of long-term benefits may lead to the development of mastery goals, rather than solely extrinsically rewarded performance goals. We further explored a range of factors that influence motivation, such as intrinsic motivation and concordance and self-set goals. This culminated in the presentation of a five-stage motivation model that illustrates sources of motivation through the GFC process.

11 Questioning and Listening Skills

Aims

- To explore the role of questions in the goal-focused coaching process;
- To examine why listening is an important skill for the goal-focused coach.

Many coaching texts highlight the use of both questions and listening, and position them as central to the art and practice of coaching. Typically though, coaching texts fail to distinguish between the differing objectives of questions and their suitability to the various coaching paradigms, or to consider how listening may have a different emphasis in different coaching settings. In this chapter, we discuss how questions and listening, while always important in any coaching paradigm, have subtle but significant variations depending on what the coaching primarily aims to achieve.

The chapter has two main sections. The first looks at questions, exploring the purpose and different types of questions as they relate specifically to GFC. The second section discusses listening, particularly the difference between active listening and what we call holistic listening.

Questions in Goal-focused Coaching

Questions in GFC are intended to achieve two main purposes: to raise coachee awareness, and to secure clarity about goals. Hawkins and Smith (2010 p. 239) focus on awareness raising when they emphasise how questions "enable the coachee to explore the situation from different standpoints and generate new perspectives and possibilities." Bresser and Wilson (2006 p. 18) highlight the clarity-generating quality of questions, and therefore describe questions as "the precision tools in the coach's toolkit." Other writers on coaching view questions as having a deeper role. Kemp (2008b p. 42), for example, discusses 'insight-driven questions' that stimulate deeper personal awareness and reflection. He suggests that questions such as "If you were to change your view of the current situation, what would that allow for?" and "What may be possible if you were to make the change you are describing?" invite coachees to free themselves from self-limiting beliefs and thought processes. Oliver (2010), too, gives examples of questions that are useful in generating reflexivity in a coaching context. These conceptions of questioning are consistent with GFC.

Drawing on Argyris and Schön's levels of learning, Skiffington and Zeus (2003) describe three types of questions. Single loop questions, they suggest, are those that explore issues on a superficial level. These questions concentrate on the actions the coachee performs to resolve a problem. Double loop questions look at deeper assumptions in order to question why a situation has occurred and what factors may have contributed to them. These questions promote reflection and may highlight issues such as the status of the coachee in the organisation, or the inherent structures of the organisation that can indirectly impact on coachee performance. Triple loop questions explore the underlying values that shape the coachee's sense of being that guides choices. The first two question loops are typical of GFC.

Since GFC is generally not intended to help with the more existentialist or identity concerns of the coachee, questions in GFC are mostly designed to create an empty space into which coachees can pour their thoughts in a semi-structured manner. Therefore, coaching questions need to be 'vacant,' to provide an opportunity for coachees to structure and clarify their own thoughts. By definition, then, effective questions are ones in which the voice of the coach is as silent as possible, allowing for the thoughts of the coachee to be expressed.

The Goal has a Question

Inherent in the theory of GFC is the self-regulatory quality of goals, as discussed earlier. Once he or she commits to a goal, the coachee's self-regulation system will normally trigger a series of questions, checking the current level of attainment, what level of activity is being expended, and what further activity is required to meet the goal. These are questions that the system naturally asks of itself in order to ascertain what action (or not) is required. GFC seeks to give explicit voice to these questions, and to sharpen them through carefully targeted questioning, to optimise the self-regulation systems goal pursuit.

However, what GFC also offers is a widening of the questioning to address issues that the instinctive self-regulation mechanism may not explore. Coaching provides an opportunity to explore potential obstacles before they arise, using 'forethought' (Bandura, 1986, 2001; Cleary & Zimmerman, 2004) to pre-empt problems ahead of time. Targeted questioning can also help to ensure that less dominant but more adaptive responses are not ignored, which is the primary function of self-regulation (Mischel & Ayduk, 2007). Coaching also provides an opportunity to consider whether the coachee's goals conflict with other goals the coachee has or with the goals of other actors within the coachee's immediate environment. In other words, coaching questions can enhance the naturally generated questions in many important ways. Moreover, they can inculcate in the coachee a habit of broadening his or her questioning purview to include these wider considerations. It may be said therefore, that in GFC the coach is merely giving voice to the questions that the coachee should be asking him or herself.

People are used to questions being asked either to gather information or to interrogate, and are accustomed to being asked questions that have a right and a wrong answer. In coaching, however, questions are asked to stimulate deeper thought, foster creative ideas and to raise awareness. There are no right or wrong answers – only honest and dishonest ones. The coachee is not meant to answer questions from the perspective of the coach – as is often the case in education – but from his/her own perspective (Whitmore, 2003).

Purpose of Questions in GFC

In developmental or therapeutic paradigms of coaching, attaining knowledge is a key objective, and questions are therefore designed to generate maximum insight. By contrast, in a goal-focused paradigm generating insight is less important; the main priority is ensuring greater clarity in relation to goals. Rather than stimulating sudden flashes or perceptual reorganisations, questions in GFC aim to facilitate an increasingly effective analysis of the coachee's situation and an increasingly improving conception of how to proceed.

Questions arise because there is a gap between the need for clarity and the present state of uncertainty. However, the question arises not necessarily because the coachee senses a lack of knowledge that triggers a query, but because the coach looks to extend the coachee's cognition by bringing into consideration issues to which the coachee may not have given conscious thought. The state of 'ignorance' that the question seeks to address may not have been experienced by the coachee until the question was raised. For this reason, many coaching texts refer to the coaching as 'stretching' the coachee and expanding the coachee's horizons (Grant, 2006; O'Neil, 2007). In coaching, this 'stretching' is largely attained through the use of questions, which it is argued stimulate creative thinking and open the mind to new ideas (Whitmore, 2003).

For the GFC coach, though, questions are also the scaffold upon which to build the coaching dialogue. Some questions (particularly small questions) act as starting points – they are heuristic guides. In successful coaching new questions are generated from these original questions. Coaches use the development of their own understanding of the goal through a series of questions in order to help the coachee rethink their understanding. Thus, the coach sublimates his or her own curiosity to focus entirely on the needs of the coachee and the achievement of the coaching goal.

Asking a question is therefore always a response to an unrequited desire for knowledge about the goal, with questions generating further questions providing new opportunities for the coach to help the coachee put together his or her picture of reality and map out a new picture. Too much knowledge might hinder questioning, but having no knowledge might also hinder questioning. Adopting the mindset of an inquisitive and curious learner is necessary to ensure that vital exploration is not undermined through assumptions made by the coach. It should be noted, however, that in GFC, a position of ignorance is maintained not primarily to encourage the coach to reflect, but to avoid overlooking key considerations that could turn out to be important for helping the coachee to successfully reach his or her goals. In GFC, the coach asks, "What does the coachee need to know, consider or address to be able to effectively set and attain the goal?"

In GFC, knowledge is, as said, largely the pursuit of clarity and we would argue that the power of effective questions lies in their clarity-inducing abilities. For example, a coachee once said: "I'm pleased you asked that, as it could have come back to bite me." This is a more typical response to a GFC question than, say, "Wow, that question has really got me thinking." De Haan (2008) further distinguishes between types of questions: 'what' type questions, which are technical or objective in nature and can be supplied by a mentor or expert; 'how' type questions that address the application of skills to specific situations, which is the main domain of coaching; and 'who' type questions, which deal with the personality of the individual. GFC focuses on the 'what' and the 'how' type questions in order to promote clarity.

The mind works as a neural network in which connections are formed and reinforced to create consistent patterns of behaviour (Mischel & Ayduk, 2007). The network is the product of the person's genetic endowment and biological history combined with their social learning experiences. It is the bias inherent in this network that results in predictable behaviour. Questions can play a role in completing missing connections, or reinforcing helpful ones, thereby ensuring that the mind has drawn together vital pieces of the information and impulses necessary to work cohesively to achieve beneficial goals. The goal-focused coach uses questions to draw attention to elements of the neural network that may otherwise be overlooked, and may result in conflicting goals or internal conflict due to a lack of concordance.

Types of Questions

Whitmore (2003) argues that the context of questioning is awareness and responsibility. A question compels the person being asked to pay attention in order to be able to answer, thus generating awareness. This means that the objective of questioning is to create awareness and inspire ownership of the problem. A salient aspect of GFC is the way that questions are used not to gain information, but to prompt thought and action. The coach needs to maximise the thought-provoking qualities of a question and avoid questions that deprive the coachee of the full benefit of asking. As Fisher and Ury (1991 p. 56) argue, "statements generate resistance, whereas questions generate answers. Questions allow the other side to get their point across and let you understand them [...] Questions offer them no target to strike at, no position to attack." Similarly, Bramson (1984 p. 101) notes that by using a question format, problems are presented as "new information to be considered and not as an attack."

In our view, there are four main criteria for GFC questions:

- They are simple
- They are open
- They are challenging
- They do not lead.

In GFC, questions should be brief and to the point. Long-winded or multi-part questions confuse, and the coachee will often struggle to remember the first part of the question. There is no need to cram lots of issues into a single question; the coach can ask several smaller questions instead. Questions should also be specific. Specific questions attract a fuller, more detailed response and generate a higher level of attention, because they require an accurate answer. Telling people what to look for is not nearly as effective as asking them a question about what it is they really need to pay attention to. Leading questions, it could be argued, are not really questions at all. Rhetorical in nature, they invite a particular type of 'answer'; the expected response is written into the question. Questions like "I suppose you're sorry now?" or "Would you agree that now is not the best time to be changing jobs?" leave the coachee having to decide whether to openly disagree with the coach, rather than give unbiased consideration to the matter at hand. For this reason, leading questions are widely acknowledged to be totally inappropriate in coaching (Nicholson, Bayne & Owen, 2006; Hawkins & Smith, 2010).

One of the more challenging aspects of questioning is the use of open or closed questions, which we now discuss.

Open and Closed Questions – Questions must have empowering and awareness-raising qualities in order to be effective. As Whitmore (2003 p. 44) suggests, "telling, or asking closed questions, saves people from having to think; asking open questions causes them to think for themselves." Open questions provoke fuller responses and exploration of the issues and, importantly in coaching, allow for a follow-up question. They are better at raising the all-important awareness and responsibility. Conversely, asking a closed question will elicit a yes or no answer, or even a defensive answer if the coachee feels threatened. "Are there any problems?" prompts a yes or no answer. "What other problems may there be?" calls for more thought. Questions that begin with 'do,' 'have,' 'has,' 'is' and 'are' tend to produce closed questions, whereas questions that begin with 'who,' 'what,' 'when,' 'how' and 'where' tend to produce open questions. Openings such as 'tell me' or 'describe to me' also prompt fuller answers. Typically, the coaching questions that work best begin with 'what' and are succinct. Closed questions require recall of fact, experience or expected behaviour, and so prompt a decision between a limited selection of choices and no response at all. By contrast, open-ended questions encourage speculation and trial and error, and offer potential for sustained, shared thinking and talking.

However, before coachees feel able to answer an open question, for example, "What's important to you about ...?" they need to perceive the coach as trustworthy. Only when trust has been established can the coach use open questions to maximum effect. Trust is established not through asking the right questions as much as through practicing effective listening, a topic that we address later in this chapter.

Graesser, Person and Magliano (1995 p. 511) propose six types of questions that are particularly suited to GFC, as they are focused on the clarification of information and lead to effective decision making:

(1) Antecedent questions ('why?', 'how?') What caused an event? What logically explains or justifies a proposition? These questions need to be used cautiously in coaching since exploring causation or justifying actions can frequently be non-productive.

(2) Consequence questions ('what if?', 'what next?') What are the causal consequences of a state or event? What are the logical consequences of a proposition? These are useful questions to use both retrospectively and hypothetically.

(3) Goal orientation ('why?') What are the goals or motives behind certain actions? Looking at motivation for the task is useful at various points in the alliance, as it allows coachees to revisit their original impetus in the light of ongoing learning and change.

(4) Enablement ('why?', 'how?') What object, state or resource allows an agent to perform an action? What state or event allows another state or event to occur?

(5) Instrumental-procedural ('how?') What instrument or plan allows an agent to accomplish a goal?

(6) Expectational ('why not?') Why did an expected state or event not occur? Why didn't an agent do something? This use of the 'why?' question may sound accusational, and should therefore be used carefully.

Included in this typology is the 'why' question. Some coaches (Berg & Szabo, 2005; Brockbank & McGill, 2006; Nicholson et al., 2006) have cautioned against the use of questions that commence with 'why?', as they are said to trigger defensiveness. In trying to answer such a question the coachee tries to justify the problem or behaviour with the effect of possibly reifying it. According to Sintonen (2004), 'why?' questions indicate that questioners' expectations have been disappointed in some way.

However, understanding the reasons behind actions is a relevant tack to take, particularly in goal-focused coaching, as the cause and the possible assumptions underpinning the cause often need to be uncovered. A 'why' question reaches the 'heart' of the answer – pulling out the true goal/value from the coachee, whereas a less penetrating question may result merely in a list of preconditions for the goal, rather than shedding light on the goal. The 'why' question uncovers 'strategic principles'; it may be better to ask "Why have you come to coaching?" rather than "What do you want to achieve through the coaching?" Similarly, when trying to understand underlying motives it may be useful to ask, "Why does this matter?" In a therapeutic coaching paradigm, it is more understandable that coaches would be apprehensive about asking a question beginning with 'why,' as the coaching style is less penetrating and more exploratory. However, with GFC we would suggest that the concern with 'why' questions is somewhat exaggerated.

Choice of questions must also be guided by the stage in the coaching process. So, for example, in the GROW model (Alexander, 2006) reality questions need to generate objective facts, and therefore need to generate answers that are descriptive rather than evaluative, such as "What would you say is missing at the moment?" By contrast, questions in the options stage need to be upbeat and creative in order to inspire a dynamic problem solving work mode. So for example, "What could you do to move yourself forward just one step right now?" will help to shrug off coachee apathy. An important feeling that needs to be conveyed is a sense of trust and acceptance. By asking, for example, "What could you do if you didn't have to explain what you were doing or be answerable to anyone?" encourages coachees to feel that they are entitled to their opinion and go a long way towards providing a secure environment for productive work to be done. By contrast, the 'will' stage must ensure that ideas are acted upon, so questions need to be action oriented. Thus, a typical 'will' question would be, "What are you going to do?" or "Which of these alternatives are you going to act on?" Questions at this stage must tie the coachee down to a specific time, and intervals between actions should also be set. Thus closed questions can be used for closing down actions, as what is needed is a definite yes or no or a concrete date, time, and so forth.

Factual and conceptual questions – We suggest that when considering questions in GFC, it is helpful to distinguish between factual and conceptual questions. Factual questions seek to collate relevant information, often stored deep in the coachee's memory. These questions can often be probing and challenging, as they are asking coachees to draw deeply on the inner recesses of the mind to recall rarely accessed data about themselves or their environment. For example, the coach may ask "What event in your life made you feel most alive?" This is a question that does not get asked on a day-to-day basis, and may require some serious thought and reflection. Higher order memory processes are needed to answer them (Munch & Swasy, 1983). However, it is still fundamentally a factual question, seeking to gain as much useful information as possible for both coachee and the coach to use in plotting a future course of action.

This type of question is referred to by Tomm (1988) as a 'lineal question,' which seeks clearly defined causes of explanations of actions, events or feelings. More than in other coaching paradigms, lineal questions are a central feature of GFC. Lineal questions are useful for extracting information, but because the questioner is overtly directing them, the answers are reactive. Factual questions also include what Tomm terms 'circular' questions, which while aiming to gather information are more exploratory. They assume that everything is connected and so aim to reveal recurring patterns rather than lineal causality. They involve a more systemic approach, by drawing in information from a variety of angles or the perceptions of a wider range of participants, such as asking about the views of other work colleagues.

Significantly, because these questions seek clarity, lineal questioning might also include a number of closed questions. For the same reason selective use of 'why' questions may also be necessary, to enable the coach to clarify a chain of events relevant to understanding the coachee's situation.

By contrast, conceptual questions are largely creative and call upon the coachee to imagine possibilities that are not currently a reality. For example, a coach may ask, "What do you think would happen if you stood up for yourself?" Here, the coachee is being asked to 'speculate' on the likely reaction to a course of action, which cannot be answered purely factually. Another example may be, "How do you think you'll feel if you were to cancel your holiday?" Here, again, to answer this question the coachee needs to make an assessment of the most likely outcome, even if the assessment is based on how he or she has handled such things in the past. A final example: a coach may ask the coachee, "What obstacles might you meet along the way?" This question would be asked to pre-empt the possibility of obstacles, both internal and external, from impeding progress. The coach needs to understand that the coachee cannot defend his or her assertions on such questions in the same way that is possible for factual questions. Therefore, it would typically be inappropriate during this line of questioning to ask closed questions, as they require a level of definitiveness that is not expected when considering future outcomes. Similarly, greater care should be given to using 'why' questions when addressing more conceptual issues, so as not to discourage the coach from sharing her or his 'guesswork' about the situation.

In Tomm's (1988) classification, 'strategic' questions build on the information revealed by answers to lineal or circular questions. Questions such as "What would happen if you stood your ground?" or "Who do you think would back you?" are strategic, as they seek to generate predictions to aid planning a future course of action. Tomm suggests that strategic questions are useful when the process becomes stuck.

More conceptual still are what Tomm calls 'reflexive' questions, which marshal the coachee's problem solving resources. Reflexive questions allow coachees to reframe their thoughts by reflecting on beliefs, asking questions of themselves and making new connections. In GFC, reflexive questions are used to help ensure that the goal is concordant with the coachee's core interests or values, or to check that the coachee has the internal resources to implement a particular course of action. They are not typically deployed in the therapeutic sense of exploring inner feelings and sensitive psychological concerns.

An additional approach is to ask incisive questions that encourage creative thinking when the coachee is stuck, since when trying to get someone to consider a new idea, there is often the danger that it will be vehemently rejected as unworkable. Bramson (1984 p. 123) suggests the use of what he terms 'detours' that suspend the negative view for long enough for the positive view to avoid suffocation. An example of creating a detour in a coaching scenario is to say, for example: "I realise that this probably won't be what we'll end up with, but could we take a few minutes to see if there may be anything useful there at all?" Incisive questions ask the coachee to suspend judgement and to think uninhibitedly.

According to Tomm's (1988) theory, lineal and circular questions have an orienting purpose, whereas strategic and reflexive questions have a more influencing purpose, which fits our framework of distinguishing between factual and conceptual questions.

Listening

Many coaching texts emphasise the necessity of good listening skills, describing how they help to build trust and rapport between coach and coachee (Rogers,

2008; Skiffington & Zeus, 2003). Goleman (1998 p. 140), talking about the development of emotional intelligence, also states that "those who cannot or do not listen come across as indifferent or uncaring, which in turn makes others less communicative." In this section, we want to explore what listening in coaching actually achieves and, more specifically, what its role is in a GFC context.

We want to argue that the beginning of listening is silence. If we are talking, we cannot listen properly. Listening can only occur in a vacuum, a vacant and inviting space for the other to be heard, what Berg and Szabo (2005 p. 74) call "the power of silence." Silence, however, means more than not speaking. The 'noise' in the coach's head can as effectively block out external stimuli as can the noise omitted by his or her mouth. Effective listening, as opposed to more casual hearing, is about emptying the mind when speaking to others to allow sufficient concentration on what they are saying. To be properly focused on the coachee, the coach needs to put aside his or her own thoughts – whether serious or trivial. When the coachee is talking the coach should not, for example, be thinking of the next question instead of paying attention to the coachee. Similarly, when the issue at hand is one the coach has experience of, the coach needs to remember: "This is not my issue" or "Concentrate on the coachee." Greene and Grant (2003) argue that the coach should be listening 70% to 80% of the time. These admonitions are standard across all forms of coaching, and GFC is no exception.

So listening requires emptying the mind of all thoughts, and surrendering the mind solely to absorbing the gift of speech from the coachee. Often when we listen, we are actually listening to ourselves – to our inner dialogue, our response to what is being said, rather than what we are actually being told. We often verbally, or at least mentally, finish another's sentence. The coach needs to adopt a posture of 'not knowing' (Anderson & Goolishian, 1992), in recognition of the reality that the coach does not know what the coachee is thinking or what is best for him or her. In coaching, we have to imagine that we really do not know anything (which is all too often the case): only through listening can the coach gain the knowledge and understanding of the coachee.

Thus, a vital part of listening is silence. Not just silence when the coachee is talking, however. Coaches need to cope with long pauses and resist the temptation to break the silence; Greene and Grant (2003 p. 128) urge the coach to "hold the silence." If unsure whether the coachee needs explanation, the coach should ask rather than rush in. This gives the coachee the time to reflect and dig deeper for fuller and more meaningful answers. Not rushing the coachee has the added benefit of making the coachee feel relaxed and accepted. When looking to obtain an honest answer from a coachee, silence is also one of the best weapons, according to negotiating experts Fisher and Ury (1991 p. 112):

> The best thing to do is sit there and not say a word. If you have asked an honest question to which they have provided an insufficient answer, just wait. People tend to feel uncomfortable with silence, particularly if they have doubts about the merits of something they have said.

So GFC coaches need to ask a question but not hasten to break the silence.

However, there are also levels of listening, mostly distinguished by what the coach is listening to. Whitworth et al. (2007 pp. 34–39) identify three incremental levels of listening:

(1) 'Internal' listening is concerned with the content of speech and what it means to us personally. In coaching, this may mean the coach is listening to inform what he or she is going to ask next.
(2) 'Focused' listening, in which the focus is totally on the coachee. The listener will act like a mirror, reflecting back what comes from the coachee, but also maintaining an awareness of the impact the listening is having on the coachee. Whitworth et al. also suggest that at this level "the mind chatter virtually disappears" (p. 36) in order to facilitate complete focus on the coachee.
(3) 'Global' listening, which involves "noticing the temperature, the energy level, the lightness or darkness" (p. 39), and also the use of intuition.

Typically, GFC only requires focused listening, although clearly the more profoundly the coach listens, the better.

Hawkins and Schwenk (2010 p. 208) also list four increasing levels of listening, which have some overlap with the levels described by Whitworth et al. (2007): attending, accurate listening, empathic listening and generative empathic listening. In GFC, only the first two of these aspects of listening are truly essential, although again it is not possible to listen too well. In our view, GFC does not require "deep generative listening" (Drake, 2010 p. 126), but prioritises the need to listen accurately to ensure effective communication.

Pemberton (2006 p. 74) distinguishes between type A and type B listening. Type A listening is "where the listener signals that they are giving the other person their full attention." By contrast, type B listening "is focused on understanding what extra information the other person holds that could be helpful to the conversation, which they may not articulate" (p. 82). In type B listening, the focus shifts from understanding content to such areas as emotions, personality and beliefs. In goal-focused coaching, more emphasis is placed on type A listening and, in particular, on ensuring complete and detailed responses from the coachee.

Active and Holistic Listening

Listening alone, however intently, is insufficient. By truly listening, the coach gains maximum insight into the thoughts of the coachee, but the coachee does not necessarily experience fully the experience of being 'listened to.' Active listening, on the other hand, is primarily about taking active measures to ensure that the coachee knows that he or she is being listened to, and feels that the coach values the listening experience. Brockbank and McGill (2006 p. 177) say that active listening means making the coachee aware of the listening. We therefore suggest that active listening means ensuring that the coachee does in fact feel listened to.

Active listening has two main features. First, it involves adopting postures and making gestures that demonstrate that we as listeners are fully engaged – what Hawkins and Schwenk (2010 p. 208) term 'attending.' Drake (2010 p. 126) describes such listening as "a method of change," in which listening and being listened to becomes the experience. When coaching in person, this means demonstrating a high level of interest in what the coachee is saying through appropriate eye contact, through focused attention, and through verbal and hand gestures that encourage open communication.

The second aspect of active listening is ensuring that we have been listening correctly, that we understand the message of the coachee. To be certain of this, it is necessary to summarise and reflect back to the coachee (Cox, 2012c). For example, if the coach asks: "Am I right in thinking that…?" it also ensures that the coachee feels understood. The coach therefore needs to display what Mason (2005) terms 'authoritative doubt,' which involves taking the risk of venturing an interpretation of the coachee's words while leaving it wide open for the coachee to correct or clarify.

Actively listening in this way ensures that the coach understands what is being said and simultaneously ensures that the coachee feels understood (Bramson, 1984). The aim is to test listeners' understandings of their message and arrive at mutual understanding. Goleman (1998 p. 141) summarises active listening as "going beyond what is said by asking questions, restating in one's own words what you hear to be sure you understand." Similarly, according to Collins and O'Rourke (2008 p. 10), active listeners ask questions in order to clarify understanding: "they reflect their interpretations of what's being said back to the speaker so that the speaker feels heard and has a chance to correct misunderstandings". Passmore and Whybrow (2007 p. 165) refer to this latter element as 'reflective listening' where "the coach checks, rather than assumes, the meaning of what the coachee has said."

In addition to listening gestures and paraphrasing, an effective goal-focused coach will take a broader view of what is going on with the coachee. We term this 'holistic listening.' This involves looking out for verbal and non-verbal clues, so, for example, a coach needs to be alert for changes in tone and language patterns: a monotone may indicate repetition of old ideas, excitement usually suggests the emergence of a new idea, negative terms indicate disbelief, while childish language could mean lack of confidence. Patterns of speech or throwaway lines often reveal a great deal about the coachee's state of mind. Body language is also a good indicator and is a more reliable source of information about how coachees are feeling than possibly their words. Furthermore, the coach needs to listen to the surrounding issues that may appear irrelevant to the coaching, for example that "the commitment the person makes in coaching has to fit into the whole array of commitment she is already in the middle of fulfilling" (Flaherty, 2005 p. 120).

When coaching on the telephone, some of these options are not available, which put an even greater onus on verbal cues. If the coachee has to ask, "Are you still there?" then the coach has failed to listen sufficiently actively. Grant and Cavanagh (2010) suggest that phone coaching can be effective, as in a paradoxical way it drives the coach to listen even more intently. Our own experience as coaches, and the information we have received from coachees, suggests that this is indeed the case.

Gaining an understanding of the coachee involves listening closely to what is being said. But it is as much about listening for what is not being said. Collins and O'Rourke (2008) describe active (in our definition, holistic) listening as requiring engagement and an understanding of the underlying emotions behind what the speaker is trying to say. It is also about drawing conclusions about what the speaker is not explicitly stating. Going a step further, Whitworth et al. (2007 pp. 32–33) describe active listening as "clarifying what the other person says, noticing body language, increasing […] awareness of the feeling behind the words, and sharpening […] sensitivity to the context of the conversation."

The main function of active listening can be viewed as a way in which to generate trust, understanding and the feeling of being heard (Myers, 2000). It is therefore surprising that Hawkins and Smith (2010 p. 238) suggest that active listening means "interrupting the pattern of delivery" to offer an alternative perspective. As a non-directive approach to coaching, in which the coach manages the process but not the content of the coaching, such an approach to listening would be alien and counterproductive.

Some authors emphasise the need for an entirely new level of listening, often referred to as empathetic listening. However, although it may be useful in the counselling or therapy relationship, empathic listening has, we would argue, limited utility in coaching. For GFC, in particular, this kind of listening is inappropriate. The purpose of GFC is not to gain an understanding of the coachee, but to help the coachee progress towards goals. It may be further argued that insofar as empathetic listening is designed to garner insight into the psychological state of mind of the coachee, it is unsuited for any form of coaching that is not intended to achieve a diagnosis of the coachee. GFC has as its priority the understanding of the task and how it may be best achieved. To fulfil this role, it is necessary to understand the coachee's perspective, but not to turn understanding of the coachee into a primary aim.

Hawkins and Schwenk (2010 p. 206) argue that "it is important that the coach lets the coachee know that they have not only heard the story, but have also 'got' what it feels like to be in their situation." Besides it being questionable for a coach to ever claim to truly know what it feels like to be in the coachee's position, this level of empathy is not required in GFC, and is a distraction from the main objective – namely, ensuring that the information shared is suitable for achieving a positive outcome.

Summary

To conclude this chapter we would add that 'active listening' should incorporate encouragement and motivation of the coachee. There are numerous approaches to fostering enthusiasm or determination in the coachee, but fundamentally the coach needs to exude a spirit of positivity and confidence in the coachee. We noted earlier that the coach needs to adopt a stance of 'authoritative doubt,' but in GFC it is equally important that the coach displays what we term 'authoritative belief,' namely presenting a high level of confidence in the potential of the coachee, to support the possibility of identifying a suitable solution and in overcoming likely obstacles.

However, the 'authoritative belief' should be tempered by 'authoritative doubt,' such that the coach does not saddle the coachee with his or her belief in what is possible when the coachee is convinced it is not. For example, a coach may say, "You've overcome a much greater challenge last year, so you have proven what you are capable of. How do you think your department could handle the restructuring?" If the coachee expresses self-doubt about his or her ability to execute a particular strategy, the coach may respond, "I can see that this is going to be challenging and I can see why you doubt this, but are you underestimating your abilities? Can we have another look at this?"

12   The Complete GFC Process

Aims

*   To highlight the key GFC-related issues addressed in this book;
*   To present a new 20-part map of the complete goal-focused process with commentary and advice on each stage;
*   To provide examples of where GFC may be applied in practice.

In this chapter, we first highlight some key issues in relation to GFC that have been addressed in previous chapters of this book. In section two, we present the complete cycle of GFC in the form of a process map. At the end of the chapter, by way of conclusion, we outline four areas where GFC has recently been applied.

Key Issues in GFC

GFC is coaching-centred around facilitating effective goal pursuit, and the focus is on practical issues. However, while GFC is comparatively less coach- and relationship-centric, it still relies heavily on the role of the coach, and is underpinned by the coaching relationship. Additionally, the coachee's relationship with the coaching itself is of equal importance to the relationship with the coach.

Consequently, GFC should not focus so heavily on the core goal-related activity that it ignores the contextual issues that can present barriers to coaching. Where the coachee's personal or organisational life is in turmoil, it is unrealistic to jump right into goal-focused work. It is incorrect to separate the goal-activity part of the coaching from its relationship aspects, as a significant part of the coaching may be unavoidably consumed by these latter issues.

Coaching Formats

On occasions, individual coaching requires expansion to involve other key stake-holders, as individual coaching alone may not be effective. Group coaching may be the only realistic approach when the individual goals of members of a single organisation overlap or are intertwined, or if important tasks require a combined effort. However, group coaching may be unable to address individual needs, in which case the group coaching should be supplemented by individual coaching. Furthermore, group coaching is best suited for the earlier stages of goal setting and action planning, but as the plan becomes more specific it will need to be tailored to the circumstances and needs of the individual.

Significantly, managing the group dynamic is central to this coaching format, and it is essential to acknowledge interpersonal relations within the group. GFC poses particular challenges to relationship management. Coachees' diverse needs, the conflicting interests of the group and individuals, and the tendency for social loafing, may all hinder the formation of group goals. It is therefore necessary to dedicate ample time to establishing an effective working relationship for group coaching to be effective.

Peer coaching is even more problematic, for often in practice the peers will not take to peer coaching and will not support each other with their individual tasks. Even if the coachee has experience of peer learning, and despite significant experience of coaching, the coachee may still not feel sufficiently confident to practice coaching. For peer coaching to succeed, the coachees will require ample training in coaching skills and preparation for a coaching orientation. Furthermore, it must be embraced willingly by those involved, and should only be attempted where the resources to make it a success are securely in place.

Coaching in Challenging Situations

Coaching can succeed under unusually challenging conditions. The coaching context may be characterised by distrust and frustration, or the coachee may be quite unclear about what he or she is aiming for or how to achieve it, or may display a highly dependent attitude. However, while such problems will divert a large amount of coaching time to address, fortunately they do not need to prevent the coaching from progressing.

Significant efforts may need to be expended addressing what we have termed 'barriers to coaching.' The coachee may be fearful and suspicious about the impact coaching can have on them, by transferring pressure from the organisation onto them. They may be resentful at the unfulfilled promises by their organisation and reluctant to assume greater responsibility for their own development. Understandably, coachees may be despondent and apathetic. Goal work will only take off properly once these issues are addressed.

However, a challenging environment is not necessarily a threat to coaching. Solutions do not have to be perfect for the coachee to be willing to commit to them, as long as he or she is convinced that it was the best available option. Moreover, problems are to be considered normal in coaching, as new challenges can provoke new problems that shift the coachee to a new level of activity. In fact, advancement in coaching often entails progressing from one level of problem to another. In particular from a goal-focused perspective, coaching facilitates progress through various levels of goal pursuit, each requiring attention to the potential problems posed at that stage. Coaching should therefore not be presented as the ultimate solving of a problem.

Role of GFC

Through an integration of self-regulation, social cognitive and goal theories, we suggest that GFC can play an important role in the vital intersection between the social and cognitive antecedents of human activity, and the goal choices and activities that are their consequences. As described in Chapter 3, GFC is positioned as a tool for enhancing self-regulation by facilitating effective goal choices and self-regulation strategies. Real-life experiences exert the largest influence on attributions, and these in turn influence expectancies, most notably self-efficacy beliefs, that guide goal choice and self-regulatory activity. Where there has been failure or limited past success, the person becomes trapped in a cycle of poor performance and results that maintain low self-belief and motivation.

Thus, GFC is conceived as contributing to raising self-efficacy through engendering the pursuit of stretching but realistic goals that, once attained, result in improved self-concept. The role of GFC is to help the person break that cycle by setting and attaining challenging goals that create empowering antecedents that lead to adaptive attributions, and positive expectancies that sustain effective goal choices for the future. In GFC, focusing on goal-directed practical actions is the primary method of raising motivation and self-responsibility. GFC resists the temptation to delve deeply into issues about negative beliefs or low self-concept. Rather, the coach encourages the coachee to take small steps regardless of whether the coachee is experiencing self-doubt.

With GFC, crafting the goal is essential and is the main role of the coach; profound and comprehensive knowledge of this function is crucial. GFC should facilitate an ongoing process of discrepancy production and reduction, rather than a response to a particular deficiency. However, GFC does not take a highly holistic approach to addressing the full range of the issues in the coachee's life and does not aim directly to alter people's mindsets, but rather focuses on stimulating effective action and integrating that into concrete goals and tasks. GFC seeks to raise performance by focusing on the individual's situated, immediate, conscious, personal goals, rather than the underlying self-concept or psychodynamic causes of behaviour. It is 'coaching in action' (Duignan, 2007). This type of coaching is compatible with an adult-learning approach of 'learning through doing' (Caroll & Bandura, 1990; Knowles, 1984), where learning is linked to tasks. GFC is therefore unsuited for situations requiring personal transformation, as it is neither therapeutic nor focused on personal development.

Goal-related Activity

GFC is fundamentally goal-driven, and must take a broad and flexible approach in accordance with the requirement of the goal. In order to achieve its objectives, the coachees may need to make adjustments to their expected course action. Coachees will need to closely review their options to select the path most suited to the goal in question. Additionally, coachees may need to seek task-related assistance, if this is what the goal requires.

There is a conceptual and practical distinction between goal setting and action planning in GFC. These are two interrelated but fundamentally separate activities, dealing with goals at varying levels of the self-regulatory hierarchy, driven by differing types of motivation, and typically function best on divergent modes of consciousness.

Goal setting is a cognitively demanding activity when it seeks to manage the superordinate long-term goals, which need to be carefully configured to provide the requisite focus, commitment and motivation. By contrast, action planning addresses subordinate short-term goals, and is part of an ongoing process that needs to adjust to unfolding circumstantial changes, and may often occur below conscious awareness.

Goal setting is an iterative process, in which it may be necessary to first identify a general, fuzzy goal, followed by the precise, clear goal vital to guide future activity. The coach must aid the coachee to set the right combination of distal and proximal goals, strike a suitable balance of difficult but attainable goals, and ensure goals are clear and specific. In relation to action planning, the coach needs to help the coachee to break down the goal into manageable chunks that can be implemented without excessive deliberation, and must be tailored to the coachee's specific challenges and needs.

Goal setting must always be a conscious decision to ensure that the decision is not unduly influenced by dominant but maladaptive motives. Furthermore, periodic moments of self-awareness are crucial to check information is being correctly assessed. Additionally, planning the path to the goal must also be a conscious process, unless effective and well-learned habits exist or are activated.

GFC needs to manage both attentional and self-regulatory resources. Consequently, the role of planning in GFC is to relegate planned activity to automatic mode, conserving resources for higher order issues. Nevertheless, it must also help coachees to ensure cool, clear thinking when significant decisions are required, especially on occasions of heightened emotional arousal.

Motivation in GFC

Motivation activity in GFC is not a specific stage in a highly structured process, but an iterative and fluid element of the coaching. GFC needs to stimulate positive, practical actions as early as possible, which helps to secure buy-in to coaching, as a prerequisite to goal-focused activity. Focusing on practical steps reduces anxiety, makes the task seem more manageable, and leads to greater acceptance of responsibility. Practical goals direct attention towards what is attainable and its potential benefit, which engenders in the coachee a greater willingness to cooperate.

It is suggested that the motivation work in GFC functions on five levels:

(1) Before goal activity can commence in earnest, it is vital to establish engagement with and commitment to the coaching process.
(2) The act of goal-setting makes tasks more motivational. Moreover, setting an effective goal contributes significantly to the motivational impact of the goal,

and participation in goal setting helps to ensure suitability of and commitment to the goal.

(3) Creating a detailed action plan and generating effective goal strategies enhances self-efficacy, thereby increasing volitional strength for the execution of the goal.

(4) With a goal and plan in place, it is necessary to generate increased motivation and commitment to implement it. Asking the coachee to identify the benefits deriving from the goal and to articulate commitment were found to be effective in securing short-term motivation and commitment.

(5) Maintaining ongoing commitment derives from monitoring progress and periodic awareness of the end goal.

While having an intrinsic source of motivation may bring certain benefits, it is often not realistic, as the need for engagement is often not matched by intrinsic interest. However, it is essential that the goal is perceived to be concordant with a coachee's values and sense of purpose. Where goals have an external origin or locus of control, the coach should help the coachee to 'identify' the valued outcomes thereof. This will enable to coachee to undergo the process of internalisation that will foster long-term motivation. GFC should facilitate structured autonomy, rendering extrinsic tasks more motivationally sustainable through clarifying the reasons that a task is important and meaningful.

The GFC Process

We now describe a complete 20-part model of GFC. The process is illustrated in Figure 12.1, which sets out both the stages and key issues in relation to each stage, although it should be noted that not all these stages will always be necessary.

(1) *Opening for coaching* – Coaching depends on an opening (Flaherty, 2005), which is more than just an acknowledgment from the coaches that there is a need, but an acknowledgement that coaching offers a potential solution. Securing the coachee's acceptance that the coaching could be helpful is vital.

(2) *Resolve misconceptions* – Coachees may have their own wishes or presumptions and may ignore the declared purpose of coaching. Coaches need to ask coachees for their perspective to check that the coach's role is that of a facilitator rather than provider of advice.

(3) *Overcome suspicion* – The coach's independence may be crucial to the development of trust, especially as coachees could perceive the coaching as an instrument to cause them harm. It helps to maintain clear coaching boundaries and defend your own independence and that of the coaching.

(4) *Deal with resentment* – Trying to change a coachee's negative view of the situation may be inappropriate. Concentrating on what could yet be done, rather than focusing on what cannot be easily changed, mitigates criticism and complaining.

(5) *Alter dependence* – GFC is a non-directive hands-off approach. Securing

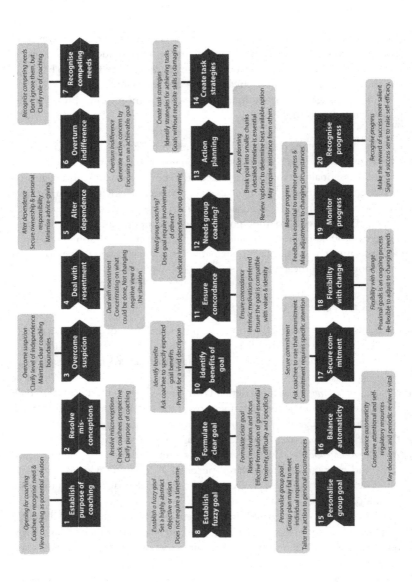

Figure 12.1 Complete GFC Coaching Process

acceptance of ownership and personal responsibility can consume significant time. Coachees with a tendency for dependency may seek to lean on the coach; however, increasing the independence of the coachee is essential to coaching.

(6) *Overturn indifference* – Under highly challenging conditions, the coachee is particularly prone to despair and may see no point in the coaching. The coach needs to help the coachee to transition from a stance of indifference to one of active concern, in particular by focusing on an achievable goal.

(7) *Recognize competing needs* – Where there are other needs, the coach cannot ignore them, but must clarify his/her position in relation to them. The coach should pre-empt the issue by clarifying the boundaries of coaching, but resist requests for direct intervention.

(8) *Establish a fuzzy goal* – It may be necessary to set a highly abstract objective, as a prerequisite to setting a more concrete goal. This high-level goal, we suggest, does not require a timeframe, for its purpose is to set out a vision.

(9) *Formulate clear goal* – In research, a clear goal was shown to raise motivation and focus. In GFC the form the goal takes is crucial. This requires a carefully considered long-term objective that is challenging but attainable and well-defined.

(10) *Identify benefits* – At this stage the goal may seem intimidating, so it may be beneficial to ask the coachee to specify the expected benefits of achieving the goal, which raises motivation in the short-term to propel the coachee forward.

(11) *Ensure concordance* – If coachees lack intrinsic interest, it may reduce their enthusiasm for the goal, but a goal that conflicts with the coachees' key values and sense of identity is usually harmful. Thus, it is vital to ensure that the coachee is concordant with the goal.

(12) *Need group coaching?* – Some goals cannot be realistically achieved as an individual goal and may require the involvement of other stakeholders. In such instances, it is necessary to dedicate enough time to establishing an interdependent dynamic for group coaching to be effective.

(13) *Action planning* – Reducing the goal into smaller chunks with a detailed timeline is essential to GFC. It may be necessary to review 'options' to determine the best available method. An action plan must address the coachee's specific challenges. Implementation may require assistance from others, which the coachee may need support in seeking.

(14) *Create task strategies* – The action planning process is likely to involve identifying strategies for achieving the coachees' tasks. For complex tasks this may require exploring unfamiliar strategies, as goals without requisite skills will falter.

(15) *Personalise group goal* – Although group coaching should ideally balance the needs of the group and the individual, these are sometimes incompatible. Thus, goals set in a group may require a tailored action plan adjusted to the circumstances and needs of the individual coachee.

(16) *Balance automaticity* – To conserve attentional and self-regulatory resources it

is beneficial to plan tasks in detail and allow them to proceed to the extent possible without conscious deliberation. However, conscious reflection on key decisions and periodic review is vital to ensure that the coachee remains on track.

(17) *Secure commitment* – Fulsome commitment will typically only be possible after a plan is in place and goal fulfilment seems attainable. Asking the coachees to rate their commitment has some impact. Commitment may not automatically rise through coaching (Moen & Skaalvik, 2009), suggesting that it requires specific attention.

(18) *Flexibility with change* – Unlike the distal goal, proximal goals (action planning) should be set on an ongoing basis, near to the time of their implementation, and must be flexible to adjust to changing needs.

(19) *Monitor progress* – Knowledge of results or feedback is essential to GFC, as this enables coachees to make adjustments to the goal or the action plan in light of the impact of their actions or in face of changing circumstances.

(20) *Recognize progress* – Advancement towards the goal is itself motivational, as it makes the reward of success more salient. Moreover, signs of success serve to raise self-efficacy.

The process just described is best suited for complex goals and in particular to challenging circumstances. According to the process map presented in Chapter 1 (Figure 1.1), the core functions of GFC are setting clear goals, putting in place a detailed action plan, and ensuring commitment to the goal. However, where the goal is perceived as highly demanding and, in particular, where organisational relations are fraught, it is necessary to address a wider range of issues for successful GFC.

Four Applications of GFC

To illustrate the diverse utility of GFC, we describe here four settings in which we have applied this approach.

Helping Singles

Being single is a prevalent and growing issue, with many people struggling to form and sustain lasting relationships, despite significant effort. For the many who want to be in a relationship, often desperately so, failure to achieve this is a cause of great frustration and distress. Our experience suggests that the main reason is not the lack of opportunity to meet people, but has more to do with outmoded behaviours and perspectives. Many young professionals, for instance, have formed views of life that get in the way of relationship success. Additionally, it would seem that many young people are bringing poor awareness of who they are, what they want out of a relationship and what it means to be in one – inadequacies that wreak havoc in their romantic lives.

From experience of working with singles, it could be suggested that five key issues dominate: (a) conflicting or confused priorities, (b) misunderstanding other people's likely reactions to their personality, (c) struggling with flexibility and inter-dependence, (d) failure to cope with disappointment or be realistic, and (e) poor conflict management.

This analysis suggests that singles do not typically require extensive and deep therapy or even developmental or therapeutic coaching. Instead they would benefit from goal-focused coaching, a challenging interaction that helps them to become more self-aware and reconsider their attitudes toward dating and relationships by setting goals and planning a course of action. Additionally, many singles have a low self-efficacy due to a series of failed relationships; GFC can help to build confidence and a track record of success through adopting a forward-focused, action-oriented approach, which is based on incremental progress instead of per-sonal transformation.

Finding a life partner is a goal for those who present themselves for singles coaching. GFC offers a useful paradigm for locating the issue and for develop-ing a solution. The coachee needs an effective and coherent goal, a realistic and robust plan of action, and the motivation and commitment to appropriate action or change.

Coaching in Prisons

Prisons are often places of despair and futility. Days and months go by with little positive progress to show, leaving all involved in the prison system feeling demor-alised and apathetic. While working as a prison chaplain, Ives began to explore how coaching may offer a way of making the prisoners' time in custody a more productive experience. Given the practical and financial constrains that prevail in prison, he concluded that training prison officers as coaches was the most realistic option.

Prisoners are often indifferent and apathetic; they may have given up on life and have very low expectations. They are also institutionalised and have a tendency to expect others to sort things out for them, rather than accept responsibility for their own fate. Most prisoners expect to achieve little of value while in prison, and see their time in custody as 'written off.'

However, the period while prisoners are in custody is the ideal time to help them to move forward, as they are quite literally a captive audience. The coaching approach helps the coachees to set challenging (but reachable) goals and to be accountable to themselves for their achievement. The coaching setup creates a supportive 'space' within which the coachee is prompted and encouraged to make continued progress towards the goal. A coaching climate within prisons helps some prisoners to assume responsibility for what they achieve while in custody, and how they prepare for their release.

In 2004, Ives introduced coaching into prisons to create a co-active and proac-tive culture of progress and achievement. The programme was piloted in Wands-worth and Lewes (medium security) prisons in the UK. The main assessment came through participant feedback. In conjunction with the prison governor, 30%

approval was set as a minimum target, with 60% considered high success. Both programmes received above the 60% mark (72.5% in Wandsworth and 67.5% in Lewes). Seminars with management teams attracted similar ratings.

Coaching in Higher Education

Ives' doctoral study (2010) investigated the potential role of GFC in an adult learning context. Within the field of education, coaching has primarily been promoted as a development tool for educators (e.g. Costa & Garmston, 2002; Lam, S., Yim & Lam, T., 2002), and has not been adopted as a method of enhancing the goal achievement of students. The work focused on the impact and relevance of coaching to student self-regulation and learning performance, and explored a coaching model that is easily implemented, but which may still have the ability to impact on student performance and motivation.

The coaching project turned out to be far more complex than originally envisaged, leading to many sobering lessons about the reality of coaching in challenging environments. Clearly, coaching in a well-run establishment with students who are reasonably clear about their purpose of study is going to be simpler than the situation that Ives found himself in when he discovered that the students were not at all certain what they expected from the programme.

However, despite (and perhaps even because of) the chaotic and confusing situation, the study demonstrated that GFC offers several benefits to students. For students unsure about what their focus should be, coaching offers a safe environment to explore and refine the goal. It can also help to build up the coachees' independence and ownership of the task. For students who struggle to organise themselves and get the best out of what they are capable of, action planning is a useful exercise. Ensuring the best options are selected, help where needed is secured, and required skills are obtained, are all key elements in successfully reaching an important educational goal. Similarly, securing commitment and raising motivation can be crucial for students who are demotivated or distracted.

The students in this study generally found coaching beneficial to achieving their goals, and moreover found the opportunity to discuss their aspirations with a coach to be helpful to them. Study is usually a long-term and challenging task, and coaching can offer students a means of being more focused and motivated to achieve their important task.

Coaching in the Workplace

Emotional literacy and resilience in the workplace is vital for organisational wellbeing and effective customer service. In an action research study undertaken within a company in the UK, a group of retail support workers took part in a tailored coaching intervention in order to address performance issues. The workers, who were charged with handling telephone complaints, resolving issues associated with logistics, and liaising with both external and internal supply chains, were caught in what could be described as an emotionally charged middle ground. They were involved with service provider-related problems in the organisation, with all the emotions that these arouse, and yet had no managerial power to resolve them.

The coaching intervention, which involved individual and group coaching, was designed so that employees could articulate their work goals in negotiation with their line manager, and so begin to develop the twin objectives of improved communication skills and enhanced emotional development. It was felt that development in these areas would enable changes in levels of assertiveness, increased ability to influence others, the establishment of useful boundaries and the ability to negotiate and resolve issues more effectively. During the intervention, employees began to recognize that they could achieve performance goals more easily if emotions were better understood and managed.

The following response demonstrates how one employee set a goal at the start of the intervention that involved not reacting to provocation, and how, following goal-focused coaching, her awareness had increased:

> One of my main goals was to hold back. I try and think about a situation before going in to it. Before, I thought I was right and that was it – and now I have started to think about other people's points of view and how they might be feeling.

The task of defining individual goals began in an initial group coaching session, following which each employee emailed their proposed goals to the coach. This was followed by individual coaching, where goals were discussed and personal coaching tasks co-constructed. One-to-one coaching sessions continued every two months for a year and enabled participants to follow up the goals they had set for themselves and assess how these were being achieved. The company already had a one-to-one process with the line manager, but an evaluation document based on the organisation's goals was also devised and each participant then reported against each action they had undertaken to improve. Both manager and worker scored themselves against each goal and then held a discussion. Creating documents such as this helped the manager, worker and coach to stay on track and introduced accountability and enough positive tension to maintain focus.

Conclusion

As we have argued throughout this book, GFC shares many features with other coaching paradigms, but differs in some important ways. While virtually all approaches to coaching view goals as central, GFC is the coaching paradigm that builds a goal focus into the heart of its theory and practice of coaching. As we have shown, emanating from a cohesive theoretical base emerge numerous important nuances that make GFC a distinctive coaching framework, whether in relation to the role of feedback, the approach to building self-efficacy, or the use of questions in coaching.

We anticipate that this book will provide a very necessary theoretical framework to support the practice of GFC, an approach that we believe is fundamental to most coaching and is the key defining feature that separates coaching from many other helping interventions. We hope that the book will help to establish goal-focused coaching as a recognized and valued paradigm alongside therapeutic and personal development approaches to coaching. Coaching is at the beginning of its development; with this book we hope to have contributed something of value towards its emergence as a mature and credible approach to getting the best out of people and helping them achieve their goals.

Notes

1 Introduction

1 Skiffington and Zeus (2008 p. xii) suggest that their behavioural coaching is "a holistic approach, in that any aspect of the individual's life can be relevant to the coaching agenda, even though the focus may be related to work." They claim that while traditional coaching models do not pay attention to unconscious forces, behavioural coaching does. It is difficult to justify these remarks. First, many so-called traditional coaching models do incorporate unconscious elements, especially therapy based models. Second, behaviourism is not an approach associated with unconscious forces, so this claim for a behavioural approach is contradictory. They argue that coaching is not a manipulative, performance focused approach. But behaviourism is just that, rendering the use of the term behaviourism inappropriate.

2 What Is Goal-focused Coaching?

1 The typology was formulated using a clustering technique and textual analysis (Miles & Huberman, 1994).
2 Classification is a popular activity among coaching writers, although they typically lack a coherent methodology and are at times rather arbitrary. For example, Barner and Higgins (2007) offer four possible roles for the coach – counsellor and therapist, advisor and trainer, systems modeller and ethnographer and narrative analyst. This would exclude the self-definition of many coaches, ourselves included, who see themselves as moderators of a coaching process, whose task is to ask challenging questions within a semi-structured process. Brockbank (2008) also distinguishes between four types of coaching approaches: functionalist, engagement, revolutionary and evolutionary, in which she adopts a questionably activist approach to coaching. De Haan (2008) posits four approaches to coaching, whether focused on the person, insight, problem or solution. While this is a generally effective taxonomy, de Haan fails to mention goal-focused coaching and his description of solution-focused coaching as 'directive' is curious. Skiffington and Zeus (2008) offer a 5-part classification that incorporates such activities that appear to have limited relation to a normative conception of coaching.

4 Goal-focused Methodology

1 However, if the person sets easy goals, although this will result short-term in high affect due to the speed at which the goal is being reached, it will quickly dissipate as the goals is reached and the discrepancy is closed (Carver & Scheier, 1998; Carver, 2007). Additionally, if the goal is very easy, the person will experience no rise in affect through progress towards the goal, as the goal will not be treated as serious.

2 Orem, Bunkert and Clancy (2007) advocate appreciative inquiry coaching, which looks to encourage a new vision of the future. In so doing, they replaced what they describe as 'problem solving' phrases such as goals, action plans, skills gaps with more visioning ones such as, affirmation, dreams, potential. However, we fail to see on what grounds goals are regarded as uniquely problem-oriented.

Bibliography

Achtziger, A. & Gollwitzer, P. M. (2008). Motivation and volition during the course of action. In J. Heckhausen & H. Heckhausen (Eds.), *Motivation and Action* (pp. 272–295). London, England: Cambridge University Press.

Addis, M. E. & Mahalik, J. R. (2003). Men, masculinity and the contexts of help seeking. *American Psychologist, 58*, 5–14.

Alexander, G. (2006). Behavioural coaching: The GROW model. In J. Passmore (Ed.), *Excellence in coaching* (pp. 83–93). London, England: Kogan Page.

Alexander, G. & Renshaw, B. (2005). *Supercoaching*. London, England: Random House.

Allan, J. & Whybrow, A. (2007). Gestalt coaching. In S. Palmer & A. Whybrow (Eds.), *Handbook of coaching psychology: A guide for practitioners* (pp. 133–159). London, England: Routledge.

Allcorn, S. (2006). Psychoanalytically informed executive coaching. In D. Stober & A. M. Grant (Eds.), *Evidence-based coaching handbook: Putting best practices to work for your clients* (pp. 129–149). Hoboken, NJ: Wiley.

Ames, C. (1992). Classrooms: Goals, structures, and student motivation. *Journal of Educational Psychology, 84*, 261–271.

Anderson, H. & Goolishian, H. (1992). The client is the expert: A not-knowing approach to therapy. In S. McNamee & K. Bergen (Eds.), *Therapy as social construction*. Newbury Park, CA: Sage.

Argyris, C. & Schön, D. A. (1974). *Theory in practice: Increasing professional effectiveness*. San Francisco, CA: Jossey-Bass.

Arriaga, X. B. & Rusbult, C. E. (1998). Standing in my partner's shoes: Partner perspective taking and reaction to accommodative dilemmas. *Personality and Social Psychology Bulletin, 24*, 927–948.

Ashton, J. T. & Wilkerson, J. (1996). Establishing a team-based coaching process. *Nursing Management, 27*(3).

Askew, S. & Carnell, E. (2011). *Transformative Coaching: a learning theory for practice*, London, England: Institute of Education.

Atkinson, J. W. (1964). *An introduction to motivation*. Princeton: Van Nostrand.

Auerbach, J. E. (2006). Cognitive coaching. In D. Stober & A. M. Grant (Eds.), *Evidence-based coaching handbook: Putting best practices to work for your clients* (pp. 103–128). Hoboken, NJ: Wiley.

Bachkirova, T. (2007). Role of coaching psychology in defining boundaries between counselling and coaching. In S. Palmer & A. Whybrow (Eds.), *Handbook of coaching psychology: A guide for practitioners* (pp. 351–366). Hove, England: Routledge.

Bachkirova, T. (2011). *Developmental Coaching: working with the self*, Maidenhead: Open University.

Bachkirova, T. & Cox, E. (2005). A bridge over troubled water: Bringing together coaching and counselling. *Counselling at Work, 48*, Spring 2005. 2–9.

Bachkirova, T. & Cox, E. (2007). Cognitive-developmental approach to the development of coaches. In S. Palmer & A. Whybrow (Eds.), *Handbook of coaching psychology: A guide for practitioners* (pp. 325–350). London, England: Routledge.

Bachkirova, T., Cox, E. & Clutterbuck, D. (2010). Introduction. In E. Cox, T. Bachkirova & D. Clutterbuck (Eds.), *The complete handbook of coaching* (pp. 1–20). London, England: Sage.

Bandura, A. (1982). Self-efficacy mechanism in human agency. *American Psychologist, 37*, 122–147.

Bandura, A. (1986). *Social foundations of thought and action: A social cognitive model.* Englewood Cliffs: Prentice-Hall.

Bandura, A. (1988). Self-efficacy conception of anxiety. *Anxiety Research, 1*, 77–98.

Bandura, A. (1989). Social cognitive theory. In R. Vasta (Ed.), *Annals of child development: Vol. 6. Six theories of child development* (pp. 1–60). Greenwich, CT: JAI Press.

Bandura, A. (1991). Social cognitive theory of self-regulation. *Organizational Behavior and Human Decision Processes, 50*, 248–287.

Bandura, A. (1996). Social cognitive theory of human development. In T. Husen & T. N. Postlethwaite (Eds.), *International encyclopedia of education* (2nd ed., pp. 5513–5518). Oxford, England: Pergamon Press.

Bandura, A. (1997). *Self-efficacy: The exercise of control.* New York, NY: Freeman.

Bandura, A. (2001). Social cognitive theory: An agentic perspective. *Annual Review of Psychology, 52*, 1–26.

Bandura, A. & Cervone, D. (1983). Self-evaluative and self-efficacy mechanisms governing the motivational effects of goal systems. *Journal of Personality and Social Psychology, 45*(5), 1017–1028.

Bargh, J. A. (1990). Auto-motives: Preconscious determinants of social interaction. In: E. T. Higgins & R. M. Sorrentino (Eds.), *Handbook of motivation and cognition: Foundations of social behaviour* (Vol. 2, pp. 93–130). New York, NY: Guilford.

Bargh, J. A. & Gollwitzer, P. M. (1994). Environmental control over goal-directed action. *Nebraska Symposium of Motivation, 41*, 71–124.

Barner, R. & Higgins, J. (2007). Understanding implicit models that guide the coaching process. *Journal of Management Development, 26*(2), 148–158.

Baumeister, R. F. (1998). The self. In D. T. Gilbert, S. T. Fiske & G. Lindzey (Eds.), *Handbook of social psychology.* (4th ed., pp. 680–740). New York, NY: McGraw-Hill.

Baumeister, R. F. & Vohs, K. D. (2007). *Handbook of self-regulation.* New York, N.Y: Guilford.

Baumeister, R. F., Schmeichel, B. J. & Vohs, K. D. (2007). Self-regulation and the executive function: The self as controlling agent. In A. W. Kruglanski and E. T. Higgins (Eds.), *Social psychology: Handbook of basic principles* (2nd ed., pp. 516–539). New York, NY: Guilford.

Baumeister, R. F., Bratslavsky, E., Muraven, M. & Tice, D. M. (1998). Ego depletion: Is the active self a limited resource? *Journal of Personality and Social Psychology, 74*(5), 1252–1265.

Bayer, U. C., Jaudas, A. & Gollwitzer, P. M. (2002). *Do implementation intentions facilitate switching between tasks?* [poster] presented at the International Symposium on Executive Functions, Konstanz, Germany.

Berg, I. K. & Szabo, P. (2005). *Brief coaching for lasting solutions.* New York, NY: Norton.

Berger, J. G. (2006). Adult development theory and executive coaching practice. In D. Stober & A. M. Grant (Eds.), *Evidence-based coaching handbook* (pp. 77–102). New York, NY: Wiley.

Biswas-Diener, R. & Dean, B. (2007). *Positive psychology coaching: Putting the science of happiness to work for your clients.* New Jersey: Wiley.

Bloisi, W., Cook, C. W. & Hunsaker, P. L. (2003). *Management and organisational behaviour.* Berkshire, England: McGraw-Hill Education.

Bluckert, P. (2005). The foundations of a psychological approach to executive coaching. *Industrial and Commercial Training, 37*(4), 171–178.

Blumenfeld, P. C., Pintrich, P. R., Meece, J. & Wessels, K. (1982). The formation and role of self-perceptions of ability in elementary classrooms. *The Elementary School Journal, 82*, 401–420.

Bordin, E. (1979). The generalizability of the psychoanalytic concept of the working alliance. *Psychotherapy: Theory, Research and Practice, 16*, 252–260.

Boud, D., Cohen, R., & Walker, D. (1994). *Using experience for learning.* Buckingham, England: SRHE & Open University.

Bramson, R. (1984). *Coping with difficult people.* New York: Ballantine Books.

Brandtstädter, J. & Renner, G. (1990). Tenacious goal pursuit and flexible goal adjustment: Explication and age-related analysis of assimilative and accommodative models of coping. *Psychology and Aging, 5*, 58–67.

Bredo, E. (2000). Reconsidering social constructivism: The relevance of George Herbert Mead's interactionism. In D. C. Phillips (Ed.), *Constructivism in education: Opinions and second opinions on controversial issues: 99th yearbook of the National Society for the Study of Education, Part 1.* Chicago, IL: The University of Chicago.

Brennan, D. (2008). Leadership coaching: The impact on the organization. In D. Drake, D. Brennan & K. Gørtz (Eds.), *The philosophy and practice of coaching* (pp. 239–260). London, England: Wiley.

Bresser, F. & Wilson, C. (2006), What is coaching? In J. Passmore (Ed.), *Excellence in coaching: The industry guide* (pp. 9–15). London, England: Sage.

Brockbank, A. (2008). Is the coaching fit for purpose? A typology of coaching and learning approaches. *Coaching: An International Journal of Theory, Research and Practice 1*(2), 132–144.

Brockbank, A. & McGill, I. (2006). *Facilitating reflective learning through mentoring and coaching.* London, England: Kogan Page.

Brookfield, S. (1986). *Understanding and facilitating adult learning,* Buckingham: Open University.

Brown, S. P., Jones, E. & Leigh, T. W. (2005). The attenuating effect of role overload in relationships linking self-efficacy and goal level to work performance. *Journal of Applied Psychology, 90*(5), 972–979.

Brown, S. W. & Grant, A. M. (2010). From GROW to GROUP: Theoretical issues and a practical model for group coaching in organisations. *Coaching: An international journal of theory, research, and practice, 3*(1), 30–45.

Burke, D. & Linley, P.A. (2007). Enhancing goal self-concordance through coaching. *International Coaching Psychology Review, 2*(1), 62–69.

Burns, D. (1990). *The feeling good handbook.* New York: Penguin Group.

Buzbee Little, P. F. (2005). Peer coaching as a support to collaborative teaching. *Mentoring & Tutoring, 13*(1), 83–94.

Cantor, N. & Fleeson, W. (1991). Life tasks and self-regulatory processes. In M. L. Maehr & P. R. Pintrich (Eds.), *Advances in motivation and achievement* (Vol. 7, pp. 327–369). Greenwich, CT: JAI Press.

Cantor, N. & Kihlstrom, J. F. (1987). *Personality and social intelligence.* Englewood Cliffs: Prentice-Hall.

Caroll, W. R. & Bandura, A. (1990). Representational guidance of action production in observational learning: A causal analysis. *Journal of Motor Behavior, 22*(1) March 1990, 85–97.

Carter, A. (2001). *Executive coaching: Inspiring performance at work.* Brighton, England: The Institute for Employment Studies.

Carver, C. S. (2007). Self-regulation of action and affect. In R. F. Baumeister & K. D. Vohs (Eds.), *Handbook of self-regulation* (pp. 13–39). New York, NY: Guilford.

Carver, C. S. & Scheier, M. F. (1998). *On the self-regulation of behaviour.* New York: Cambridge University Press.

Cavanagh, M. (2006). Coaching from a systemic perspective: A complex adaptive approach. In D. Stober & A. M. Grant (Eds.), *Evidence-based coaching handbook: Putting best practices to work for your clients* (pp. 313–354). Hoboken, NJ: Wiley.

Cavanagh, M. J. & Grant, A. M. (2010). The solution-focused approach to coaching. In E. Cox, T. Bachkirova & D. Clutterbuck (Eds.), *The complete handbook of coaching* (pp. 54–67). London, England: Sage.

Cervone, D. (1989). Effects of envisioning future activities on self-efficacy judgments and motivation: An availability heuristic interpretation. *Cognitive Therapy and Research, 13,* 247–261.

Cervone, D., Mor, N., Orom, H., Shadel, W. G. & Scott, W. D. (2007). Self-efficacy beliefs and the architecture of personality. In R. F. Baumeister & K. D. Vohs (Eds.), *Handbook of self-regulation* (pp. 461–484). New York, NY: Guilford.

Chao, A., Lee, S-L. & Jeng, S-L. (1992). Estimating population size for capture-recapture data when capture probabilities vary by time and individual animal. *Biometrics, 48,* 201–216.

Chapman, T., Best, B. & van Casteren, P. (2003). *Executive coaching: Exploding the myths,* Palgrave Macmillan, New York.

Charmaz, K. (2008). Grounded theory as an emergent method. In S. N. Hesse-Biber & P. Leavy, (Eds.), *The handbook of emergent methods* (pp. 155–170). New York: Guilford.

Chase, A. & Wolfe, P. (1989). Off to a good start in peer coaching. *Educational Leadership, 46*(3), 37.

Cleary, T. J. & Zimmerman, B. J. (2004). Self-regulation empowerment program: A school-based program to enhance self-regulated and self-motivated cycles of student learning. *Psychology in the Schools, 41,* 537–550.

Clutterbuck, D. (2005). Establishing and maintaining mentoring relationships: An overview of mentor and mentee competencies, *SA Journal of Human Resource Management, 3*(3), 2–9

Clutterbuck, D. (2007). *Coaching the team at work.* London: Nicholas Brealey.

Clutterbuck, D. (2008). Mentoring and retention. *Clutterbuck Associates Newsletter,* August 2008.

Clutterbuck, D. (2010). Team coaching. In E. Cox, T. Bachkirova & D. Clutterbuck (Eds.), *The complete handbook of coaching* (pp. 271–283). London, England: Sage.

Clutterbuck, D. & Megginson, D. (2004). *Techniques for coaching and mentoring.* New York: Butterworth-Heinmann.

Cocivera, S. & Cronshaw, S. (2004). Action frame theory as a practical framework for executive coaching process. *Consulting Psychology Journal: Practice and Research, 56*(4), 234–245.

Coghlan, D. & Brannick, T. (2001). *Doing action research in your own organization.* London: Sage.

Collins, S. and O'Rourke, J. (2008). *Interpersonal Communication Listening and Responding.* Cengage South-Western.

Cooperrider, D. L. & Srivastva, S. (1987) Appreciative inquiry in organizational life. *Research in Organization Change and Development, 1*, 129–169.

Costa, A. L. & Garmston, R. J. (2002). *Cognitive coaching: A foundation for Renaissance schools*. Norwood: Christopher-Gordon.

Cox, E. (2005). Adult learners learning from experience: Using a reflective practice model to support work-based learning. *Reflective Practice, 6*(4) January, 459–472.

Cox, E. (2006). An adult learning approach to learning. In D. Stober & A. M. Grant (Eds.), *Evidence-based coaching handbook* (pp. 193–218). New York, NY: Wiley.

Cox, E. (2009). Last things first. In S. Palmer & A. McDowall, (Eds.), *Putting people first. Understanding interpersonal relationships in coaching* (pp. 159–181). London, England: Routledge.

Cox, E. (2012a). Individual and organisational trust in a reciprocal peer coaching context. *Mentoring and Tutoring* (forthcoming).

Cox, E. (2012b). Managing emotions at work: an action research study of how coaching affects retail support workers' performance and motivation. *The International Journal of Evidence Based Coaching and Mentoring, 10*(2), 1–18.

Cox, E.,(2012c) *Coaching Understood*. London: Sage.

Cox, E., Bachkirova, T. & Clutterbuck, D. (Eds.), (2010). *The complete handbook of coaching*. London, England: Sage.

Cox, E. & Jackson, P. (2010). Developmental coaching. In E. Cox, T. Bachkirova & D. Clutterbuck (Eds.), *The complete handbook of coaching* (pp. 217–230). London, England: Sage.

Cropanzano, R. S., Kacmar, K. M. & Bozeman, D.P. (1995). Organizational politics, justice, and support: Their differences and similarities. In R. S. Cropanzano & K. M. Kacmar (Eds.), *Organizational politics, justice, and support: managing the social climate of the workplace* (pp. 2–18). Westport: Quorum Books.

D'Abate, C., Eddy, E. & Tannenbaum, S. T. (2003). What's in a name? A literature-based approach to understanding mentoring, coaching, and other constructs that describe developmental interactions. *Human Resource Development Review, 2*(4), 360–384.

DeBacker, T. K. & Nelson, R. M. (1999). Variations on an expectancy-value model of motivation in science. *Contemporary Educational Psychology, 24*, 71–94.

de Haan, E. (2008). *Relational coaching: Journeys towards mastering one to one learning*. Chichester, England: Wiley.

de Shazer, S. (1988). *Clues: Investigating solutions in brief therapy*. New York, NY: Norton.

Deci, E. L. (1995). *Why we do what we do: The dynamics of personal autonomy*. New York, NY: Putnam.

Deci, E. L. & Ryan, R. M. (1985). *Intrinsic motivation and self-determination in human behavior*. New York, NY: Plenum.

Deci, E. L. & Ryan, R. M. (2002). *Handbook of self-determination research*. Rochester: University of Rochester.

Dembkowski, S. & Eldridge, F. (2008). Achieving tangible results: The development of a coaching model. In D. Drake, D. Brennan & K. Gørtz (Eds.), *The philosophy and practice of coaching. Insights and issues for a new era* (pp. 195–211). London, England: Wiley.

Dembkowski, S., Eldridge, F. & Hunter, I. (2006). *The seven steps of executive coaching*. Oxford: Thorogood.

Diedrich, R. C. (1996). An interactive approach to executive coaching. *Consulting Psychology Journal: Practice & Research, 48*(2), 61–66.

Downey, M. (2003). *Effective coaching: Lessons from the coaches coach*, London, England: Texere.

Drake, D. B. (2008). Finding our way home: Coaching's search for identity in a new era. *Coaching: An international journal of theory, research, and practice, 1*(1) March, 15–26.

Drake, D. B. (2008). Thrice upon a time: Narrative structure and psychology as a platform for coaching. In D. B. Drake, D. Brennan & K. Gørtz (Eds.), *The philosophy and practice of coaching: Insights and issues for a new era* (pp. 55–71). London, England: Wiley.

Drake, D. B. (2010). Narrative coaching. In E. Cox, T. Bachkirova & D. Clutterbuck (Eds.), *The complete handbook of coaching* (pp. 120–131). London, England: Sage.

Druckman, D. & Bjork, R. A. (1991). *In the mind's eye: Enhancing human performance.* Washington, DC: National Academy.

Ducharme, M. J. (2004). The cognitive-behavioural approach to executive coaching. *Consulting Psychology Journal: Practice & Research, 56*(4), 214–224.

Duignan, K. (2007).Conversational learning: applying personal construct psychology in coaching. In S. Palmer & A. Whybrow, *Handbook of Coaching Psychology* (pp. 229–252). London: Routledge.

Dunbar, R. I. (2009). The social brain hypothesis and its implications for social evolution. *Annual Journal of Human Biology, 36*, 562–572.

Eccles, J. & Wigfield, A. (1993). Motivational beliefs, values, and goals. *Annual Review of Psychology, 53*(1), 109–133.

Eden, C. & Huxham, C. (1996). Action research for the study of organisation. In S. Clegg, C. Hardy & W. Nord (Eds.), *The handbook of organisation studies.* Beverly Hills: Sage.

Elliot, A. J. & Church, M. A. (1997). A hierarchical model of approach and avoidance achievement motivation. *Journal of Personality and Social Psychology, 72*(1), 218–232.

Elliot, A. J. & Harackiewicz, J. M. (1996). Approach and avoidance achievement goals and intrinsic motivation: A mediational analysis. *Journal of Personality and Social Psychology, 70*, 461–475.

Ellis, S. (1997). Strategy choice in sociocultural context. *Developmental Review, 17*, 490–524.

Emmons, R. A. (1986). Personal strivings: An approach to personality and subjective well-being. *Journal of Personality and Social Psychology, 51*, 1058–1086.

Emmons, R. A. (1992). Abstract versus concrete goals – personal striving level, physical illness, and psychological well-being. *Journal of Personality and Social Psychology, 62*, 292–300.

Evered, R. D. & Selman, J. C. (1989). Coaching sales performance: A case study. *Organisational Dynamics, 18*(2), 16–32.

Feldman, D. C. & Lankau, M. J. (2005). Executive coaching: A review and agenda for future research. *Journal of Management, 31*, 829.

Ferrar, M. (2006). Interview notes with Mark Ferrar. *Connecting for Health,* 11–14.

Fillery-Travis, A. & Lane, D. (2006). Does coaching work or are we asking the wrong questions? *International Coaching Psychology Review, 1*(1), 23–36.

Fishbein, M. & Ajzen, I. (1975). *Belief, attitude, intention and behavior: An introduction to theory and research.* Reading: Addison-Wesley.

Fisher, R. & Ury, W. (1991). *Getting to yes.* London: Random House.

Fitzsimons, G. M. & Bargh, J. A. (2007). Automatic self-regulation. In R. F. Baumeister & K. D. Vohs (Eds.), *Handbook of self-regulation* (pp. 1151–1170). New York, NY: Guilford.

Flaherty, J. (2005). *Coaching: Evoking excellence in others.* Oxford, England: Elsevier.

Ford, M. (1992). *Motivating humans: Goals, emotions, and personal agency beliefs.* Newbury Park: Sage.

Fournies, F. F. (2000). *Coaching for improved work performance: How to get better results from your employees!* (Revised Ed.). New York: McGraw-Hill.

Fredrickson, B. L. & Losada, M. (2005). Positive affect and the complex dynamics of human flourishing. *American Psychologist, 60*(7), 678–686.

Frese, M., & Zapf, D. (1994). Action as the core of work psychology: A German approach.

In H. C. Wiandis, M. D. Dunnette & L. M. Hough (Eds.), *Handbook of industrial and organizational psychology* (Vol. 4, pp. 271–340). Palo Alto: Consulting Psychologists Press.

Freund, A. M. & Baltes, P. B. (2002). Life-management strategies of selection, optimization, and compensation: Measurement by self-report and construct validity. *Journal of Personality and Social Psychology, 82*, 642–662.

Frijda, N. H. (1994). Emotions are functional, most of the time. In P. Ekman & R. J. Davidson (Eds.), *The nature of emotion: fundamental questions* (pp. 112–126). New York: Oxford University.

Fritz, R. (1984). *The path of least resistance.* Salem, MA: Stillpoint Publishing

Gallwey, T. (2002). *The inner game of work: Overcoming mental obstacles for maximum performance.* New York: Texere.

Garvey, B., Stokes, P. & Megginson, D. (2009). *Coaching and mentoring: Theory and practice.* London, England: Sage.

Gavin, J. (2005). *Lifestyle fitness coaching.* Champaign, IL: Human Kinetics.

Glaser, B. G. & Strauss, A. L. (1967). *The discovery of grounded theory.* Chicago, IL: Aldine.

Goleman, D. (1998). *Working with emotional intelligence.* New York: Bantam Books.

Gollwitzer, P. M. (1990). Action phases and mind sets. In E. T. Higgins & R. M. Sorrentino (Eds.), *Handbook of motivation and cognition: Foundations of social behaviour* (Vol. 2, pp. 53–92). New York, NY: Guilford.

Gollwitzer, P. M. (1996). The volitional benefits of planning. In P. M. Gollwitzer & J. A. Bargh (Eds.), *The psychology of action: Linking cognition and motivation to behaviour* (pp. 287–312). New York: Guilford.

Gollwitzer, P. M. & Bayer, U. C. (1999). Deliberative versus implemental mindsets in the control of action. In S. Chajken & Y. Trope (Eds.), *Dual-process theories in social psychology* (pp. 403–422). New York, NY: Guildford.

Gollwitzer, P. M. & Brandstaetter, V. (1997). Implementation intentions and effective goal pursuit. *Journal of Personality and Social Psychology, 73*, 186–199.

Gollwitzer, P. M., Fujita, K. & Oettingen, G. (2007). Planning and the implementation of goals. In R.F. Baumeister & K.D. Vohs (Eds.), *Handbook of self-regulation* (pp. 211–228). New York, NY: Guilford.

Gollwitzer, P. M. & Schaal, B. (1998). Metacognition in action: The importance of implementation intentions. *Personality and Social Psychology Review, 2*, 124–136.

Gollwitzer, P.M. & Sheeran, P. (2006). Implementation intentions and goal achievement: A meta-analysis of effects and processes. *Advances in Experimental Social Psychology, 38*, 69–119.

Goodman, R. G. (2002). Coaching senior executives for effective business leadership. In C. Fitzgerald & J. G. Beger (Eds.), *Executive coaching: Practices and perspectives* (pp. 135–253). Palo Alto CA: DaviesBlack.

Gordon, S. (2008). Appreciative inquiry coaching. *International Psychology Review, 3*(1), 17–29.

Graesser, A. C., Person, N. K. & Magliano, J. P. (1995). Collaborative dialogue patterns in naturalistic one-to-one tutoring. *Applied Cognitive Psychology, 9*(6) 495–522.

Grant, A. M. (2003). The impact of life coaching on goal attainment, metacognition and mental health. *Social Behaviour and Personality, 31*(3), 253–264.

Grant, A. M. (2006). An integrative goal-focused approach to executive coaching. In D. Stober & A. M. Grant (Eds.), *Evidence-based coaching handbook* (pp. 153–192). New York, NY: Wiley.

Grant, A. M. (2007). Past, present and future: The evolution of professional coaching and coaching psychology. In S. Palmer & A. Whybrow (Eds.), *Handbook of coaching psychology: A guide for practitioners* (pp. 23–39). London, England: Routledge.

Grant, A. M. & Cavanagh, M.J. (2004). Toward a profession of coaching: Sixty-five years of progess and challenges for the future. *International Journal of Evidence-Based Coaching and Mentoring, 2*(1), 1–16.

Grant, A. M. & Cavanagh, M. J. (2010). The person-centred approach to coaching. In E. Cox, T. Bachkirova & D. Clutterbuck. *The Sage handbook of coaching*. London: Sage.

Grant, A. M. & O' Connor, S.A. (2010). The differential effects of solution-focused and problem-focused coaching questions: a pilot study with implications for practice. *Industrial and Commercial Training, 42*(2), 102–111.

Grant, A. M. & Stober, D. (2006). Introduction. In: D. Stober & A. M. Grant (Eds.), *Evidence-Based Coaching Handbook*. New York: Wiley & Sons.

Gray, D. E. (2006). Executive coaching: Towards a dynamic alliance of psychotherapy and transformative learning processes. *Management Learning, 37*(4), 475–497.

Green, L. S., Oades, L. G. & Grant, A. M. (2006). Cognitive-behavioral, solution-focused life coaching: Enhancing goal striving, well-being and hope. *Journal of Positive Psychology, 1*, 142–149.

Greene, J. & Grant, A. M. (2003). *Solution-focused coaching: A manager's guide to getting the best from people*. London, England: Pearson Education.

Gregory, J. B., Beck, J. W. & Carr, A. E. (2011). Goals, feedback, and self-regulation: control theory as a natural framework for executive coaching. *Consulting Psychology Journal: Practice and Research, 63*(1) 26–38.

Grimley, B. (2007). NLP coaching. In S. Palmer & A. Whybrow (Eds.), *Handbook of coaching psychology: A guide for practitioners* (pp. 193–210). Abingdon, UK: Routledge.

Grimmett, P. P. & Crehan, E. P. (1992). The nature of collegiality in teacher development: The case of clinical supervision. In M. Fullan & A. Kargreaves (Eds.), *Teacher Development and Educational Change* (pp 56–85). London: Falmer.

Grolnick, W. S. & Ryan, R. M. (1989). Parent styles associated with children's self regulation and competence in schools. *Journal of Educational Psychology, 81*, 143–154.

Gruber, H. E. & Wallace, D. B. (1999). The case study method and evolving systems approach for understanding unique creative people at work. In R. Stenberg (Ed.), *Handbook of creativity* (pp. 91–115). New York: Cambridge University.

Haaga, D. A. F. & Stewart, B. L. (1992). Self-efficacy for recovery from a lapse after smoking cessation. *Journal of Consulting and Clinical Psychology, 60*, 24–28.

Hackman, J. R. & Wageman, R. (2005). When and how team leaders matter. *Research in Organizational Behavior, 26*, 37–74.

Haines, S. G. (1998). *The manager's pocket guide to systems of thinking and learning*. Amherst: HRD.

Hall, L. M. & Duval, M. (2004). *Meta-coaching: Coaching change: Vol. 1*. Clifton, CO: Neuro-Semantic Publications.

Harackiewicz, J. M., Barron, K. E., Carter, S. M., Lehto, A. T. & Elliot, A. J. (1997). Predictors and consequences of achievement goals in the college classroom: Maintaining interest and making the grade. *Journal of Personality and Social Psychology. 73*(6) 1284–1295.

Hardingham, A. (2005) A job well done? The coach's dilemma. *People Management, 11*(8), 54.

Hargreaves, A. (1994). *Changing teachers, Changing times: Teachers' work and culture in postmodern times*. London, England: Cassell.

Hargreaves, A. & Dawe, R. (1990). Paths of professional development: Contrived collegiality, collaborative culture, and the case of peer coaching. *Teaching and Teacher Education, 6*, 227–241.

Hargrove, R.A. (2003). *Masterful coaching*. San Francisco, CA: Jossey-Bass.

Harris, M. (1999). Look, it's an I-O psychologist . . . no, it's a trainer . . . no, it's an executive coach. *TIP*, *36*(3), 1–5.

Harter, S. (1990). *Manual of the self-perception profile for children*. Denver, CO: University of Denver.

Hawkins, P. and Schwenk, G. (2010). The interpersonal relationship in the training and supervision of coaches. In S. Palmer & A. McDowall, (Eds.), *Putting people first: Understanding interpersonal relationships in coaching* (pp. 203–221). London, England: Routledge.

Hawkins, P. & Smith, N. (2010). Transformational Coaching. In E. Cox, T. Bachkirova & D. Clutterbuck (Eds.), *The complete handbook of coaching* (pp. 231–244). London, England: Sage.

Heckhausen, H. (1991). *Motivation and action*. Berlin: Springer-Verlag.

Heckhausen, H. & Gollwitzer, P.M. (1987). Thought contents and cognitive functioning in motivational and volitional states of mind. *Motivation and Emotion*, *11*, 101–120.

Heffernan, T. W. (2004). Trust formation in cross-cultural business to business relationships. *The International Journal of Qualitative Marketing Research*, *7*(2), 114–125.

Herzberg, F. (1959). *The motivation to work*. New York: John Wiley and Sons.

Herzberg, F. I. (1987). One more time: How do you motivate employees? *Harvard Business Review*, *65*(5), 109–120.

Higgins, E. T. (1997). Beyond pleasure and pain. *American Psychologist*, *55*, 1217–1230.

Higgins, E. T. (2000). Making a good decision: Value from fit. *American Psychologist*, *13*, 519–554.

Hodgetts, W. H. (2002). Using executive coaching in organizations: What can go wrong (and how to prevent it). In C. Fitzgerald & J. Garvey Berger (Eds.), *Executive coaching: Practices and perspectives* (pp. 203–224). Palo Alto, CA: Davies-Black.

Hodgins, H. S. & Knee, C. R. (2002). The integrating self and conscious experience. In E. L. Deci & R. M. Ryan (Eds.), *Handbook of self-determination research* (pp. 87–100). Rochester: University of Rochester.

Hollenbeck, J. R., Brief, A. P., Whitener, E. M. & Pauli, K. E. (1988). An empirical note on the interaction of personality and aptitude in personnel selection. *Journal of Management*, *14*, 441–451.

Holyoak, K. J. & Spellman, B. A. (1993). Thinking. *Annual Review of Psychology*, *44*, 265–315.

Hubble, M. A. & Miller, S. D. (2004). The client: Psychotherapy's missing link for promoting a positive psychology. In P. A. Linley & S. Joseph, *Positive psychology in practice* (pp. 335–353). Hoboken, NJ: Wiley.

Hudson, F. M. (1999). *The handbook of coaching: A comprehensive resource guide for managers, executives, consultants and human resource professionals*. San Francisco, CA: Jossey-Bass.

Hunt, J. & Weintraub, J. (2004). Learning developmental coaching. *Journal of Management Education*, *28*(1) February, 39–61.

Hunt, J. & Weintraub, J. (2007). *The coaching organization: A strategy for developing leaders*. Thousand Oaks: Sage.

Husman, J. & Lens, W. (1999). The role of the future in student motivation. *Educational Psychologist*, *34*, 113–125.

Ives, Y. (2008). What is 'coaching'? An exploration of conflicting paradigms. *International Journal of Evidence Based Coaching and Mentoring*, *6*(2),100–113.

Ives, Y. (2010). *Goal focused coaching*. Unpublished doctoral dissertation. Oxford, United Kingdom: Oxford Brookes University.

Jackson, P. (2008). Does it matter what the coach thinks? A new foundation for professional development. In D. B. Drake, D. Brennan & K. Gørtz (Eds.), *The philosophy and practice of coaching: Insights and issues for a new era* (pp. 73–90). London, England: Wiley.

Jackson, P. Z. & McKergow, M. (2008). *The solutions focus: Making coaching and change simple.* London, England: Nicholas Brealey.

Janoff-Bulman, R. & Brickman, P. (1982). Expectations and what people learn from failure. In N. Feather (Ed.), *Expectations and actions: Expectancy-value models in psychology.* Hillsdale: Lawrence Erlbaum.

Johnson, D. & Johnson, R. (1991). *Learning together and alone: Cooperative, competitive and individualistic learning* (3rd ed.). Boston, MA: Allyn & Bacon.

Johnson, D., Johnson, R. & Smith, K. (1998). Cooperative learning returns to college: what evidence is there that it works? *Change, 30,* 27–35.

Jones, G. & Spooner, K. (2006). Coaching high achievers. *Consulting Psychology Journal: Practice and Research, 58*(1), 40–50.

Joseph, S. (2010). *Theories of counselling and psychotherapy: An introduction to the different approaches.* Hampshire: Palgrave Macmillan.

Judge, W. Q. & Cowell, J. (1997). The brave new world of executive coaching. *Business Horizons, 4*(40) 71–78.

Kanfer, R. (1990). Motivation theory and industrial and organizational psychology. In M. D. Dunnette, (Ed.), *Handbook of industrial and organizational psychology* (pp. 75–170). Palo Alto, CA: Consulting Psychologists Press.

Kanfer, R. & Ackerman, P. L. (1989). Motivation and cognitive abilities: An integrative/aptitude treatment interaction approach to skill acquisition. *Journal of Applied Psychology, 74,* 657–690.

Kanfer, R. Ackerman, P. L., Murtha, T. C., Dugdale, B. & Nelson, L. (1994). Goal setting, condition of practice, and task performance: A resource allocation perspective. *Journal of Applied Psychology, 79,* 826–835.

Karoly, P. (1993). Mechanisms of self regulation: A systems view. *Annual Review of Psychology, 44,* 23–52.

Kasser, T. (2002). Sketches for a self-determination theory of values. In E. L. Deci & R. M. Ryan (Eds.), *Handbook of self-determination research.* (pp. 123–140). Rochester: University of Rochester.

Kasser, T. & Ryan, R. M. (1996). Further examining the American dream: Wellbeing correlates of the intrinsic and extrinsic goals. *Personality and Social Psychology Bulletin, 65,* 410–422.

Katzenbach, J. R. & Smith, D. K. (1993). *The wisdom of teams: Creating the high-performance organization.* Boston, MA: Harvard Business School.

Kauffman, C. (2004). Pivot point coaching. *Annual Meeting of the International Coaching Federation.* Quebec, Canada.

Kauffman, C. (2006). Positive psychology: The science at the heart of coaching. In D. Stober & A. M. Grant (Eds.), *Evidence-based coaching handbook* (pp. 219–254). New York, NY: Wiley.

Kauffman, C. & Bachkirova, T. (2008). Coaching: An international journal of theory, research and practice: Why does it matter? *Coaching: An International Journal of Theory, Research and Practice, 1*(1).

Kauffman, C., Boniwell, I. & Silberman, J. (2009). Positive psychology coaching. In E. Cox, T. Bachkirova & D. Clutterbuck (Eds.), *The complete handbook of coaching* (pp. 158–171). London, England: Sage.

Kauffman, C. & Scouler, A. (2004) Toward a positive psychology of executive coaching. In A. Linley & S. Josephs (Eds.), *Positive psychology in practice.* Hoboken, NJ: Wiley.

Kayes, D. C. (2006). *Destructive goal pursuit: The Mount Everest disaster.* Basingstoke, UK: Palgrave Macmillan.

Kegan, R. (1982). *The evolving self.* Cambridge, MA: Harvard University.

Kegan, R. & Laskow Lahey, L. (2001). *Seven languages for transformation.* San Francisco, CA: Jossey-Bass.

Kelley, H. H., & Michela, J. L. (1980). Attribution theory and research. *Annual Review of Psychology, 31,* 457–501.

Kelso, J. A. S. (1995). *Dynamic patterns: The self-organization of the brain and behaviour.* Cambridge, MA: MIT Press.

Kemp, T. (2006). An adventure-based framework for coaching. In D. Stober & A. M. Grant (Eds.), *Evidence-based coaching handbook* (pp. 277–312). New York, NY: Wiley.

Kemp, T. (2008a). Self-management and the coaching relationship: Exploring coaching impact beyond models and methods. *International Coaching Psychology Review, 3*(1), 32–42.

Kemp, T. (2008b). Coach self-management: The foundation of coaching effectiveness. In D. B. Drake, D. Brennan & K. Gørtz (Eds.), *The philosophy and practice of coaching: Insights and issues for a new era* (pp. 27–50). London, England: Wiley.

Kets de Vries, M. F. R. (2005). Leadership group coaching in action: The Zen of creating high performance teams. *Academy of Management Executive, 19*(1), 61–76.

Khan, S. and Quaddus, M. A. (2004). Group decision support using fuzzy cognitive maps for causal reasoning. *Group Decision and Negotiation, 13,* 463–480.

Kilberg, R. (2004). Trudging towards Dodoville: Conceptual approaches towards and case studies in executive coaching. *Consulting Psychology Journal, 56*(4).

Kilburg, R. (1997). Coaching and executive character: Core problems and basic approaches. *Consulting Psychology Journal: Practice and Research, 53*(4), 251–267.

King, P. & Eaton, J. (1999). Coaching for results. *Industrial and Commerical Training, 31*(4), 145–151.

Kinlaw, D. C. (1989). *Coaching for commitment.* San Diego: Pfeiffer.

Klein, H. J., Wesson, M. J., Hollenbeck, J. R. & Alge, B. J. (1999). Goal commitment and the goal-setting process: Conceptual clarification and empirical synthesis. *Journal of Applied Psychology, 84*(6), 885–896.

Klinger, E. (1975). Consequences of commitment to and disengagement from incentives. *Psychological Review, 82,* 1–25.

Kluger, A. N., & DeNisi, A. (1996). The effects of feedback interventions on performance: A historical review, a meta-analysis, and a preliminary feedback intervention theory. *Journal of Applied Psychology, 119,* 254–284.

Knowles, M. S. (1975). *Self-directed learning.* Chicago, IL: Follet.

Knowles, M. S. (1984). *Andragogy in action.* San Francisco, CA: Jossey-Bass.

Koestner, R. & Losier, G. F. (1996). Distinguishing reactive vs. reflective autonomy. *Journal of Applied Social Psychology, 64,* 465–494.

Koestner, R., Losier, G. F., Fichman, L. & Mallet, M. (2002). Internalisation and adaptation: Finding personal meaning in school activities. In E. L. Deci & R. M. Ryan (Eds.), *Handbook of self-determination research* (pp. 101–121). Rochester: University of Rochester.

Kolb, D. A. (1984). *Experiential learning: Experience as the source of knowledge and development.* Englewood Cliffs: Prentice-Hall.

Kuhl, J. (1984). Volitional aspects of achievement motivation and learned helplessness: Toward a comprehensive theory of action control. In B. A. Maher (Ed.), *Progress in experimental personality research: Vol. 13* (pp. 99–171). New York: Academic.

Ladyshewsky, R. (2010). Peer coaching. In E. Cox, T. Bachkirova & D. Clutterbuck (Eds.), *The complete handbook of coaching* (pp. 284–296). London, England: Sage.

Lam, S., Yim, P. & Lam, T. (2002). Transforming school culture: Can true collaboration be initiated? *Educational Research, 44*, 181–195.

Latham, G. P. (2007). *Work motivation: History, theory, research, and practice.* London, England: Sage.

Latham, G. P., Almost, J., Mann, S. & Moore, C. (2005). New development in performance management. *Organizational Dynamics, 34*(1) 78–87.

Latham, G. P., Erez, M. & Locke, E. A. (1988). Resolving scientific disputes by the joint goal-setting design of crucial experiments: Application to the Erez-Latham dispute regarding participation in goal setting [monograph]. *Journal of Applied Psychology, 73,* 753–777.

Latham, G. P., Winters, D. & Locke, E. (1994). Cognitive and motivational effects of participation: A mediator study. *Journal of Organizational Behaviour, 15*, 49–63.

Lave, J. & Wenger, E. (1991). *Situated learning: Legitimate peripheral participation.* New York, NY: Cambridge University Press.

Lawrence, J. W., Carver, C. S. & Scheier, M. F. (2002). Velocity toward goal attainment in immediate experience as a determinant of affect. *Journal of Applied Social Psychology, 32*(4), 788–802.

Lee, G. (2010). The psychodynamic approach to coaching. In E. Cox, T. Bachkirova & D. Clutterbuck (Eds.), *The complete handbook of coaching* (pp. 23–36). London, England: Sage.

Lee, T. W., Locke, E. A. & Latham, G. P. (1989). Goal-setting theory and job performance. In L. A. Pervin, (Ed.), *Goal concepts in personality and social psychology.* Hillsdale: Erlbaum.

Lenz, B. K., Ellis, E. S. & Scanlon, D. (1996). *Teaching learning strategies to adolescents and adults with learning disabilities.* Austin: Pro-Ed.

Levene, L. & Frank, P. (1993). Peer coaching: Professional growth and development for instruction librarians. *Reference Services Review, 21*(3), 35–42.

Lewin, K. (1946). Action research and minority problems. *Journal of Social Issues, 2*, 34–46.

Lewin, K., Dembo, T., Festinger, L. & Sears, P. (1944). Level of aspiration. In J. Hunt (Ed.), *Personality and the behavior disorders* (Vol. 1). New York: Ronald Press.

Libri, V. (2004). Beyond GROW: In search of acronyms and coaching models. *International Journal of Mentoring and Coaching, 2*(1).

Linder-Pelz, S. & Hall, M. (2008). Meta-coaching: a methodology grounded in psychological theory. *International Journal of Evidence-Based Coaching and Mentoring, 6*(1), 43–56.

Linley, P. A. (2006). Coaching research: Who? what? where? when? why? *International Journal of Evidence-Based Coaching, 4*(2), 1–7.

Linnerbrink, E. A. & Pintrich, P. R. (2002). Achievement goal theory and affect: An asymmetrical bidirectional model. *Educational Psychologist, 37*, 69–78.

Little, B. R. (1993). Personal projects and the distributed self: Aspects of a conative psychology. In J. M. Suls (Ed.), *The self in social perspective: Psychological perspectives on the self* (Vol. 4., pp. 137–185). Hillsdale: Erlbaum.

Locke, E. A. (1996). Motivation through conscious goal setting. *Applied and Preventative Psychology, 5*, 117–124.

Locke, E. A., Alavi, M. & Wagner, J. (1997). Participation in decision-making: An information exchange perspective. In G. Ferris, (Ed.), *Research in personnel and human resources management* (Vol. 15, pp. 293–331). Greenwich, CT: JAI.

Locke, E. A. & Latham, G. P. (1990). *A theory of goal setting and task performance.* Englewood Cliffs: Prentice-Hall.

Locke, E. A. & Latham, G. P. (2002). Building a practically useful theory of goal setting and task motivation: A 35 year odyssey. *American Psychologist, 57*, 507–717.

Locke, E. A. & Latham, G. P. (2006). New directions in goal-setting theory. *Current Directions in Psychological Science, 15*, 265–268.

London, M., Smither, J. W. & Adsit, D. J. (1997). Accountability: The Achilles' heel of multisource feedback. *Group & Organization Management, 22*(2), 149–161.

Lowman, R. L. (2007). Coaching and consulting in multicultural contexts: Integrating themes and issues. *Consulting Psychology Journal: Practice and Research, 59*(4), 296–303.

Luebbe, D. M. (2005). *The three-way mirror of executive coaching.* ProQuest: Dissertation Abstracts International.

MacCoon, D. G., Wallace, J. F. & Newman, J. P. (2007). Self-regulation: Context-appropriate balanced attention. In R. F. Baumeister & K. D. Vohs (Eds.), *Handbook of self-regulation* (pp. 275–306). New York, NY: Guilford.

Manderlink, G. & Harackiewicz, J. M. (1984). Proximal versus distal goal setting and intrinsic motivation. *Journal of Personality and Social Psychology, 47*, 918–928.

Margolis, H. & McCabe, P. (2006). Improving self-efficacy and motivation: What to do, what to say. *Intervention in School and Clinic, 41*(4) 218–227.

Markus, H. & Ruvolo, A. (1989). Possible selves: Personalized representations of goals. In L. A. Pervin, (Ed.), *Goal concepts in personality and social psychology* (pp. 211–241). Hillsdale: Erlbaum.

Mason, B. (2005). Relational risk-taking and the therapeutic relationship. In C. Flaskas, B. Mason & A. Perlesz (Eds.), *The space between: Experience, context and process in the therapeutic relationship.* London: Karnac.

Mathieu, J. E. & Button, S. B. (1992). An examination of the relative impact of normative information and self-efficacy on personal goals and performance over time. *Journal of Applied Social Psychology, 22*, 1758–1775.

McCroskey, J. C., Richmond, V. P. & Daly, J. A. (1974). Toward the measurement of perceived homophily in interpersonal communication. *The Convention of the International Communication Association*, New Orleans.

McDowall, A. & Millward, L. (2009). Feeding back, feeding forward and setting goals. In S. Palmer & A. McDowall (Eds.), *The coaching relationship: Putting people first* (pp. 55–78). Hove, England: Routledge.

McKergow, M. W. & Korman, H. (2009). In between – neither inside nor outside: The radical simplicity of Solution-focused Brief Therapy. *Journal of Systemic Therapies, 28*(2), 34–49.

McNiff, J. & Whitehead, J. (2005). *Action research for teachers.* London, England: David Fulton.

Mezirow, J. (2000). *Learning as transformation: Critical perspectives on a theory in progress.* San Francisco, CA: Jossey Bass.

Miles, M. B. & Huberman, A. M. (1994). *Qualitative data analysis: An expanded sourcebook.* Thousand Oaks: Sage.

Miller, R. B. & Brickman, S. J. (2004). A model of future oriented motivation and self-regulation. *Educational Psychology Review, 16*, 9–33.

Miller, R. B., Greene, B. A., Montalvo, G. P., Ravindran, B. & Nichols, J. D. (1996). Engagement in academic work: The role of learning goals, future consequences, pleasing others, and perceived ability. *Contemporary Educational Psychology, 21*, 388–422.

Miller, W. R., Benefield, R. G. & Tonigan, J. S. (1993). Enhancing motivation for change in problem drinking: A controlled comparison of two therapist styles. *Journal of Consulting and Clinical Psychology, 61*, 455–461.

Miller, W. R. & Rollnick, S. (2002). *Motivational interviewing: Preparing people for change.* New York: Guilford.

Mischel, W. (1996). From good intentions to willpower. In P. M. Gollwitzer and J. A. Bargh (Eds.), *The psychology of action* (pp. 197–218). New York: Guilford.

Mischel, W. & Ayduk, O. (2007). Willpower in a cognitive-affective processing system. In R. F. Baumeister & K. D. Vohs (Eds.), *Handbook of self-regulation*. (pp. 99–129). New York, NY: Guilford.

Moen, F. & Skaalvik, E. (2009). Coaching and the effects on performance psychology. *International Journal of Evidence-Based Coaching and Mentoring, 7*(2), 31–49.

Mone, M. A. & Shalley, C. E. (1995). Effects of task complexity and goal specificity on change in strategy and performance over time. *Human Performance, 8*, 243–262.

Munch, J. & Swasy, J. (1983). A conceptual view of questions and questioning in marketing communications. In R. Bagozzi & A. Tybout (Eds.), *Advances in consumer research* (Vol. 10, pp. 209–214). Ann Abor: Association for Consumer Research.

Muraven, R. F., Tice, D. M. & Baumeister, R. F. (1998). Self control as a limited resource: regulatory depletion patterns. *Journal of Personality and Social Psychology, 74*, 774–789.

Myers, S. (2000). Empathic listening: Reports on the experience of being heard. *Journal of Humanistic Psychology, 40*(2), 148–173.

Nadler, D. & Tushman, M. (1989). Organisational framebending. *Academy of Management Executive, 3*, 194–202.

Nakamura, J. & Csikszentmihalyi, M. (2002). The concept of flow. In C. Snyder & S. Lopez (Eds.), *Handbook of positive psychology*. Oxford: Oxford University Press.

Natale, S. M. & Diamante, T. (2005). The five stages of executive coaching: Better process makes better practice. *Journal of Business Ethics, 59*, 361–374.

Neal, D. T., Wood, W. & Quinn, J. M. (2006). Habits – a repeat performance. *Current Directions in Psychological Science, 15*, 198–202.

Neenan, M. (2006). Cognitive behavioural coaching. In J. Passmore (Ed.), *Excellence in coaching* (pp. 1110–1122). London, England: Kogan Page.

Newell, A. & Simon, H. A. (1972). *Human problem solving*. Englewood Cliffs: Prentice Hall.

Newman, R. S. (1998). Adaptive help-seeking: A role of social interaction in self-regulated learning. In S. A. Karabenick, (Ed.), *Strategic help-seeking: Implications for learning and teaching* (pp. 13–37). Mahwah: Erlbaum.

Nicholson, P. Bayne, R. & Owen, J. (2006). *Applied psychology for social workers* (3rd ed.). Basingstoke, England: Palgrave.

Nielson, T. R. & Eisenbach, R. J. (2003). Not all relationships are created equal: Critical factors of high-quality mentoring relationships. *The International Journal of Mentoring and Coaching, 1*(1).

Nuttin, J. (1984). *Motivation, planning, and action: A relational theory of behavior dynamics*. Hillsdale, NJ: Erlbaum.

O'Broin, A. & Palmer, S. (2006). The coach-client relationship and contributions made by the coach in improving outcome. *The Coaching Psychologist, 2*(2), 16–20.

O'Broin, A. & Palmer, S. (2007). Reappraising the coach–client relationship: The unassuming change agent in coaching. In S. Palmer & A. Whybrow (Eds.), *Handbook of coaching psychology: A guide for practitioners* (pp. 295–324). Abingdon, England: Routledge.

O'Broin, A. & Palmer, S. (2009). Co-creating an optimal coaching alliance: A cognitive behavioural coaching perspective. *International Coaching Psychology Review, 4*(2), 184–194.

O'Connell, Bill (2005). *Solution-focused therapy* (2nd edition). London: Sage.

O'Connell, B. & Palmer, S. (2007). Solution-focused coaching. In S. Palmer & A. Whybrow (Eds.), *Handbook of coaching psychology: A guide for practitioners* (pp. 278–292). London, England: Routledge.

O'Hanlon, W. (1998). Possibility therapy: An inclusive, collaborative, solution-based model of psychotherapy. In M. F. Hoyt, (Ed.), *The handbook of constructive therapies: Innovative approaches from leading practitioners* (pp. 137–149). San Francisco, CA: Jossey-Bass.

Oliver, C. (2010). Reflexive coaching: linking meaning and action in the leadership system. In S. Palmer & A. McDowall (Eds.), *The coaching relationship: Putting people first* (pp. 101–120). Hove, England: Routledge.

Ommundsen, Y. (2006). Pupils' self-regulation in physical education: The role of motivational climates and differential achievement goals. *European Physical Education Review, 12*(3), 289–315.

O'Neill, M. B. (2007). *Executive coaching with backbone and heart.* San Francisco, CA: Jossey-Bass/Wiley.

O'Neill, M. B. (2000). *Executive coaching with backbone and heart: A systems approach to emerging leaders with their challenges.* San Francisco, CA: Jossey-Bass.

Orbell, S., Hodgkins, S. & Sheeran, R. (1997). Implementation intentions and the theory of planned behaviour. *Journal of Personality and Social Psychology, 23*, 945–954.

Orem, S., Binkert, J. & Clancy, A. L. (2007). *Appreciative coaching: A positive process for change.* San Francisco, CA: Jossey-Bass Business & Management.

Palmer, S. (2007). Practice: A model suitable for coaching, counselling, psychotherapy and stress management. *The Coaching Psychologist, 3*(2), 71–77.

Palmer, S. & Panchal, S. (2011). *Developmental coaching: Life transitions and generational perspectives,* Abingdon, England: Taylor and Francis.

Palmer, S. & Szymanska, K. (2007). Cognitive behavioural coaching: An integrative approach. In S. Palmer & A. Whybrow (Eds.), *Handbook of coaching psychology: A guide for practitioners* (pp. 86–117). London, England: Routledge.

Palmer, S. & Whybrow, A. (2007). Coaching psychology: an introduction. In S. Palmer & A. Whybrow (Eds.), *Handbook of coaching psychology: A guide for practitioners* (pp. 1–20). Abingdon, England: Routledge.

Parker, P., Hall, D. T. & Kram, K. E. (2008). Peer coaching: A relational process for accelerating career learning. *Academy of Management Learning & Education, 7*(4), 487–503.

Parsloe, E & Wray, M. (2000). *Coaching and mentoring,* London, England: Kogan Page.

Passmore, J. (2005). The heart of coaching: A coaching model for managers. *The Coaching Psychologist, 1*(2), 6–9.

Passmore, J. (Ed.). (2006). *Excellence in coaching.* London, England: Kogan Page.

Passmore, J. (2007). Addressing deficit performance through coaching: Using motivational interviewing for performance improvement in coaching. *International Coaching Psychological Review, 2*(3), 265–279.

Passmore, J. & Whybrow, A. (2007). Motivational interviewing: A specific approach for coaching psychologists. In S. Palmer & A. Whybrow (Eds.), *Handbook of coaching psychology: A guide for practitioners* (pp. 160–173). London, England: Routledge.

Peltier, B. (2001). *The psychology of executive coaching: Theory and application.* New York: Brunner-Routledge.

Pemberton, C. (2006). *Coaching to solutions: A manager's toolkit for performance delivery.* Oxford: Butterworth-Heinemann.

Pervin, L. A. (1982). The stasis and flow of behaviour: Toward a theory of goals. In M. M. Page (Ed.), *Nebraska symposium on motivation* (pp. 1–32). Lincoln: University Press.

Pervin, L. A. (1992). Transversing the individual environment landscape: A personal odyssey. In W. B Walsh, K. H. Craik. & R. H. Price (Eds.), *Person-environment psychology: models and perspectives* (pp. 71–88). Hillsdale: Lawrence Erlbaum.

Peterson, C., Maier, S. F. & Seligman, M. E. P. (1993). *Learned helplessness: A theory for the age of personal control.* Oxford, England: Oxford University Press.

Peterson, D. B. (2006). People are complex and the world is messy: A behavior-based approach to executive coaching. In D. Stober & A. M. Grant (Eds.), *Evidence-based coaching handbook* (pp. 51–76). New York, NY: Wiley.

Peterson, D. B. & Hicks, M. D. (1996). *Leader as coach: Strategies for coaching and developing others.* Minneapolis, MN: Personnel Decisions International.

Pintrich, P. R. (2000). Multiple goals, multiple pathways: The role of goal orientations in learning and achievement. *Journal of Educational Psychology, 92,* 544–555.

Pintrich, P. R. & Schunk, D. H. (1996). *Motivation in education: Theory, research, and application.* Englewood Cliffs: Prentice-Hall.

Pintrich, P. R. & Schunk, D. H. (2003). *Motivation in education: Theory, research, and application* (2nd ed.). Upper Saddle River: Merrill.

Pooley, J. (2006). Layers of meaning: A coaching journey. In H. Brunning (Ed.), *Executive coaching systems-psychodynamic perspective* (pp. 113–130). London: Karnac.

Powers, W. T. (1973). *Behavior: The control of perception.* Chicago, IL: Aldine.

Raynor, J. O. & Entin, E. E. (1982). *Motivation, career striving, and aging.* New York: Hemisphere.

Rawsthorne, L. & Elliot, A. (1999). Achievement goals and intrinsic motivation: A meta-analytic review, *Personality and Social Psychology Review, 3,* 617–630.

Reding, P. & Collins, M. (2008). Coaching the human spirit. In D. B. Drake, D. Brennan & K. Gørtz (Eds.), *The philosophy and practice of coaching: Insights and issues for a new era* (pp. 1787–1194). London, England: Wiley.

Reeve, J. (2002). Self-determination theory applied to educational settings. In E. L. Deci & R. M. Ryan (Eds.), *Handbook of self-determination research* (pp. 183–202). Rochester: University of Rochester.

Reeves, D. B. & Allison. E. (2009). *Renewal coaching.* San Francisco, CA: Jossey-Bass.

Rogers, C. (1959). A theory of therapy, personality and interpersonal relationships as developed in the client-centered framework. In S. Koch (Ed.), *Psychology: A study of a science: Vol. 3. Formulations of the Person and the Social Context.* New York: McGraw Hill.

Rogers, C. (1980). *A way of being.* Boston, MA: Houghton Mifflin.

Rogers, J. (2008). *Coaching skills: A handbook.* New York, NY: Open University Press.

Rosenzweig, S. (1936). Some implicit common factors in diverse methods of psychotherapy. *American Journal of Orthopsychiatry, 6,* 412–415.

Rothman, A. J., Baldwin, S. & Hertel, A. W. (2007). Self-regulation and behaviour change: Disentangling behavioural initiation and behavioural maintenance. In R. F Baumeister & K. D. Vohs (Eds.), *Handbook of self-regulation.* New York: Guilford.

Rothwell, J. D. (2004). *In the company of others.* New York: McGraw-Hill.

Rotter, J. B. (1954). *Social learning and clinical psychology.* New York: Prentice-Hall.

Rubin, R. S. (2002). Will the real SMART goals please stand up? *The Industrial-Organizational Psychologist, 39*(4), 26–27.

Saporito, T. J. (1996). Business-linked executive development: Coaching senior executives. *Consulting Psychology Journal: Practice and Research, 48*(2), 96–103.

Scamardo, M. & Harnden, S. (2007). A manager coaching group model: Applying leadership knowledge. *Journal of Workplace Behavioral Health, 22*(2), 127–143.

Schein, E. H. (2006). Coaching and consultation revisited: Are they the same? In M. Goldsmith & L. Lyons (Eds.), *Coaching for leadership.* San Francisco: Pfeiffer.

Schmeichel, B. J. & Baumeister, R. F. (2007). Self-regulatory strength. In R. F. Baumeister & K. D. Vohs (Eds.), *Handbook of self-regulation.* New York, NY: Guilford.

Schmeichel, B. J., Vohs, K. D. & Baumeister, R. F. (2003). Intellectual performance and ego depletion: Role of the self in logical reasoning and other information processing. *Journal of Personality and Social Psychology, 85,* 33–46.

Schön, D. (1983). *The reflective practitioner.* Basic Books: New York.

Schön, D. (1991). *The reflective practitioner: How professionals think in action.* Aldershot: Arena.

Schunk, D. H. (1984). Enhancing self-efficacy and achievement through rewards and goals: Motivational and informational effects. *Journal of Educational Research, 78,* 29–34.

Schunk, D. H. (1989). Self-efficacy and achievement behaviors. *Educational Psychology Review, 1,* 173–208.

Schunk, D. H. (1991). Self-efficacy and academic motivation. *Educational Psychologist, 26,* 207–231.

Schunk, D. H. & Pajares, F. (2002). The development of academic self-efficacy. In A. Wigfield & J. Eccles (Eds.), *Development of achievement motivation* (pp. 16–31). San Diego: Academic Press.

Schwartz, N. (1990). Feelings as information: Informational and motivational functions of affect. In E. T. Higgins & R. M. Sorrentino (Eds.), *Handbook of motivation and cognition: Foundations of social behaviour* (Vol. 2, pp. 527–561). New York: Guilford.

Seijts, G. H. & Latham, G. P. (2001). The effect of distal learning, outcome, and proximal goals on a moderately complex task. *Journal of Organizational Behavior, 22,* 291–302.

Shah, J. Y. (2005). The automatic pursuit and management of goals. *Current Directions in Psychological Science, 14,* 10–13.

Sheldon, K. M. (2002). The self-concordance model of healthy goal striving: When personal goals correctly represent the person. In E. L. Deci & R. M. Ryan (Eds.), *Handbook of self-determination research* (pp. 65–86). Rochester: University of Rochester.

Sheldon, K. M. & Elliot, A. J. (1998). Not all personal goals are personal: Comparing autonomous and controlled reasons as predictors of effort and attainment. *Personality and Social Psychology Bulletin, 24,* 546–557.

Sheldon, K. M. & Elliot, A. J. (1999). Goal striving, need satisfaction, and longitudinal well-being: The self-concordance model. *Journal of Personality and Social Psychology, 76,* 482–497.

Sheldon, K. M. & Kasser, T. (1998). Pursuing personal goals: Skills enable progress but not all progress is beneficial. *Personality and Social Psychology Bulletin, 24*(12), 1319–1331.

Sheldon, K. M., Kasser, T., Smith, K. & Share, T. (2002). Personal goal and psychological growth: Testing an intervention to enhance goal-attainment and personality integration. *Journal of Personality, 70,* 5–31.

Sherrin, J. & Caiger, L. (2004). Rational–emotive behavior therapy: A behavioral change model for executive coaching? *Consulting Psychology Journal: Practice and Research, 56*(4), 225–233.

Showers, J. & Joyce, B. (1996). The evolution of peer coaching. *Educational Leadership, 53*(6), 12–16.

Siegel, P. H. (2000). Using peer mentors during periods of uncertainty. *Leadership and Organization, 21*(5), 243–253.

Sieler, A. (2010). Ontological coaching. In E. Cox, T. Bachkirova & D. Clutterbuck (Eds.), *The complete handbook of coaching* (pp. 107–119). London, England: Sage.

Simon, H. A. (1953). *Models of man.* New York: Wiley.

Sintonen, M. (2004). Reasoning to hypotheses: Where do questions come? *Foundation of Science, 9,* 249–266.

Skiffington, S. & Zeus, P. (2003). *Behavioral coaching: How to build sustainable personal and organizational strength.* Sydney: McGraw-Hill Australia.

Slater, C. L. & Simmons, D. L. (2001). The design and implementation of a peer coaching program. *American Secondary Education, 29*(3), 67–76.

Slavin, R. (1990). Research on cooperative learning: Consensus and controversy. *Educational Leader, 47*, 52–54.

Sloman, S. A. (1996). The empirical case for two form of reasoning. *Psychological Bulletin, 119*, 3–22.

Smith, C., Hofer, J., Gillespie, M., Solomon, M. & Rowe, K. (2006). How teachers change: A study of professional development in adult education. In P. Villa (Ed.), *Teacher change and development* (pp. 11–155), New York: Nova Science.

Smither, J. W., London, M. & Reilly, R. R. (2005). Does performance improve following multisource feedback? A theoretical model, meta-analysis and review of empirical findings. *Personnel Psychology, 58*, 33–66.

Smolensky, P. (1998). On the proper treatment of connectionism. *Behavioral and Brain Sciences, 11*, 1–23.

Snyder, A. (1995). Executive coaching: The new solution. *Management Review, 84*(3), 29–32.

Spence, G. B. (2007). GAS powered coaching: Goal attainment scaling and its use in coaching research and practice. *Coaching Psychology Review, 2*, 155–167.

Spence, G. B. & Grant, A. (2007). Professional and peer life coaching and the enhancement of goal striving and well-being: An exploratory study. *The Journal of Positive Psychology, 2*, 185–194.

Spencer, L. (2011). Coaching and training transfer: A phenomenological inquiry into combined training-coaching programmes, *International Journal of Evidence Based Coaching and Mentoring*, Special Issue 5, 1–18.

Sperry, L. (1993). Working with executives: consulting, counseling and coaching. *Individual Psychology: Journal of Adlerian Theory, Research & Practice, 49*(2), 257–266.

Spinelli, E. (2010). Existential coaching. In E. Cox, T. Bachkirova & D. Clutterbuck (Eds.), *The complete handbook of coaching* (pp. 94–106). London, England: Sage.

Spinelli, E. & Horner, C. (2007). An existential approach to coaching psychology. In S. Palmer & A. Whybrow (Eds.), *Handbook of coaching psychology: A guide for practitioners* (pp. 118–132). Abingdon, England: Routledge.

Stacey, R. D. (2000). *Strategic management and organisational dynamics: The challenge of complexity.* Essex, UK: Pearson Education Ltd., Prentice Hall.

Starr, J. (2007). *The coaching manual: The definitive guide to the process, principles and skills of personal coaching.* Upper Saddle River: Prentice Hall.

Stern, L. R. (2004). Executive coaching: A working definition. *Consulting Psychology Journal: Practice and Research, 56*(3), 154–162.

Stewart, L. J., Palmer, S., Wilkin, H. & Kerrin, M. (2008). The influence of character: Does personality impact coaching success? *International Journal of Evidence Based Coaching and Mentoring, 6*(1) 32–43.

Stober, D. (2006). Coaching from the humanistic perspective. In D. Stober & A. M. Grant (Eds.), *Evidence-based coaching handbook* (pp. 17–50). New York, NY: Wiley.

Stober, D. & Grant A. M. (2006). Toward a contextual approach to coaching models. In D. Stober & A. M. Grant (Eds.), *Evidence-based coaching handbook* (pp. 355–366). New York, NY: Wiley.

Stober, D., Wildflower, L. & Drake, D. (2006). Evidence-based practice: A potential approach for effective coaching. *International Journal of Evidence-based Coaching, 4*(1),1–8.

Strauss, A. & Corbin J. (1990). *Basics of qualitative research: Grounded theory procedures and techniques.* London, England: Sage.

Sullivan, M. F., Skovholt, T. M. & Jennings, L. (2005). Master therapists' construction of the therapy relationship. *Journal of Mental Health Counseling*, Jan 2005, *27*, 1.

Summerfield, J. (2006). Do we coach or do we counsel? Thoughts on the "emotional life" of a coaching session, *The Coaching Psychologist*, *2*(1), 24–27.

Szabo, P. & Meier, D. (2009). *Coaching: Plain and simple*. New York, NY: Norton.

Thach, L. & Heinselman, T. (1999). Executive coaching defined. *Training & Development*, March, 35–39.

Thompson, T., Purdy, J. M. & Summers, D. B. (2008). A five factor framework for coaching middle managers. *Organization Development Journal*, *26*(3), 63–72.

Tomm, K. (1988). Inventive interviewing part III: Intending to ask lineal, circular, strategic or reflective questions. *Family Process*, *27*(1), 1–15.

Truijen, K. J. P. & Van Woerkom, M. (2008). The pitfalls of collegial coaching: an analysis of collegial coaching in medical education and its influence on stimulating reflection and performance of novice clinical teachers. *Journal of Workplace Learning*, *20*(5), 316–326.

Vallacher, R. R. & Kauffman, J. (1996). Dynamics of action identification: Volatility and structure in the representation of behavior. In P. M. Gollwitzer & J. A. Bargh (Eds.), *The psychology of action: linking motivation and cognition to behaviour* (pp. 260–282). New York, NY: Guilford Press.

Vallacher, R. R. & Wegner, D. M. (1985). *A theory of action identification*. Hillsdale: Erlbaum.

Vallacher, R. R., Wegner, D. M., McMahan, S. C., Cotter, J. & Larsen, K. A. (1992). On winning friends and influencing people: Action identification and self-presentation success. *Social Cognition*, *10*, 335–355.

Vallacher, R. R., Wegner, D. M. & Somoza, M. (1989). That's easy for you to say: Action identification and speech fluency. *Journal of Personality and Social Psychology*, *56*, 199–208.

Waddell, D. L. & Dunn, N. (2005). Peer coaching: The next step in staff development. *The Journal of Continuing Education in Nursing*, *36*(2), 84–89.

Wageman, R., Nunes, D. A., Burruss, J. A. & Hackman, J. R. (2008). *Senior leadership teams: What it takes to make them great*. Boston, MA: Harvard Business School.

Wagner, J. A. III (1994). Participation's effect on performance and satisfaction: A reconsideration of research evidence. *Academy of Management Journal*, *19*, 312–330.

Walsh, K., Bartunek, J. M. & Lacey, C. A. (1998). A relational approach to empowerment. In C. L. Cooper & D. M. Rousseau (Eds.), *Trends in organizational behaviour* (pp. 103–126). Chichester, England: Wiley.

Waring, P. A. (2008). Coaching the Brain. *The Coaching Psychologist*, *4*(2), August 2008.

Wasik, B. (1984). *Teaching parents effective problem-solving: A handbook for professionals*. Unpublished manuscript. Chapel Hill: University of North Carolina.

Wasylyshyn, K. M. (2003). Executive coaching: An outcome study. *Consulting Psychology Journal: Practice and Research*, *55*(2), 94–106.

Weiner, B. (1986). *An attributional theory of motivation and emotion*. New York, NY: Springer-Verlag.

Weldon, R. & Yun, S. (2000). The effects of proximal and distal goals on goal level, strategy development, and group performance. *Journal of Applied Behavioural Science*, *36*(3), 336–344.

West, L. & Milan, M. (Eds.), (2001). *The reflecting glass*. London, England: Palgrave.

Whitmore, J. (2003). *Coaching for performance*. London, England: Nicholas Brealey.

Whitmore, J. & Einzig, H. (2006). Transpersonal coaching. In J. Passmore (Ed.), *Excellence in coaching* (pp. 119–133). London, England: Kogan Page.

Whitworth, L., Kimsey-House, H. & Sandhal, P. (2007). *Co-active coaching: New skills for coaching people toward success in work and life*. Palo Alto, CA: Davies-Black.

Wigfield, A. & Karpathian, M. (1991). Who am I what can I do: Children's self-concepts and motivation in achievement situations. *Educational Psychologist*, *25*, 233–261.

Williams, K., Kiel, F., Doyle, M. & Sinagra, L. (2002). Breaking the boundaries: Leveraging the personal in executive coaching. In C. Fitzgerald & J. Garvey Berger (Eds.), *Executive coaching: Practices and perspectives* (pp. 119–134). Palo Alto, CA: Davies-Black.

Williams, P. (2008). The life coach operating system: Its foundations in psychology. In D. B. Drake, D. Brennan & K. Gørtz (Eds.), *The philosophy and practice of coaching: Insights and issues for a new era* (pp. 3–26). London: John Wiley & Sons.

Williams, S. L. & Cervone, D. (1998). Social cognitive theories of personality. In D. F. Barone, M. Hersen. & V. B. Van Hasslet (Eds.), *Advanced personality* (pp. 173–207). New York, NY: Kluwer.

Wild, T. C. & Enzle, M. E. (2002). Social contagion of motivational orientations. In E. L. Deci & R. M. Ryan (Eds.), *Handbook of self-determination research* (pp. 141–157). Rochester: University of Rochester.

Wolters, C. A., Pintrich, P. R. & Karabenick, S. A. (2003). Assessing academic self-regulated learning. In K. A. Moore & L. H. Lippman (Eds.), *What do children need to flourish?* (pp. 251–270). New York, NY: Springer.

Wong, M. M. & Csikszentmihalyi, M. (1991). Motivation and academic achievement: The effects of personality traits and the quality of experience. *Journal of Personality, 59*, 539–574.

Yontef, G. (2005). Gestalt therapy theory of change. In A. M. Woldt & S. M. Toman, *Gestalt Therapy: History, Theory and Practice*. Sage, London.

Zajonc, R. B. (1965). Social facilitation. *Science, 149*, 269–274.

Zeus, P. & Skiffington, S. (2007). *The coaching at work toolkit*. Roseville, NSW: McGraw Hill.

Zimmerman, B. J. (1989). A social cognitive view of self-regulated academic learning. *Journal of Educational Psychology, 81*, 329–339.

Zimmerman, B. J. (2000). Attaining self-regulation: A social cognitive perspective. In M. Boekaerts, P. R. Pintrich & M. Zeidner (Eds.), *Handbook of self-regulation* (pp. 13–39). San Diego, CA: Academic.

Zimmerman, B. J. & Kitsantas, A. (1996). Self-regulated learning of a motoric skill: The role of goal setting and self-monitoring. *Journal of Applied Sport Psychology, 8*, 69–84.

Index

Printed in the United States
by Baker & Taylor Publisher Services